CW01498525

The Only Way I Know

The Only Way I Know

The Autobiography

ANDY FARRELL

with Gavin Mairs

SANDYCOVE

an imprint of

PENGUIN BOOKS

SANDYCOVE

UK | USA | Canada | Ireland | Australia
India | New Zealand | South Africa

Sandycove is part of the Penguin Random House group of companies
whose addresses can be found at global.penguinrandomhouse.com

Penguin Random House UK,
One Embassy Gardens, 8 Viaduct Gardens, London s w 1 1 7 b w

penguin.co.uk

Penguin
Random House
UK

First published 2025

001

Copyright © Andy Farrell, 2025

The moral right of the author has been asserted

Set in 13.5/16pt Garamond MT Std
Typeset by Six Red Marbles UK, Thetford, Norfolk
Printed and bound in Great Britain by Clays Ltd, Elcograf S.p.A.

The authorized representative in the E E A is Penguin Random House Ireland,
Morrison Chambers, 32 Nassau Street, Dublin D 0 2 Y H 68

A CIP catalogue record for this book is available from the British Library

ISBN: 978–1–844–88678–4

Penguin Random House is committed to a sustainable future
for our business, our readers and our planet. This book is made from
Forest Stewardship Council® certified paper.

To my wife, Colleen, and to our children,
Owen, Elleshia, Gracie and Gabriel:
you mean the world to me.

Contents

CONTENTS

1. The Coin

I found the two-pence coin on the floor behind the old wall bars of the school basketball court. Moments later I would be wishing I had left it where I found it.

I had barely given it a thought before I decided to roll it across the varnished wooden floor towards my teammate Lee Penny. He would go on to play rugby league for Warrington and Scotland, but you wouldn't have guessed it that day. He was just an over-excited kid, like the rest of us. We wished we were running around outside on the pitch, not stuck in an old gym because our playing fields – on Bankes Avenue in Orrell, on the outskirts of Wigan – were frozen.

The coin rolled in an arc towards the feet of our coach, Haydn Walker. Even before it began to wobble, he knew the culprit. He had been trying to bring a rabble of noisy ten- and eleven-year-olds to order and talk through the training session that lay ahead of us.

I guess I knew I would get myself in trouble, just not how deep. It was not like I had been the only one messing around.

It was my first full season playing for the Orrell St James junior rugby league club. I may have been a chubby ten-year-old kid with everything still to learn, but I was confident enough in my ability to expect I would be playing in the team every weekend. Perhaps that is why Haydn singled me out. We were still rugby league infants, taking our first baby steps in a hard-man's world.

Haydn was not some over-eager parent coaching an

age-group side. Orrell St James were just establishing a junior section at the time, so we were one of the new sides coming through. Even back then it was clear that Haydn had a burning desire to build a club where boys could expand their rugby skills and knowledge.

Haydn always kept up to date with what the senior Wigan team were doing and became part of their academy set-up. While other teams in our age group would be playing games in their training sessions and messing around, we would be doing drills the whole time to hone our skills.

We may have only been Under-11s, but we acted as though we were a professional outfit. That attitude was reflected in our results. Our training session in the basketball court was preparation for meeting Leigh Rangers in the cup final of the North West Counties League the following weekend. Paul Rowley, who went on to play for Halifax, Huddersfield and England, and is now head coach of Salford, was in the Leigh team we were facing.

There was tremendous rivalry with local clubs like Blackbrook, Thatto Heath and Leigh. If you are not from the north-west of England, it is hard to describe how territorial it is. Let's just say it was a big enough decision for my parents to move from Delph Street, off Park Road in the middle of town, where my older sister Catherine was born, to what would be our family home in Goose Green, a fifteen-minute drive from the town centre. Shaun Edwards, my future Wigan teammate, had been a neighbour about six doors down on the opposite side of the street from their first home. Yet moving was the best decision they made. The house was a tight fit at the start but would be extended over the years. Mum and Dad still live there today, in the same house, and I love going back.

You can only imagine what it was like when you went out

of town. There would have been pure hatred between Wigan and Warrington. We were just trying to get one up on each other. It was pride, really. The rivalry was fierce, and it mattered. Boy, did it matter.

Haydn's commitment to our team exceeded convention too. In order to ensure that he had the right boys in his team, he had bought a clapped-out minibus and every Tuesday and Thursday he would drive around Wigan, battling through traffic on a two-hour journey to pick us all up so that no one would miss training, and then another two-hour journey afterwards to drop us all home.

I didn't know any different, so I just thought it was normal. It was only when I became a parent that I looked back and realized it was anything but. Haydn was a guy who cared passionately about giving everyone the opportunity to train and play because he knew that not everyone's mum and dad had a car or the time to take their kids to training or matches.

Yes, I knew that I was at the right club, and I loved the trips in the minibus almost as much as the rugby sessions. It was about four miles from our house to the club. I would usually be among the last to get picked up and one of the first to be dropped off afterwards. The banter on the bus was such that I would often ask Haydn if there was any chance he could drop me off last instead so I could enjoy it a bit longer. Those sessions were what I lived for.

And it was now all about to come to a shuddering halt. Silence swiftly replaced the chatter as Haydn's stare fixed first on the coin and then firmly on me. What on earth had I been thinking?

* * *

My first passion had been football, not rugby. Manchester City, to be precise. My dad used to take me to the Platt Lane

Stand at Maine Road whenever they played at home, and sometimes to away matches too. Trevor Francis and Kevin Bond were the first posters on the wall of my bedroom in our small three-bedroom house on Freshfield Road in Goose Green.

We were lucky enough to have a corner plot. Our street was off the main road and led onto a cul-de-sac so there was very little passing traffic. For me, it was the best street ever to grow up in. There were about ten other kids living nearby and every afternoon we would meet up after school to play games.

When I was around ten, there were three or four lads who were a few years older than me, and another who was older still. We were a tight group. Somebody would always be knocking on your door to ask if you were coming out, or I would look through the window and see people out playing and dash outside. It was like having a gang of older brothers. We share a WhatsApp group to this day.

The problem with being the youngest in the group was that every night I would be the first to be called in by my mum. It would do my head in. I would trudge back with a burning sense of injustice and watch the others all still play-ing around under the lamppost from my bedroom window.

I used to share a room with my brothers Chris and Phil, twins just under five years younger than me. I was in a single bed and they were in bunk beds. The room seemed spacious at the time, but when I go back now, I shudder to think how we all squeezed in. It was usually chaos in there. Like most big brothers, I would tease my younger siblings, and they would taunt me back. There were constant fights. I don't think we got much sleep.

For me, it was an idyllic childhood. Wigan is a former

mining town and near to our house was a vast stretch of ground layered with stones that we called 'the tips'. There was a lake too. We used to spend hours each day of the summer playing there. One year we decided to construct a BMX track using the stones. It became so popular that people came from all over town to ride on it. During the winter we would skate on the lake when it froze over.

After part of that land was sold, JCB diggers arrived and a new housing estate was built. The banter we had on the building site was brilliant, jumping out of windows and landing in sandpits. Mum and Dad were not strict parents and I am very lucky to have grown up in that era when children had so much more freedom. Kids today seem to spend their free time on their phones or gaming, but we were always outside, always active. I wouldn't say we were feral, but we were gone first thing in the morning and back last thing at night. All we needed were our bikes.

My wife Colleen pointed out recently that you never see dogs roaming the streets any more. When we were kids, it was a common sight to see dogs on the loose around town. Colleen remembers one day seeing her two dogs running around the school playing field after jumping the fence. Our dog Shandy, an English springer spaniel, would also like to roam. When we saw her out, we would shout, 'Shandy, go home!' She would scurry off looking guilty and we would carry on with what we were doing. She was a lovely dog. We would later have two boxers as well, Fergie and Holly, and all three were a big part of our family life.

Messing around with older lads gave me the same kind of street toughness that they had. Rugby league was not played at my primary school, St Paul's in Goose Green. We mostly played football in the winter and cricket in the summer, or British Bulldog, where one team had to stop the other crossing the road by tackling them. Then one year the council put gravel down on the tarmac after it was resurfaced, and we were gutted. The gravel cut us to pieces. Still, we played on.

Playing football for the age-group Wigan town sides, physically at least, was easy in comparison, but I was hardly a superstar at football. I was happy to be the workhorse in the middle of the field, trying to galvanize the team. I had a decent left foot, and taking corners and free-kicks definitely contributed to my skills later as a goal-kicker in rugby league. Some kids become obsessed with goal-kicking because they think they can do it. Others tend to shy away from it because it seems too difficult. I was firmly in the former camp. I knew straight away I could strike a ball.

I was intrigued by rugby league because I was aware of how important it was to my dad, but he never really pushed me to play it. As a teenager he had played for Wigan Colts, an Under-19s side. He later became a baker, and had to rise at 2.30 a.m. every day. On Saturday mornings he would go straight from work to the rugby club and have a sleep on the bench before the game. He was associated with the St Patrick's Club, a famous amateur club that has produced some of the biggest names to come out of Wigan.

Rugby league was cut-throat in those days. Dad had been a decent boxer at school, but when he broke his jaw playing rugby he lost his nerve, and with it his dream of playing 'for the town', as we say in Wigan.

His passion for the game did not die, however. Whenever we drove from our house in Goose Green to my grandma's house about three miles away in Aspull, a village on the outskirts of Wigan, he made a point of always driving past Central Park,

Wigan's stadium. 'In two minutes, Andrew, we will be going past heaven,' he would say, every time we approached the stadium.

The first game I went to was Wigan against Widnes in the Challenge Cup final at Wembley in May 1984. It felt like the whole town had been transported to London. I didn't know it then, but Keiron O'Loughlin, who was playing for Widnes that day and scored a try, would later be my father-in-law. I also didn't know that Colleen was somewhere in the crowd, as a Wiganer supporting Widnes and her dad. Two other Wigan lads, Joe Lydon and Andy Gregory, were also in their side, Joe scoring two tries in a 19–6 victory for Widnes. The defeat was tough to take, but what an occasion! It was one of those childhood moments that stay with you.

* * *

When the Graeme West rugby league summer camp at Robin Park was advertised in the local newspaper the summer after that final at Wembley, Dad wondered if I might like to go. I was nine years old.

West, a giant New Zealander, was a Wigan club legend and his camp was in high demand. But I was not sure if I wanted to go. I was shy and none of my friends were going as they all played football. In the end I went along, probably to keep Mum and Dad happy. I made sure I wore a football top, though, a baggy Blackpool shirt.

Yet almost from the first moment I got the ball in my hands, I knew this was the game for me. I was a big lad for my age, and I loved the physical contact, both in carrying the ball and making tackles. It was during the camp that I first met Haydn, who was in charge of our group. I started off as a prop forward, because of my size and the fact that I didn't know the game, but the exhilaration of making line-breaks and scoring tries quickly got me hooked. And once you get a bit of success, the hunger goes through the roof.

Haydn put up a reward of a Mars Bar for the player who won man-of-the-match or for anyone who made three tackles in a row. After our first game, I came away with two Mars Bars. Yes, this was the game for me.

At the end of the camp, Haydn invited me to join Orrell St James. It was then that my shyness returned. I had surprised myself by how much I had enjoyed the week, but I told Haydn no.

Haydn refused to give up. Later in the week he came by our house to ask Mum and Dad whether they could persuade me. Dad was excited that I had made an impression on one of the coaches, but in my mind, moving to Orrell St James was unthinkable. All my friends played football: why would I want to go there and play a new sport? But Haydn was persistent. He told my parents I had a special talent. Eventually, I said I would give it a go. It was not the first time I would wrench myself out of my comfort zone, and not the first time I would live to be thankful that I did.

The easy decision would have been to stay with my mates playing football. Had I done that, I suspect I would have continued to take the easy path through life. But I decided to commit to rugby league, and ever since then I have looked for challenges to broaden my experience.

We won a pre-season game by over fifty points, and I got a buzz from scoring tries and kicking conversions. Under Haydn's guidance, we went on a winning streak that made us the envy of our rivals. But he kept challenging us to develop our skills further. One day he introduced a rule that anyone who scored more than three tries during a match would be substituted to give someone else a chance. I never wanted to come off, so there were times when, if I made a break having already scored three, I would wait for the support to come and pass to make sure someone else scored.

I still played football, but when I was picked for the town's Under-11s rugby league team by Mick Mullaney, who ran it, it was not long before I had to make a decision about which sport to commit to. The rugby and football sessions clashed on a Saturday and Orrell St James was on a Sunday. It was a no-brainer for me because I was enjoying rugby so much and making rapid progress through the ranks. I was quickly becoming aware that the sport was treated like a religion in Wigan. My dad's passion was starting to make sense.

Then one day the frost came, and we had to train inside. And for some reason I rolled a coin at Haydn . . .

* * *

'Farrell, you are out of this session,' he boomed. Suddenly Haydn had my attention as silence fell over the school's basketball court. At first I thought he was joking. It was just a stupid coin. Ah, come on! I was not happy, but things were about to get worse.

After the session Haydn took me to one side.

'Andy, you are not playing against Leigh in the cup final next Saturday,' he told me.

On the journey home on the minibus that evening, everyone was silent. The others hadn't seen me cry. I made sure of that. I don't think I have cried since. That's how much it meant to me.

I was the last stop that day. Haydn called into the house to tell my parents what had happened. My mum, being softer, probably thought Haydn had been a bit harsh, while my dad told me he had done the right thing.

I was devastated. I couldn't believe the severity of the

punishment. Haydn had taken away everything that I looked forward to during the week. Even now I can remember the burning sense of injustice. And anger. Why me? Others were up to mischief too, but they didn't seem to get punished. How could he do this to me?

In my eyes Haydn was now the worst person in the world. I went to the game the following Saturday and stood on the sidelines, still seething. As if to rub it in, Haydn asked me to run onto the pitch with the sand to make a mound for the goal-kicker to kick from.

I supported my teammates as best as I could, trying to prove a point. But what I didn't realize was that the point had already been made. I guess I must have played over 150 games for Orrell St James. I don't remember them all, but I'll never forget the one game that I missed.

As a coach I am all in favour of putting a bit of discipline into someone who is getting above their station and I now recognize that Haydn was trying to make a statement not just to me but to everyone else. A line had been drawn in the sand. He knew that making an example of one of the team's better players would send a strong message to the others. He ran a tight ship. It was one reason people wanted to come to Orrell St James and why we won so many trophies.

I know now that it might seem like a trivial moment, a coach berating a petulant child at a training session, but it had a lasting impact on me. I knew that if I wanted to keep doing what I loved, I would have to act appropriately rather than messing around. From then on, discipline would become something I prided myself on. I vowed I would never again give anyone an excuse to drop me.

2. The Signature

You could always tell a scout by the way he dressed. The standard attire was a big puffer coat emblazoned with the name of the club they represented. Every time I ran out onto the pitch I looked to see if there were any of them on the sidelines. There would always be an extra buzz ahead of a match if you knew you were being scouted. Often there were as many as six of them patrolling the touchline on a Saturday or Sunday morning, and I was desperate to impress. Especially the ones from Wigan. Only the ones from Wigan, in fact. The truth is, even back then I only ever wanted to play for the town.

Wigan is a working-class town of 330,000 people located between Liverpool and Manchester. It first made its name in textiles, coal and industry. But it is rugby league that has long been the town's DNA. Plenty of sportswriters have tried to get to the bottom of the phenomenon, but to me there is no secret. It is founded in the tightness of the community. We look after our own and are proud of each other, no matter what they are doing.

As a boy I loved the sense of belonging and was a real homebird. People might have seen a different side to me on the pitch, but away from it I could be painfully shy at times and didn't like to travel. I was the type of kid who, if I went away for the weekend with a friend, would soon be on the phone to my mum asking her to come and pick me up, even if we had only gone thirty-odd miles up the road to Blackpool.

In rugby union in England, you might have a school producing brilliant teams in one part of the country, but their main competition is hundreds of miles away. In Wigan, we were surrounded by fierce competition, so many clubs, so many rivals. I live in Dublin now, and I see something similar in the rivalry between the schools in rugby union and the burning desire to play for Leinster and Ireland. I recognize the pressure.

That pressure was incredible, even at age-group level in Wigan. I felt it the first time I pulled on the treasured cherry-and-white shirt when I represented the town Under-11 side. The jerseys were handed out on match days, and even though we had to return them after the game to get washed, I remember thinking, *Wow, this is what it is about!*

It's what drove me on. I couldn't bear the thought of not being selected the following year. That shirt represents all of us. If you are lucky enough to pull it on, you know the weight of responsibility that comes with it. You know about the people who have gone before you and are under immense pressure to do well.

That pride seeped through to my desire to play for Lancashire and pull on their famous red jersey with a white 'V'. But at time it felt like the trials for the town team were harder than the county ones. You were up against players from St James, St Pat's, St William's and St Jude's amateur clubs, and some great players missed out.

When I was growing up, the focal point of the town was Central Park. The stadium was located right in the middle of town, which meant that fans could travel by bus or walk to the game and have a beer or two.

It was there that my deep bond with the Wigan senior team was cemented, the night of 7 October 1987. I still remember it like yesterday. Manly Warringah Sea Eagles had come to town for the inaugural World Club Challenge match. There had been an unofficial game between the domestic champions of England and Australia in 1976 involving St Helens and Eastern Suburbs at the Sydney Cricket Ground. After Wigan had won the RFL Championship and John Player Special Trophy in the 1986/87 season, the club chairman Maurice Lindsay resurrected the concept by inviting Manly to play in a winner-takes-all game in Wigan.

Australia has dominated rugby league for as long as I can remember, so to have the opportunity to watch their champion club side go head-to-head with ours was beyond my wildest dreams. To make sure of a good vantage point, I went straight to the stadium as soon as school finished at 3.30. There was terracing in the stadium in those days, and I remember running down to the front and jumping up to sit on the wall, where I stayed, swinging my legs, until the kick-off at 7.45. What else would I be doing?

It was the only way I was guaranteed to see the action. The official capacity of the ground was around 35,000 but afterwards it was said that over 50,000 made it in.

Before the kick-off, fireworks lit up the sky over the old stadium, but it was the pyrotechnics on the pitch that I found utterly compelling. The Wigan team that night boasted eleven Great Britain internationals and one New Zealander, and we won 8–2 in a ferocious contest with an atmosphere that you would not believe. I knew then that I could never play for another rugby league club in England. No way. I just hoped they would have me.

I am as passionate now about coaching the Ireland rugby union side as I was playing for Wigan, but that passion was forged in the town. Whatever I do outside Wigan, it is because of what the place means to me.

* * *

The town Under-11 side had fixtures almost every weekend against sixteen other towns across the north. The home games were at Robin Park, an athletics stadium with a rugby field in the middle of it.

The inter-town games led to selection for the Lancashire Under-11s to face Yorkshire. My birthday is in May, so I spent most of my age-grade career playing with boys who were older than me. I was always driven by a desire to keep up. I wanted to prove to other people that I could do what they expected of me. And to keep testing myself against the best.

Iain McCorquodale, the Lancashire coach, sensed that in me early on, and used it to fast-track my development. After a couple of training sessions, he named the squad to face Yorkshire. I hadn't made the cut. It was my first setback, and I could not hide my disappointment as I trudged from the changing rooms back to Dad's car.

Suddenly Iain was on my shoulder. 'Andrew, what's up, you look a little bit disappointed?' he asked me. Back then it was always Andrew. It's funny, I've been called Andy for years, but even now my close family and friends still call me Andrew. Colleen sometimes calls me Drew.

'I know I could have done better,' I replied.

'OK then, come with me, let's go back to the gym.'

When we got to the gym, Iain proceeded to throw down some mats on the floor and called in two county players who were a couple of years older than me. 'OK, let's see how you go now.'

It was a tackling drill, and I took out all my frustration at being left out of the squad on those two lads. After ten minutes, Iain stopped the session. 'That's enough. Andrew, you are in the team to play against Yorkshire.' Wow! I couldn't believe it.

I was fortunate that there were so many people willing to help with my development at that time, and it felt like my life was changing quickly. I started to slim down as my junior career progressed through to the Under-13s. Haydn started to see me as a ball-playing type and I moved to second row and then loose forward, the equivalent of No. 8 in rugby union. It was the position I would play for the vast majority of my rugby league career, and it suited me to be the link between forwards and backs.

What I loved was the challenge of unlocking a game. Even now, I wouldn't have a clue about my scoring record. If you spoke to Martin Offiah, the Wigan and Great Britain winger, he could tell you every try that he scored, no matter who it was against, or if it was in a cup final or at the start of a season. It means so much to him because that is what his job was, to score tries. He was a speedster like Jason Robinson. That was their thing.

It wasn't mine. I loved goal-kicking, but it never bothered me how many points I scored. I wanted to be the player who unlocked the game when the contest was still on the line, and that didn't always mean scoring a try.

One of the hardest things to do in rugby league is to keep running into defensive brick walls again and again, just to set the tone of a game. The first twenty minutes are always the most brutal. I wanted to be the player who made the break to turn a game or found a way to put a teammate in space. Could I be the player to unlock the game?

* * *

The competition in the representative sides was fierce. There were at least half a dozen players who were tipped to make it.

You would hear stories of players who did not make the town or the Lancashire team and then gave up playing. Others stuck with it and worked hard even if they had been overlooked at first and developed later to enjoy successful careers. Kris Radlinski, a future teammate of mine in the senior Wigan squad, who is now the club's chief executive, never made it as a regular for the town team as a boy, but became one of the best players to have ever played for the club.

They were the days before academies had been established and clubs were starting to spend considerable sums to secure young talent. One club had signed five junior players from one of the successful sides, but none of the players came through, so much more 'due diligence' was now being carried out. Scouts would watch players they were interested in for a number of games. There were constant rumours about who might have signed for whom. Often, I found myself in the centre of it all. At one game away at Leigh, who were our biggest rivals at the time, one of the parents came over and started shouting abuse at me. Thankfully, Dad was there, but it wasn't pleasant to hear.

It was crazy, looking back, and I can understand why some people must worry about the impact of the pressure and expectation on such young shoulders. For many people rugby, like football, was an escape route. The financial rewards on offer were life-changing for working-class families who were struggling to make ends meet.

It was different for me. We weren't from a privileged background, but I never felt under any pressure from my mum and dad. The pushing came from me. I couldn't imagine wanting to do anything else. As my commitment to rugby league intensified, it was matched by the support from my family. I was in a hurry, desperate to keep getting better. I was always thinking about the game. (I still am.) Every day had to count, and the next game could never come quickly enough.

***

I grew up in awe of my parents. Mum worked full-time managing children's nurseries, and Dad always left for the bakery every morning hours before we had even stirred.

Every school morning, my grandparents on my mum's side of the family, George and Annie Heyes, were up at about 5 a.m. to catch a bus from Aspull, first to Wigan town centre and then on to us in Goose Green, so that my mum could get off to work. Every morning, it was they who woke us up. It's what family means. I guess we took it for granted at the time, but not now. I used to love going up to their house at the weekend as well. There was always fizzy pop and a packet of crisps for us. Whenever my sister Cath or I got into trouble with Mum or Dad, they were always on our side too.

When the twins arrived, Mum took time off work. It became incredibly hard for her, handling four unruly kids in the morning. Then, when she had to go back to her job, Grandma and Grandad took over.

I would have been grumpy enough in the morning and they were kind, good-hearted people. Being kids, we would try to take as many liberties as we could. It must have been bloody hard work for them, but they were a big part of our lives. Having two babies in the house was a big change for Cath and me, but an exciting one. It was a happy home. The twins grew up to love their rugby too; both made the Wigan academy, and both would later sign for Oldham in the first division. Chris made the decision fairly early on that he did not want to pursue the game as a professional. It was a good decision for him. He joined the police and has moved up through the ranks. Phil was more stubborn and clung tightly to his dream of being a professional, playing late into his twenties. He now has a successful career as an electrician.

My involvement with Orrell St James encouraged Dad to take up coaching, and he started running the Under-9s side. He reckons he only got to see about fifty of my games during my entire time at the club. Like Haydn, he ran a shuttle, picking up and dropping off kids, and it led to my first encounter with my future wife. One of the players in my dad's team was Colleen's younger brother Kevin, who would, years later, sign for St Helens. When we dropped him off, my dad asked their dad, Keiron O'Loughlin, if we could go inside to see the shirt he had worn for Widnes in their Challenge Cup final victory over Wigan at Wembley.

My shyness gripped as I entered the house, and it seems that Colleen felt the same way, as she shot up the stairs upon my arrival. I didn't think much of it, but she would remember the incident vividly. (She remembers everything. Her auntie used to live across the road from me and she reckons she used to see me acting feral, running around the streets.) I started to notice Colleen at matches, as she would sometimes come to watch Kevin play.

One day we were all at Central Park and I was watching some of my Orrell St James teammates play in a match against Colleen's school in a final. She didn't recognize me at first because by the age of thirteen I had shot up in height and lost the puppy fat. She asked one of her friends who I was, and it quickly became schoolkid gossip. She was asked if she liked me and somehow it got back to me, and I was keen to see what she looked like.

I saw her again at a May Day event. She was looking after her little brother Sean, as her parents had taken her grandparents on a trip to Lourdes. When I got back home, I decided to ring her. I didn't know what to say really, and Colleen said later I sounded really moody! It was not a great start to our relationship.

We agreed to go to the pictures the following weekend in town, but on the Saturday morning Colleen's mum and dad asked if she could mind Sean again as they were going to buy a new car. Those were the days before mobile phones, and I had already left the house, so I knew nothing of this change of plan. I sat nervously at the cinema, waiting. And waiting. Back at Colleen's house, her parents had returned late, and even though it was just a fifteen-minute walk into town, she begged her dad for a lift. She hadn't told them she was meeting a boy as she was worried that her mum wouldn't approve.

'Why are you getting so worked up about meeting some friends?' her mum asked.

When she arrived over an hour late, I was in a mood, but Colleen would later say that the fact that I had waited for her proved it was meant to be. She was right, of course. Our first date might not have got off to the best of starts, but we quickly became the best of friends. We never stopped talking. One day Colleen's dad burst into their house after work and was steaming because he had been trying to ring home for over an hour, but we had been chatting on the phone. We were always in trouble for being on the phone too long and running up bills.

Colleen's dad took a real interest in helping me develop as a player and became a massive influence on my career.

Perhaps he saw something in me. He had a makeshift gym in a shed out the back and players used to come to the house to do extra training. 'That gym is my insurance policy,' he would joke. 'Time in the gym is money in the bank when it comes to looking after yourself.'

He took me under his wing. I was incredibly fortunate to have someone of his stature and experience in the game helping me out. Keiron had a brilliant attitude to conditioning. He had been influenced at Widnes by the late Vince Karalius, who was a coach far ahead of his time.

Keiron had been given an insight into what professional rugby would look like in the future, and now I was benefiting from his advice as a thirteen-year-old. It was like Christmas Day, every day.

I trained in the mornings before school and afterwards, and would run the two-mile track along the River Douglas up to Haigh Hall, a country house surrounded by woodland, where I would do hill sprints. Colleen's family would have a big influence on what I ate, too. I didn't have the healthiest diet at the time and preferred simple foods like beans on toast.

I can still remember the first time I went to Colleen's house and her mum asked me if I wanted to stay for tea. I politely accepted but was a bit concerned at what was cooking on the Aga.

'What's that?' I asked Colleen.

'It's chilli con carne, Andrew,' she replied.

I almost ran out of the house.

'I can't eat that!' I had never even eaten rice or pasta before, let alone chilli con carne.

Her mum offered to make me sandwiches instead, but I tried the chilli and actually liked it! It was the first step towards improving my eating habits.

I played for Wigan every Saturday morning, and for my club on Sundays, while also playing rugby and football for my school during the week. The county games for Lancashire were predominantly against Yorkshire, with the home games played at Leigh, Wigan or Widnes, and away games at Wakefield, Hull or Leeds.

Haydn took Orrell St James on a tour of Australia along with some guest players from Leigh, and it was an eye-opening experience. We were away for six weeks and stayed in digs, only coming together for training. I loved the challenge of taking on the Aussies. We played a district side in Townsville on the Queensland coast. It was a ferocious game as they were a year ahead of us, but despite their physical edge and the heat and humidity, we won the match with a try in the final minute.

When I was fourteen, I was picked for the England Under-16s schools side to play against France in Paris. When you played for England Schools, all the scouts would be there, from every club. It was what I had been working towards since I first broke into Haydn's team.

It was the first time I can honestly say that I felt a sense of trepidation taking the field. Playing for the England Schools side had felt like a distant dream, and getting called up two years early left me wondering if I was ready for it. They matured early, the French, and some of their players had full-on beards, prompting suspicions that they were more like Under-18s. That was no use to us. I might have been scared but I drew confidence from the fact that in our pack we had some mature boys who were also big strong lads.

I played at centre on my debut and knew that I had a forward pack that would back me up. It made me feel bulletproof, at least fleetingly. I was out of my comfort zone, way out of it, and I knew this was one of those moments that could make or break me.

We had a brilliant coach called Dennis McHugh, who was a hard taskmaster but knew how to get the best out of us.

'We have got something for you,' he said. 'It is a drink with a secret ingredient that is going to make you play really well.'

I was intrigued. I took a sip but almost spat it out. The taste was putrid, but I drank it anyway, hoping in my innocence that it would work its magic. It turned out I had just drunk my first coffee. A double espresso, in fact. It may not have gone down well, but I was happy with my performance. From that moment on, before every game throughout my career, I would drink a double espresso.

* * *

People think of rugby league as a professional sport that broke away from rugby union, which remained amateur. But for most of its history rugby league was not what we would recognize today as a professional sport. Match fees were paid only to the top players at the top clubs to compensate for the work they missed. It did not become a full-time professional sport in England until the 1990s, when the Super League was established.

There was a distinction between 'professional' clubs, like Wigan, and 'amateur' clubs, like Orrell St James. The scouts who were coming to watch me were from the professional clubs. Officially you had to wait until your sixteenth birthday to sign for a club. But it was possible to make a 'pre-contract' deal at a younger age, and when I was fourteen, my parents decided that was the right thing to do. They felt that attaching me to a professional club would take the pressure off me and let me get on with playing.

If it had been left to me I would have signed for Wigan straight away, but Dad did a good job in talking to everyone. Salford made a strong bid for me. Iain McCorquodale, who in addition to his Lancashire role was also assistant coach at Salford, invited me down to the club.

Dad, who went on to become a scout for Wigan, St Helens, Leeds and Warrington, did a great job by making out that signing for Wigan wasn't the be-all and end-all for me, even though it was. Back in the late eighties, some of the figures that were being paid to the top players were astronomical, so clubs were looking to sign juniors, as a cheaper investment in the future.

'Dad, when are you going to let me sign?' I asked him.

'When they pay you what you are worth,' he replied.

He held his nerve, and we were extremely happy with what we got in the end. We signed a contract on 19 January 1990. I received a lump-sum payment of £25,000, which was a massive amount of money for a fourteen-year-old kid from Wigan. My parents wisely put it straight into an investment for me, having taken advice from a financial advisor. In the end, four of us from the Orrell St James side signed pre-contract agreements.

When I turned sixteen, I was invited into the Wigan boardroom to sign the proper contract. The boardroom was a sacred place in those days. The board ran the club back then, not the head coach. I wore a Benetton T-shirt, and a photo of me and my Orrell St James teammate Paul Stevens was published in the *Lancashire Evening Post*.

The report said, 'Farrell is a 6ft 2ins 14 stone second row or loose forward and he has scored 168 tries in 172 appearances for St James and he has been described as the most explosive young talent since Shaun Edwards. His physique and fitness are astonishing for a 16-year-old – what a prospect alongside or behind Denis Betts and Andy Platt in the pack! He has won every junior representative honour available and is the current captain of Wigan Under-16s town team.'

Dad made sure I couldn't touch the money for a number of years, but I managed to buy Colleen some roses to celebrate.

My biggest fear was always of not meeting people's expectations of me. The word had already been out for a while that I had been offered a big signing-on fee by Wigan. But I had seen other outstanding young players fall by the wayside because of a lack of commitment or dedication. I knew I had everything to prove. I couldn't wait to get started.

3. The Debut

Ellery Hanley was my childhood idol. He had signed for Wigan from Bradford Northern for a record transfer fee of £150,000 in 1985 and finished his career as a club legend. He captained Great Britain and won everything he could with Wigan, including four Challenge Cup winner's medals and a World Club Challenge winner's medal. I kept all sorts of videos of him scoring tries or of the work that he did during games.

Ellery would have been twenty-nine when I turned up for my first training session with Wigan as a fourteen-year-old. All I could do was pinch myself. I quickly discovered that he set the standards. He didn't drink or smoke and was incredibly disciplined.

It is one of my regrets that I never got to play in the same team as Ellery, as he left the club to sign for Leeds not long after I joined. But training with him was a huge honour for me and it left a lasting mark. I got to see exactly how someone becomes the best player in the world. It is not just because of talent; it's also about preparation, commitment and dedication. I saw several talented players in my peer group fall by the wayside, some because they thought they had already made it, others because they didn't want it enough. Training with Ellery was a window to the world of excellence, even if only for a few months.

Maurice Lindsay, the chairman, told me when I signed for the club that Ellery trained on Christmas Day to gain an edge on his rivals. No one else would be training then, Ellery reckoned. That was good enough for me. From then on, I would train every Christmas Day too. When I speak to players about training now as a coach, I often ask them what they are doing extra that no one else is doing. The answer tells me all I need to know about them. It is what the best players have always done.

Before pre-season training started, players got a four- or five-week break. But I would have no break. I was always desperate to put extra work in, not to try to outdo anyone but just to show my teammates that I was committed. The competition was fierce.

It was no hardship because I loved rugby so much. It never felt like work to me as a player. It still doesn't now that I am coaching. I loved training two or three times a day. People think it is a cliché, but I know it is true, because I played with players who hated it. They only played rugby because they were good at it. Some probably resented the amount of time and work it took to play at the top level.

I was fortunate in that, for me, it was a dream to get up and train. Even now I like to try to squeeze in half an hour of gym work most days because I like how it makes me feel. I never saw hard physical work, or working on the technical details of the game, as a burden. I couldn't pull a rabbit out of the hat with individual brilliance the way someone like Jason Robinson could. I had to immerse myself in every part of the game and understand the workings of it, and make sure I was fit enough and strong enough to deliver what was expected of me.

My relentless approach would eventually catch up with me: my rugby union career finished at thirty-three not because of my age but because of what I had put my body through.

It was then that I regretted not taking more time off to give my body a chance to recover. But I didn't because I loved it at the time.

Somewhere in there was a fear of failure, too. Big time. I felt it first when I played for Wigan Under-11s. You might think it was only junior rugby, so not a big deal, but to me it was the only thing that mattered, and I carried a fear that everything could be taken away from me. What would I do if I was dropped? I tried to protect myself psychologically by assuming the worst: telling myself that I would be dropped, or, when I became captain, that I was going to lose it to someone else at the start of the following season. Every year I said as much to Colleen. My glass was always half empty. She would tell me I was being stupid, but it was my way of making sure that I stayed hungry.

Even after Ellery left, I was desperate to earn his respect. Later, when I played against him, I decided that if I got the ball, I would deliberately veer off in attack to make sure that I could run at him just so that he could tackle me. I thought I might start to earn respect from both him and my team. Respect from your peers was the only currency that mattered. It was a principle that would stay with me throughout my career.

When I first played against Jonathan Davies when he was at Warrington, I ran at him all afternoon. Towards the end of the game he turned to me and shouted, 'Hey kid, would you fuck off and hit somebody else?' I loved the comment because I had only run at him because he was a magical player, a man I had huge respect for. And I had caught his attention.

* * *

As there were no academies in those days, anyone who was on the books – around forty or fifty of us – trained with the first team. It was sink or swim.

The most obvious thing for a child entering this hard-man's world was the physicality. There is a major step-up in intensity from junior to adult football, too, but rugby is on a different level. At fourteen, I may have been a big lad for my age at six foot two and over fourteen stone, but I am not ashamed to say that at times I found those early sessions scary. The intensity was like nothing I had ever even imagined. I can only guess how my parents felt.

The likes of Andy Gregory, a born-and-bred Wiganer who had done it all in the game, would call anyone out who was even a few inches out of position. It was tough love, all right, but I didn't mind getting stuck in when things boiled over at times.

What I soon learned was that the quickest way to earn the respect I craved was to bring maximum physicality to the basics of the game. It has been known for a player to make sixty tackles in a rugby league game. It sounds like a remarkable feat, given that the record total in rugby union Test matches is thirty-eight. But I would ask: why are the opposition allowing you to make sixty tackles? Is it because they're not too bothered by them?

I would prefer to have a solid twenty-five tackles, all of them hard: that would probably save you making another thirty-odd because of the impact you had made. That is the mentality I learned from those very early sessions at Wigan. Make everything count. Do the unseen work that only your peers will appreciate. Make a line-break when the game is in the balance; don't worry about scoring tries once the game is won.

John Monie, our head coach, used to say that there were

twenty ways to tackle someone, so just make it happen. Bring them down. Any way you could, it didn't matter how. Get it done. I loved the challenge of trying to get it done.

* * *

By the time I started training with Wigan, I had switched from prop to loose forward. In rugby league, the loose forward wears the No. 13 shirt, but the closest equivalent in rugby union is No. 8. Some sides choose to effectively play a grafting forward, but more often it is an additional playmaker who can also perform forward duties. It is the position that best suited my skillset and athletic capabilities.

It takes a mix of talents to put together a rugby league team. You need players who can carry the ball hard to the defensive line, ball players at the line, players who score tries and players who set up tries. You need some players with a high work rate and others who have the ability to beat people two or three times a game and finish tries. I loved loose forward because it required a little bit of everything.

I was not quick or explosive enough to play in the backs, but as a forward I had a bit of subtlety about how I played rather than just crashing the ball up all the time. Later in my career I played some games at stand-off, even for Great Britain, not because of my flair but because I knew how to organize and navigate a game plan. To a rugby union fan, it might be strange to imagine a No. 8 switching to fly-half, but it is not that big a leap because of the number of touches rugby league players get in a game and in training.

As a fourteen-year-old my focus was straightforward: how to survive the Tuesday and Thursday night training sessions at Wigan, when the first team and the A team would all train together, along with a handful of fifteen- and sixteen-year-olds who had also been signed but were not part of the A-team squad. I was the youngest there. It was mad. You can only imagine how much I was shitting myself being out there with that lot. The physicality was eye-opening. I immediately got an insight into why Wigan were so successful. From the outside, people assumed it was because we had the finances to sign up the big stars, but it was so much more than that. The competition within the first-team squad was fierce. Nothing came easy to these guys. I saw up close what it would take to be a professional, and their ferocious work ethic behind the scenes soon made me realize that their success was no accident.

Despite the harshness of the regime, I always felt part of things, even as a kid. It was pretty special that senior players with heaps of international caps were happy to include me. It made me feel bulletproof when I went back to play for the age-group sides. It was just as well because, when word got out that I had signed forms with Wigan, it didn't always go down too well.

It was dog eat dog. There were plenty of lads keen to have a pop at me when I was playing for Orrell St James, and it was the same for others who were linked with professional clubs. Once, when I was playing for Orrell St James Under-15s, my mum came onto the pitch with her umbrella when I was involved in a brawl, shouting 'Get off him!' and giving the opposition players a whack. That was as embarrassing as it could get. Still, you can't stop mothers sometimes, can you?

I was full of testosterone, and I simply loved the combative nature of the sport. I had grown up watching an amateur rugby league competition in Wigan called the Ken Gee Cup, named after the Wigan legend Ken Gee, who played for Great Britain in the 1940s and '50s. The competition was made more intense by the fact that each club was allowed to play one professional in their side. You would think any pro would be crazy to go from playing for Wigan, Widnes or Warrington to playing in the Ken Gee Cup because the games were pure thuggery. Brutal. This was an opportunity for the amateur player to have a go at the professionals. Colleen's dad used to love playing in it, and as a boy I loved watching those games. They shaped my attitude.

There had been some concern about how signing for Wigan would affect my school work, but I wasn't too bothered. Rugby wasn't a big deal at my secondary school, Hawkley Hall High School. Jeff Clare, who had played for Wigan and been a discus thrower for the Great Britain team, did join our school from Colleen's school, St Peter's Catholic High School, which at the time was seen as a big transfer. But my development came in the evenings and weekends at the club. I knew what I wanted to do. I enjoyed my time at school, but my goal was making the Wigan first team. The rest would look after itself.

* * *

Looking back, I can't believe how fortunate I was to have so many good people helping me to develop and reach my potential. From almost my first day, Bob Lanigan, the club's Australian strength-and-conditioning coach, took me under his wing. He was happy to spend hours with me during one-on-one sessions.

Every morning I got up at the crack of dawn to do a training session with Frano Botica and Sam Panapa from the first team. Dean Bell and Andy Platt would be in the gym too. Sometimes Frano and Sam would pick me up if I needed a lift. As I got home in the afternoon, I would go out to train again. I couldn't believe it. I would have paid to go training with those guys.

Colleen's dad was brilliant too. He told me that I needed to put on weight if I was going to play in the forwards. Between the ages of eleven and thirteen, I had slimmed down after a growth spurt that took me over six feet. I was now doing proper weights, but Keiron told me that no matter how much strength work I was doing, I needed to bulk out if I was going to manage myself in the men's game. 'It doesn't matter how strong you think you are; you need weight on you, Andrew,' he said.

I remember when the late Va'aiga Tuigamala, the former All Blacks winger, joined the club. He was a bull of a man, weighing almost eighteen stone. Yet he had hardly done any weights before joining Wigan. I remember him trying to do the bench-press, and he was wobbling all over the place. But when he got onto the pitch, he would throw me around like a rag doll.

Keiron was right. If I wanted to play in the forwards, I needed weight to survive. We had a plan to put on a couple of stones in weight in my teenage years to enable me to absorb the pressure, and I could lose it when I was older and had a man's strength and the know-how to navigate the professional game. If you look at the photographs of me in my mid-teens, you can see I am carrying extra pounds.

The club's approach to nutrition was changing. One day a dietician came into the club to talk to us about it. She got to the point pretty quickly. 'Can anyone honestly say here that they eat purely for rugby purposes?' she asked the room. Most faces looked to the floor. Only about three lads put their hands up. Phil Clarke was one. He was way ahead of his time. He understood what it took and where he wanted to go and how to get there. The fact that most of the squad had not put their hands up was telling.

The days when you were told to have a steak the night before a game were coming to an end. Now all the talk was about 'carb loading', with spaghetti bolognese replacing steak and chips.

There was a pecking order, and I used to see it as a responsibility to play my part in it. There were the senior players – Shaun Edwards, Dean Bell, Andy Platt and Andy Goodway – and I could see the impact they were having on the generation below them, the likes of Phil Clarke and Denis Betts. What was cool about it was that Phil and Denis would then pass down those benefits to the likes of me, Mick Cassidy, Jason Robinson and Barrie-Jon Mather. I understood it would be my responsibility to pass them down the ladder as well. Phil and Denis remain good mates of mine to this day because of all the hard graft we went through together. For now, my aim was to challenge the nineteen- and twenty-year-olds who had been in the system for a couple of years. They were my first target.

I was signed for Wigan not just as a loose forward, but as a loose forward who could kick. In rugby league there was never an assumption that the stand-off, the No. 6, would be the goal-kicker. It was done by whoever was best at it, and I think rugby union should be more open-minded about this.

Frano had joined Central Park in 1990 after switching codes from rugby union. He had played for the All Blacks seven times, and would have had many more caps if he had not spent most of his international career behind the legendary Grant Fox. Fox was a kicking fly-half, whereas Frano had been seen in union as more of a running and creative player, but the irony was that it was his kicking ability that set him apart. Frano was the best kicker I have ever seen in either code. He had clearly learned a lot from Fox. I latched onto him straight away and loved working with him.

Frano would come to training at 6 a.m. and stay on afterwards to practise his kicking. He was phenomenal. He could kick touchline conversions with his eyes closed, because he did so many times in practice. I lapped it all up. He taught me more of an advanced kicking technique. When I first started kicking, I would have dug twice into the ground to try to get the turf to come up a bit to place the ball on. Frano was already ahead of everyone else by using a mound of sand and angling the ball forward: this makes it easier to find the 'sweet spot' in the ball.

Outside of club training, I spent hours at the Little Lane playing fields, about a mile from my house, practising my kicking. It comprised four or five football pitches and became a sporting playground for me. The football goals had to do for my kicking: I would kick the ball over the top of them. I would pick a small target at the back of the stand to aim at, so that the posts became irrelevant. It is the same in golf. If you aim at a branch in the distance when you hit your drive, and miss it by five metres, you still land in the middle of the fairway. That was my logic, anyway.

* * *

John Monie's philosophy was always to rotate one or two youngsters into a good team because he knew they would get looked after, rather than throwing a lot of youngsters in together because you want to give everyone else a rest. That could damage young players. Wigan could tolerate a sixteen-year-old coming into the team because of the strength that was placed around that sixteen-year-old. It is a philosophy that I have taken with me now that I am a head coach.

Part of the process of preparing me to play for the first team involved making my debut for the A team. Back then the A-team league was a very tough competition, and a lot of sides featured experienced players. At times I thought I was sinking, dark moments when self-doubt dominated my thoughts. I was terrified of letting everyone down. But my overriding feeling was that I had to take my opportunity and push on. Graeme West, the former club captain whose summer camp was where my rugby career had begun, was now the A-team coach, and played for them well into his forties just to look after everyone. He was the toughest player I had seen, and that toughness shone through in how he looked after the youngsters on the field, acting as our father figure when it all kicked off.

My A-team debut came against Castleford at home. I am sure my mum and dad must have been terrified.

Self-doubt gnawed at me on the journey to the stadium. When I got there, I went straight across to Bob Lanigan, who had put so much time into me. I trusted his opinion.

'Are you sure I am ready for this?' I asked him.

'One hundred per cent, Andy,' he replied.

What else could I do but take that faith he had shown in me and get on with it? There was no other way. If Bob and John Monie and Graeme West thought I was ready, then who was I to disagree? We won the game 28–2, our opening game of the Alliance League, and I was name-checked in a report of the game in the *Lancashire Evening Post*.

When I came off the pitch I told Dad that I had never played in a game before with such pace. I was still sweating hours after the final whistle.

I was picked for another A-team game against Warrington at their old Wilderspool stadium, which was nicknamed

'The Zoo'. Their A team was stacked with players who were not quite good enough to make their first team but would have been good enough at most other clubs. And as my name had been in the papers, I was expecting a warm welcome.

A couple of their players – Paul Cullen, who was one of the nicest blokes you could meet except on the rugby pitch, and Paul Darbyshire, who went on to coach at Munster and tragically died at the age of forty-one from motor neurone disease – battered the hell out of me. But worse was to come when a skirmish broke out at the corner of the pitch where my mum and dad were watching.

I found myself at the bottom of a pile of players. Graeme West was trying to pull everyone off me, grabbing them by the neck and thumping them. It was the normal sort of skirmish that tended to happen every second week in the amateur game.

I had a lot of that when I first signed. Harvey Howard was an ex-rugby union player who had joined Widnes from Waterloo. I can remember one game when he kept shouting at me to run at him. I should have just ignored him, but that's exactly what I did. I ran all day at him.

Anyone picked for the Wigan A team was deemed in contention to make the senior side that weekend, so the competition was fierce. The subs for the first team were not picked until the second team had played on a Friday night, so some players would be doubling up over the weekend.

Years later, when I was coaching with the Lions or Ireland on tour, there would be the issue of managing midweek fixtures. For example, when Ireland went to New Zealand on tour in the summer of 2022, we had midweek fixtures against the Māori All Blacks, trained the next day and then played a few days later against the All Blacks. That was seen as a big deal.

Yet at Wigan, if you played well enough for the A team on a Friday night, you were picked in the squad for the first-team match on the Saturday or Sunday. At Wigan we would often be on the hunt for five trophies at the business end of the season, which could mean playing seven games in twenty-eight days. That might sound ridiculous now. But it depends where you put your mind. Whatever you have to do becomes the norm, and it was the norm for us.

* * *

Playing for the second team helped boost my finances. After each match we would get a brown envelope containing £100 cash. For a teenager it was massive money in those days. I still couldn't believe I was being paid to do something that I loved and would have done for nothing.

Now that I was part of the second team, it was compulsory to go out on Friday night after the game to the Riverside club in town, made famous by the entertainer and singer John Martin, who went on to become a director at Wigan. It was the place to go.

I might have only been sixteen, but I was playing against men, so I guess it was OK for me to go too. I loved being part of it, but I never let the social side of things get in the way of training. I saw some lads fall by the wayside because they thought they had made it, and the social side became too big for them.

It was not like there would have been any extra attention for me. In Wigan, everyone knows everyone, so it was never a problem for me. You wouldn't be bothered. It is another trait that stayed with me. Some players I know would use a different name when booking a restaurant, but I have never understood that. Whether living in Wigan then, or now in Sandymount in Dublin, I have always wanted to get out there and be part of the community. In Dublin people see the Farrells as part of the furniture, like everyone else. And if you are involved in the local community, people tend to give you the space to be yourself.

* * *

John Monie learned his trade in Australia as the assistant to the legendary Parramatta Eels head coach Jack Gibson, whose nickname was simply 'Supercoach'. He had won Australian Rugby League (ARL) Premierships before he joined Wigan a couple of years earlier and it was regarded as a massive signing for us. It was his predecessor Graham Lowe, a New Zealander, who had first pulled Wigan out of the doldrums in the mid-1980s, but Monie had driven it on. He had given the club a great structure and was intent on bringing through a core group of young players including Jason Robinson and Mick Cassidy.

But it was a tough environment too. John was brilliant, but also absolutely ruthless. He kept tight control over the superstars at the club. They could have run riot under a weaker coach, but not under John. He had seen it all at Parramatta. He knew how to manage the personalities and egos. He humbled them all and made them hungry. The senior players might have seen it differently, but I didn't feel the squad were like a family or a band of brothers. There was a lot of infighting to be top dog.

John created an environment where everyone wanted to earn everyone else's respect, whether they liked them or not. It was an attitude that fired up the young players like me too. His main weapon was the post-match reviews on Monday mornings. They were brutal. Nothing was held back. Any player who got a few things wrong in a game would be shitting himself all day Sunday.

One Monday morning, Steve Hampson, our full-back who had played for Great Britain and was a big personality in the squad, came bouncing into the review after scoring a hat-trick of tries in the game.

'He's not going to get me today,' he said on the way in, only to find that the whole review was based around his performance and how poor he had been.

It left me thinking that if John Monie could lay into Steve Hampson after he'd scored a hat-trick, what could he do to me? I was in no doubt about what was at stake when John handed me my senior debut less than six months after my sixteenth birthday.

The Regal Trophy match against Keighley on Sunday, 24 November 1991, was a game we were expected to win comfortably. The Regal Trophy was not as prestigious as the Challenge Cup, which we had held since 1988, and in a hectic season the match represented an opportunity for John to rotate his squad and rest some of his big-name players. I was not stupid. I knew that was why he had included me on the bench for the game.

Even so, the team sheet still included legends such as Andy Gregory, Joe Lydon, Shaun Edwards, Dean Bell and Andy Platt. The journey from my house up the Warrington Road to Central Park felt longer than usual. I had to get a lift because I was not old enough to drive. A few weeks earlier I had been named player of the month for the A team, which had earned me a cheque for £100, but I couldn't help asking myself on the journey if I was ready for the first team. Two days earlier I had been playing for the A team in Halifax and John had only told me about my selection for the first-team squad the following morning. But the reassuring message from John, Graeme and Bob was unanimous. Be yourself, Andy. It is something I use now, years later, as Ireland head coach. When I sense that players are anxious, I tell them that all I want them to be is themselves. That is what has got them here. Be the best version of yourself.

It was a concept that was challenged as I stood in the tunnel at Central Park, waiting to run onto the pitch as an early sub against Keighley.

Steve Hampson warned me that Andy Gregory was going to be all over me when I came on. 'Andy is going to give you a right bollocking today,' said Hampo. 'But don't worry about it, he does it to everyone.'

And he did. At least I had been given a heads-up. Gregory was one of the best scrum-halves ever to have played. He barked at me all through the game, But, as Steve had said he would, he also gave everyone else a bollocking. It didn't matter if you were sixteen or thirty-six. And ultimately, I *had* been ready, thanks to the environment at Wigan, even if I also had so much still to learn.

Looking back, it seems ridiculous that I played first-team rugby at sixteen. I look at my son Gabriel playing a year ahead for his school in Dublin and see how strict things are in terms of player safety. It was a different world back then.

I can honestly say, though, that I was never pushed into something I didn't want to do. I always felt that I was being looked after and that everything was done in the right manner. I loved the physical challenge. It was all that I knew.

When people ask me how I coped with playing for Wigan so young, I tell them that I had nothing to compare it with. I reckon playing for England Schools Under-16s as a fourteen-year-old was as tough as playing for the Wigan A team against men for the first time. Those two experiences helped prepare me for the experience of first-team rugby.

Was I good enough? Would I let anyone down? The game was going to be on TV, so there was nowhere to hide. Everyone was going to have an opinion. Dealing with all that was as daunting as the physical challenge. If I seemed confident, it was only because I didn't know any better. But you only get to that stage if someone thinks you are good enough.

The speed of the game was incredibly challenging. So too the strength and skill level of the players. First-team rugby was a very big step up. It was the step I was hoping it would be, even though I didn't know exactly what that step entailed. I always think people wrongly set their own limits. If a game of rugby is played at what you think is the highest level, and you put a marker down at that level, then you are going to get stuck. There will always be a game that is tougher.

And I just loved the challenge. I loved pushing myself harder in training and meeting the physical demands head-on. At one stage Wigan were looking at signing Australian or New Zealand loose forwards and my dad asked what I thought of moving to prop. I said to him, 'Dad, how do you fancy going and working down the pit? If I can't make my way through and prove that I am better than them, I might as well pack it in now.'

The game itself flashed by. I came on for Mike Forshaw – who became a great friend of mine and is now coaching in rugby union – and played for around sixty minutes. Naivety, adrenaline and fear were enough to allow me to keep pace with the game.

I was asked about my performance by a local reporter after the game. 'Not bad!' I said. 'I thought I played all right and was trying hard. I suppose I did some good things, but

I thought I could have done better. It was a big experience for me, and I enjoyed it, but to be honest I never noticed the crowd.'

I held my own and finished the game with a burning desire to stay at this level. It meant that when I went back to the A team, I could draw on the experience of playing at a higher level.

Later in the season I got another great boost to my confidence when I came on as a sub in the final league game of the season, against Warrington. With the experience of another big game under my belt, I headed into the off-season with extra determination to target a first-team place during my summer preparations.

But it was not just about my personal ambition any more. I had new responsibilities off the pitch now too, which sharpened my focus. I was playing for my own family now.

4. The Father

Colleen had just rung from a phone box in Wigan town centre. She was laughing, even though it felt like both our worlds had just ended.

'Why are you laughing?' I asked her. 'It's not funny.'

But Colleen wasn't laughing because it was funny. It was a nervous reaction. She, like me, was terrified. Colleen was pregnant.

We were far too young to deal with this. Trying to break into the Wigan squad was one thing, but this was something completely different.

The pregnancy test had confirmed our worst fears. Colleen had been late, and we had been trying to figure it out and work out dates. I was on the phone to Colleen when I called out to my mum to ask her how many weeks it had been since they had gone for a night out in town. They didn't do that very often. Colleen was worried that the question would make my mother suspicious.

One day after school she decided to go to the chemist with her friend Charlotte to take a pregnancy test. When the test was positive, the pharmacist urged her to go to the maternity clinic. She rang me instead. I wasn't any help. I think all I managed to say was, 'What are we going to do?' She took the bus home with Charlotte and said nothing to anyone else. Neither did I. The only thing Colleen was sure about was that she couldn't tell her parents. I didn't blame her. I was terrified of her telling them. I was terrified of telling mine too.

For a while we both stuck our heads in the clouds and pretended nothing had changed. I got on with my training. Colleen was a fantastic athlete and even more competitive than me. She loved her team sports, netball and hockey, but excelled at running. She ran for Wigan Harriers and was up at the track every night. Her strength was middle-distance running: 800 metres and 1,500 metres. One day someone pulled out of the 200 metres, and she was invited to join the sprinters' group. Everyone wanted to sprint, but you had to be invited. She was that good.

We couldn't avoid the reality of the new situation for very long. Everything went through our heads. Should we get an abortion? Should we run off together? We were so young we didn't know what we were thinking. We were meant to be studying for our GCSE exams, while I was also edging towards making my senior debut for Wigan. How were we meant to cope with this? It was some secret to carry.

Eventually we worked up the courage to go to the maternity unit at Billinge Hospital. I sat outside as Colleen went in to speak to the health visitor. She asked Colleen if she was going to tell her mum and dad. Colleen said she couldn't. The health visitor advised her to have a think about things. She wrote 'no home correspondence' on her notes, and asked Colleen to come back and see her.

Colleen and I were at my house a few weeks later when the phone rang. It was Colleen's dad. 'He wants to speak to you,' I said and passed her the phone. Moments later, her face dropped. She kept asking, 'Why, Dad?' When the conversation finished, she turned to me. 'Dad wants me to come home, immediately,' she said. 'But he wouldn't say why.' We both knew something was up, so I decided to go with Colleen for support.

We caught two buses to get to her house on the other side

of town. Her mum was standing at the front door, waving a letter. On the front of it was a stamp with a stork and the words 'Billinge Maternity Unit'.

'Colleen, are you pregnant?' she asked.

'No, I'm not,' Colleen replied.

'Colleen, I am going to ask you one more time. Are you pregnant?'

'No.'

'Well, what's this then?' she asked, holding up the letter.

'It is my friend Anna, she has used my name,' Colleen replied.

'Colleen, I am going to ask you one more time . . .'

With that, Colleen burst into tears. She couldn't take it any more. I had one foot inside the door and didn't know what to do. Maybe I should just leave?

Then Keiron boomed at me, 'Andrew, get inside now.'

I was not going to argue.

* * *

It was an awful day. Colleen tried to defend me, saying that I didn't know she was pregnant. It was typical of her. Emotions understandably ran high, but at least our secret was finally out. It was such a relief that we didn't have to cope with the burden of it all on our own.

It was remarkable how quickly her parents' reaction turned from shock and anger to support. I look back now, as a parent, and understand what they must have been feeling. Their disappointment and worry must have been terrible. Keiron had been brilliant at helping me with my rugby development. Now his daughter was pregnant. We had been so naive. Years later, as parents, Colleen and I both made sure we were very open with our kids about taking precautions.

In the living room of the house where just a couple of years earlier I had been so excited to see Keiron's framed 1984 Wembley shirt, Colleen's parents went into crisis management mode, drawing up an action plan. Keiron had given up tea for Lent, but the shock broke his resolve. He went into the kitchen to brew himself a cup. I was surprised he didn't pour himself something stronger.

'Right, the first thing you need to do is get back on the bus and go and tell Andrew's mum and dad,' he said.

Instead of going straight back to my house, we first stopped off in the town centre to see Cath, who was working at a library at the time. After telling her the news, I asked if she would come with us for support. My mum was still at work when we got home but my dad was there. We walked in with our heads down.

'Andrew and Colleen have got something to tell you,' my sister said to him.

'What's that,' asked my dad.

'Colleen's pregnant.'

'Oh,' he replied. He seemed to be struggling to take it all in, and didn't say much more.

But it was a different story when my mum got back. She had been working in a family centre at the time. She would later say that she knew what the news was just by looking at Colleen's eyes when she walked in through the door. She was furious and gave me a good slap across the head. She told me in no uncertain terms that there had been 'no need for it in this day and age' and that we should have used contraception. But once everyone calmed down, Mum and Dad too became incredibly supportive.

Colleen's dad made her go to see his parents and let them know. Her grandad Joe was fine and gave her a hug. Sadly, he did not live to see the baby arrive. But Colleen's nan,

Annie, took to her bed to cry when she heard our news. She blamed Colleen's dad for letting us see too much of each other. Colleen's grandparents on her mum's side took it well.

Colleen later wondered if the hospital had sent the letter deliberately so that her parents would find out. In the end, though, it was for the best. Remarkably, years later during a game at Twickenham, the same health visitor recognized Colleen and came over to say hello in very different circumstances. It really is a small world.

Before the pregnancy, we had had a plan to go to Leeds University to train as physical education teachers in case my rugby career didn't work out. Now we had to reassess everything. Colleen had wanted to keep going with all her sporting activities, but her school, in consultation with her doctor, said that, while she could still play netball, she had to stop hockey and athletics.

When I turned sixteen, I left school and got a job as an apprentice carpenter for Wigan council. We were fortunate to know that our parents would help us look after and support our baby. Taking the job was more about keeping myself busy and doing something useful as I strove for a full-time contract with Wigan.

I loved it, spending time in the van with the lads, putting a shift in. But I was a dreadful carpenter. When I signed my first full-time rugby contract, I remember happily handing my tools over to my mates. And the prospect of a baby coming only made me more determined to succeed at Wigan.

* * *

I think Colleen's parents had been planning to add an extension anyway, but Colleen's bedroom was something of a box room and her pregnancy accelerated things. Keiron was a joiner and lots of people were able to help out with the building work.

We received our GCSE results while Colleen was still pregnant, which led to an embarrassing moment. Even late in pregnancy she didn't really show, and when she went back into school to get her results, a month before Owen was born, she was wearing a loose T-shirt. Some of the girls thought she'd had the baby already.

We hadn't been told the sex of the baby, so were discussing names for both boys and girls. For a boy, Colleen's mum suggested William, after her dad, and at first Colleen wanted to name the baby Andrew, after me. But we settled on Owen after Colleen had heard the name when a little boy came into the hairdresser's where she worked on Saturdays. She really liked the name, but we had to settle on the spelling. A lot of Colleen's family have Irish names and some of them wanted her to spell it 'Eoghan'. There were already names like Siobhan and Sinead in their family and one of Colleen's brothers is called Sean. But her mum, who is not from the Irish side of the family, insisted on the English version.

'For goodness' sake, Colleen, just make it simple for him while he is at school and don't spell it the Irish way,' she said. So, Owen it was.

At one stage it looked like my debut for the Wigan second team would clash with Colleen's due date. By the time she was five days overdue, her family were starting to get concerned. Her mum, who was a district nurse, kept popping in to see if she was OK and telling her that if she felt anything she must ring her. It was when Colleen's auntie Marie called in with a cake that she first started feeling some twinges. When Colleen couldn't eat the cake because she was feeling sick, Marie rang Colleen's mum. Soon her other auntie,

Aileen, arrived, and they went to the hospital together. I arrived soon after.

Colleen's mum didn't want to be in the room with her when she went into labour, so Aileen stayed with Colleen and me for the birth. Meanwhile, the room outside was quickly filling up. My mum and dad, sister and brothers, and Colleen's dad and brothers turned up, so there was quite a crowd to see Owen enter the world. There had been a slight scare during the birth as his umbilical cord got caught around his neck and his heart rate started to drop, so they'd had to speed up the delivery. After he was born, they took him away to help him with his breathing and clear his airways. But thankfully he was fine.

The date was 24 September 1991. I had become a father, even though I was still a boy myself.

When Colleen had gone into labour, I hadn't known what to do with myself. I wasn't used to holding a baby – probably no sixteen-year-old boy is. But the amazing thing was that as soon as he was born, the first time I held him, it felt entirely natural. I was instantly obsessed with my son. They both had to stay in hospital for five more days and I was up every day to see them.

When Colleen returned to her parents' house, I often spent the night there, though I wasn't allowed to sleep in the same room as her and the baby.

I had to learn fatherhood pretty quickly. Colleen's family was much bigger than mine and with her family it felt like there was always a baby around. It was different for me. But I loved it.

It was a tough time for Colleen. Owen was a terrible sleeper from the start – in fact he didn't sleep through until he was five! One night, Colleen was so desperate she went to her mum and dad's bedroom in floods of tears because she couldn't settle him down. Her dad said to bring him up, but her mum said no, that Colleen had to learn, and went with her to get him off to sleep.

I was not much use at nights. As I had to get up early for training, I rarely helped her with him. It was an old-fashioned approach. A few times when Colleen was really exhausted we would swap places; she would come up and sleep in her brother's room and I would go downstairs with Owen. But Colleen will tell you she could count the number of times that happened on one hand.

Despite my inexperience, I had no trouble looking after Owen during the day. I didn't mind changing nappies and feeding him with a bottle. I used to hate it when I came over to Colleen's after training and Owen wasn't there. Colleen's aunties would sometimes take him for a walk to let her sleep and I would go mad as I just wanted to see him.

I bought myself a second-hand Honda 50 motorbike so I could get to see Colleen and Owen more easily from work and training. I had to bump-start it down the road every time, but at least I was mobile. Colleen's parents were out at work all day, so I'd turn up at her house on the bike. It was while I was doing the apprenticeship, which was supposed to involve going to college for several hours a week. Sod that! I wanted to see Colleen and my son.

After work I would always ride over to Colleen's house to give Owen a cuddle before going off to training in the evenings. And I would pop in again on my way home if I wasn't staying at hers, to say goodnight. When I went full-time with Wigan, it made it easier to see more of Owen because we were training during the day.

As we were not married at the time, Colleen's mum asked

her what surname we were going to give Owen. Understandably, there was concern from her family about what would happen if we didn't stay together. Colleen suggested a compromise: we would name him Owen O'Loughlin for now, but 'If we get married, I'll let him be a Farrell,' she said with a smile.

As if to soften the blow, she said we would give him the middle name Andrew. Fair enough. And so, on the original birth certificate, his name was registered Owen Andrew O'Loughlin. And my occupation? Apprentice joiner. God help us all! It was just as well my rugby was going well as I am not sure too many people would have wanted me doing their joinery.

With Owen to support now, I was even more determined to break into the Wigan senior squad. But Colleen sacrificed a lot. She took a year out, then sat her A levels at Wigan Tech before studying to become a fitness trainer.

She lost a lot of her school friends in the process. I guess they didn't really know what to say to her now that she had a baby to look after, and soon they would be going off to university anyway. Years later one of her old friends, who ended up living in Berkhamsted in Hertfordshire, reached out to Colleen and they met up when we were living nearby in Harpenden. It was a nice touch, but it was also a reminder to her of the friendships that were lost at the time. Colleen had to put up with the judgemental attitudes of strangers too. It was tough for her as such a young mum to walk into places for the first time, and things were said to her that were out of order.

With the support of our families, we got on with our new life as best we could. Our parents would look after Owen so we could go out after a game, or when I travelled with

Wigan. Of course, it was a different life from that of most sixteen- or seventeen-year-olds, but the magnificent support from our parents enabled us to still be teenagers. As Owen became a toddler and developed into a real character, I spent more and more time with him at Colleen's. By that point I was living there almost full-time, but would still bring my washing home to my mum.

Every Saturday we visited my mum and dad. Ever since I had started playing rugby on Sundays, Mum had been making her Sunday lunch on Saturdays and invited her parents, Annie and George, over too. It became something of a tradition, and we went without fail. After Owen was born, we brought him along too. The grandparents loved it. Colleen also loved helping my sister Cath get ready to go out on a Saturday night. We never really went out on Saturdays because I was often playing on a Sunday, but our parents were great at looking after Owen so that we could go to club social nights. And when Wigan's first-team games started being played on Friday nights, it meant we could go out on Saturdays too.

When Owen was around a year old, we decided to go on our first holiday together. Colleen's mum insisted that we go by ourselves, and she would look after Owen for the week. Colleen and I jumped at the offer, as we had not been away together before.

We went to Tenerife, but Colleen ended up missing Owen too much to enjoy it. Every day she would call home from a phone box and cry, saying she wanted to go back. We must have looked like a strange pair of teenagers. We had never really been out clubbing together, because of my rugby and then having Owen so young. We did like to go out, but we would go for a nice meal and a few drinks and then back to the apartment around 11 p.m. – just as everyone else was heading out! It was a long week, missing Owen.

* * *

Rugby league was also at a crossroads at this time. A power struggle between Rupert Murdoch and Kerry Packer for control of the sport and broadcasting rights in Australia drove rugby league in the UK headlong into full-time professionalism, and there was a flood of big contract offers.

Shortly after I made my Wigan senior debut, the agreement that I had signed as a fourteen-year-old was replaced by a full-time professional one. When I turned eighteen, the ARL offered me a deal to go to Canterbury or Parramatta. But we were too young to move to Australia, and it would have taken Owen away from our support network.

Instead, one day my teammate Shaun Edwards took me to Bradford to see his agent, who was a lawyer. Shaun said he was looking after me because one day I would look after him. I asked him years later what he had meant, and he said that he thought he would go on to coach Wigan while I was still playing.

Effectively there was a battle between Murdoch's Super League and Packer's ARL. Everyone knew through agents which players had been contacted. Murdoch already owned the broadcasting rights to the First Division in the UK, and he would later pay £87 million for the establishment of the Super League in the UK too. Wigan offered me a one-off payment to stay rather than move to an ARL club in Australia – a mind-blowing amount of money. The ARL were doing the same, offering one-off payments to keep players in their clubs.

The salary wasn't anything like what the seniors were getting paid, and I lost almost half of the one-off payment to tax, but it meant that Colleen and I were able to buy our first house together. Colleen at first was reluctant to leave her parents' house because of the help she had been getting there, but it helped that the house we bought was only a mile away. It was a lovely new build. As it was the showhouse of the development, it came fully fitted out and decorated, which made moving into it very easy. It cost £90,000, which was a lot of money in those days. We still drive past it every time we go back to Wigan.

Buying a house and moving in together added another layer of responsibility. When I had been living at home, all the bills had been paid. Before we moved, I sat down with Mum and Dad and tried to work out what the outgoings were going to be. Mortgage payments, utility bills, food shopping . . . Colleen and I were panicking.

'We will have no money left after we have paid for all that,' I said to my dad. 'We can't buy the house with that mortgage. If we buy the house, all my money is gone, every month.'

My dad reassured me. 'Don't worry, Andrew, you will have money left.'

My new reality focused my mind 100 per cent. I was just so lucky to have my dream job. It was not long after we had bought the house that I proposed to Colleen. We had planned to get married when we were twenty-one, but I decided to pop the question a year early. We had been together since we were fourteen, so it was hardly a surprise. I decided to keep the proposal low key, but that suited us both. Walking down an alley after a night out in Wigan, I turned to Colleen.

'Shall we get married, then?' I asked her.

'Yeah, all right,' she replied.

'Shall I go and get a ring then, soon?'

'Yeah.'

That was us. No glitz and glamour, just simple and straightforward, and we couldn't have been happier.

The hard part was finding a date for the wedding. When you are part of a squad, it is not always straightforward. It was not just a matter of finding a gap in the fixtures; there were already quite a few weddings planned that year among the Wigan squad. But finally we found a date, and it was a grand affair. Colleen's family is a big one, and we invited a lot of the Wigan players too.

We were married, in a Catholic church that was linked to Colleen's school, by an Irish canon who knew Colleen's nan and grandad well and often came to their house for tea. Her family had decided that it should be a nuptial mass. The canon didn't mention at the time that this was not normally allowed if the marriage was to a Protestant. My family were Church of England.

In our ignorance, we went ahead anyway, which was fine until the point when the canon said that anyone who wasn't a Catholic could come up to the front of the church to receive a blessing instead of communion. Well, my grandma was having none of that. She insisted on receiving communion anyway. In the commotion Colleen got the giggles, only to be told off by the canon. In the end we all burst out laughing. It was a great day.

There were more nerves at the reception afterwards, which was held at the Park Hall Hotel in Charnock Richard, a small village about eight miles north of Wigan. I don't think I have ever seen Colleen's dad so nervous. Here was a guy who had played for Wigan, Workington Town, Widnes, Salford and Leigh but he ended up crying during his speech.

Gary Connolly, my Wigan teammate, was my best man and, shall we say, I think he needed a few drinks to get through his speech. When I got up to speak, Colleen told me later I'd had an air of confidence about me and had spoken well. In truth, I had been absolutely petrified.

Once we were married, we got a new birth certificate for Owen. Both he and Colleen were Farrells now. Colleen's profession was now 'fitness instructor'. And the apprentice joiner was now a 'professional rugby league player'. That was more like it. Living the dream, and with a family all of my own.

We decided to try for another baby, and Colleen became pregnant again just before her twenty-first birthday with our first daughter, Elleshia. Gracie was born a couple of years later. I always wanted to make sure we had something to fall back on if my rugby career did not work out, so with the money I was earning from Wigan I set up two children's nurseries in the town. My mum and my sister helped us massively from the start, as they had experience in that field, and my sister Cath still runs the business for us to this day.

We also decided we wanted to get into property. Some of the senior players at the club had started buying houses and doing them up. We bought a house that needed to be renovated and we moved in six weeks before Elleshia was born. Another teammate, Terry O'Connor, and I, along with a few of the lads, also renovated a few cottages on a farm, so at least my carpentry skills were put to some use.

* * *

Owen might not have been a good sleeper, but at least attending his birth had been relatively straightforward. The same could not be said for Elleshia, Gracie, or later when we had Gabriel. There was always something going on – a tour, a press conference, a game or training session – and Colleen went past the due date for all of them.

Although Gracie was overdue, on the day Colleen was booked into Billinge Hospital she arrived earlier than expected. 'I might as well go training now,' I said to Colleen. It was a different world then. Our training facility was just round the corner and off I went. Two weeks later I went off on a six-week tour with Great Britain. I got my comeuppance when I came back from the tour. When I picked Gracie up, she bawled her head off. 'She is probably thinking to herself, *Who on earth is this guy?*' said Colleen, laughing.

Players' attitudes nowadays are very different. Some won't go on tour because a baby is due, or will miss matches after one is born. I played at a time when rugby came first, and in our family that was possible only because of Colleen's support and understanding. I guess she had grown up in that environment too.

* * *

Most players choose to have their kids near the end of their playing careers, but Owen was part of the furniture at Wigan from the age of four. He would come into the club with me, and everyone was brilliant at accepting him. There was support for Colleen from the other wives too.

Owen grew up on the touchlines, watching training and matches, and it was not long before he wanted to get involved. The players were fantastic with him. The only time his presence became a bit of an issue was during the celebrations after our Challenge Cup victory over Leeds in 1995. On the way back from London, our coach stopped just before we got back to Wigan and then everyone got onto an open-top bus for the drive into the town and to Central Park for the celebrations with the fans.

The journey took us past my mum and dad's house, and when it stopped nearby, where some fans had gathered, mum came over to the bus with Owen and passed him to me. Colleen was furious because I'd had a few beers on the way back from Wembley. I think she was petrified that I was going to drop him off the top deck. When we got to Central Park, it was like a pop concert, with a stage erected on the pitch for us to sing songs to the supporters. There was me, with a three-year-old Owen in his Wigan replica kit on my shoulders, singing my heart out. Eventually, Colleen snatched him off me.

Owen loved being at the heart of the club. I never forced him into it. He couldn't wait to come to training with me and would fetch the balls when we were doing kicking practice. Before long, he was doing the kicking himself. Every child is different. Owen made a decision to commit to the game and then off he went: it became part of his life, as it was mine. He, like me, grew up only wanting to play the game for the love of it. Not to be a big personality off the pitch or revel in the celebrity of it all. Being a character on the field and earning the respect of your peers is what mattered to us both. The apple definitely didn't fall far from the tree.

5. The Breakthrough

Making my senior debut for Wigan did nothing to alter the pecking order in the dressing room. I had learned my lesson early on. One day I found that my clothes had been thrown outside in the corridor after I had mistakenly taken the seat of one of the senior players.

The dressing room was a minefield. You could sit down and someone would say, 'Sorry, mate, that's Shaun Edwards' seat,' or, even worse, 'That's Andy Gregory's seat.' I was shitting myself, even if half the time they were only joking. After I had sat in the wrong seat four or five times, I decided it was easier just to stay in the second-team dressing room. I was still there two years after I had made my debut against Keighley, out of respect. And fear.

It was the culture at the time. The young players were unbelievably respectful of the senior pros. Sometimes I would go and sit in the kit room just to get away from the adults for a bit.

The first time one of the kit men cleaned my boots and handed me a towel, all I could think was: *Wow, this is a dream come true!* Looking back at that environment, there is much I would change – it was of its time. But I think the balance is not where it should be in today's game, either. Some young players think they have made it when they join a club's academy and are integrated into the first-team's training. They seem happy just to be rubbing shoulders with the first-team players, eating together, driving into training together. They lose a bit of that drive and ambition because they are having a great time. A bit more of the old-school approach, of earning the right to be there, would rebalance that.

I never felt comfortable. Never. I guess there must have been a moment when I was accepted as an established player, but I was never aware of it at the time. Statistically I could look back and say, well, I played thirty games for Wigan that year. Or forty games the next year. But I was always striving for the respect of my teammates, and only found peace of mind if I knew I had not rested on my laurels. If I had faith in my ability, I was always driven by the fear that everything could be taken away from me, at any time.

I was not alone. Seeing what it meant to the senior players shaped my mentality. Some guys would do 200 press-ups before a game and rip the toilet door off every time they went out on the field. Some players would be sick because of the nerves.

The standout moment for me came when I was selected in the Wigan squad for the Challenge Cup final in 1993 against Widnes at Wembley. I couldn't wait to tell my parents. Mum was working in a family centre at the time, and on my lunch break I called over to see her. She told me afterwards she could tell by my face that something had happened. 'Mum, he's put me on the bench!' I said. 'I am going to Wembley!' I was seventeen. It was only nine years since I had stood on the terraces watching Wigan beat Widnes, the day I fell in love with the game.

* * *

The only thing any of us wanted to do was play at Wembley. I think it was more iconic then. The final was always live on BBC, with the classic commentators Ray French and Eddie Waring. I always find it remarkable, now that I am living in

Ireland, the number of people who tell me about watching those finals.

It was the early days of rugby league coverage on Sky Sports in 1993, but with the final shown on BBC you knew the whole nation would be watching. In the week before the game every shop in Wigan would be covered in cherry and white, and on the day of the game itself the whole town would travel to London. If you were a burglar and you fancied making a bit more money, then all you would have to do was go to Wigan, because it was deserted. Everyone was on the way to the final.

The closest thing I've seen elsewhere was the All-Ireland hurling final in 2016, the year I moved to Ireland to start coaching with the national team. It felt like the entire counties of Kilkenny and Tipperary had emptied to be at the final. Everyone was in their county colours, and the final had the same sort of pageantry and traditions, such as walking the pitch beforehand.

There was never much razzmatazz in rugby league ordinarily, but the cup final was a different story. We were measured up for suits to wear on the day, just like footballers ahead of an FA Cup final. And we always stayed in the best hotels. The night before my first final, we travelled down to Sopwell House hotel in St Albans.

John Monie had decided that I should share a room with Dean Bell, our captain. That was typical of John, pairing me with an experienced pro. But if he had been hoping that Dean would be a reassuring presence for me, it backfired. Bell, a hard-as-nails New Zealander, had already won the Challenge Cup on five occasions and had previously won the 'Man of Steel' award, but that night I found him in the toilet in our room being sick because of the nerves.

Roles reversed, it was up to me to comfort him. With the naivety and cockiness of youth, all I could say was, 'Don't worry, Dean, we'll be all right; we'll batter them tomorrow.' I don't know who I was kidding. Dean, as one of the elder statesmen of the team, knew what a big occasion it was. And Widnes were stacked with hard men themselves, including Bobbie Goulding, who had won the Challenge Cup with Wigan in 1990 and 1991. I knew Bobbie from training when I had first joined the club as a fourteen-year-old.

He was one of the first players I saw after our coach had driven up to the back of the Wembley Stadium tunnel and dropped us off around ninety minutes before kick-off. The tunnel sloped up towards the pitch and ended behind the posts as you crossed the greyhound track. The atmosphere hit me like a sonic boom – quickly followed by a blast from Goulding, who was returning to the tunnel. Before I could even mutter, 'Hi Bobbie, how are you doing?' he told me in no uncertain terms that he was going to kill me that day. Bloody hell!

My parents and grandad George were in the crowd. They had driven down from Wigan that morning. Mum, by her own admission, does not enjoy dressing up, but when she got to the car park at Wembley, she went into the public toilets and put on a smart skirt and top, before they went up to their seats in the stand. The two sides were lined up facing each other, not the crowd, as the national anthem was played. My mind shot back to my second trip to Wembley as a fan, to see Wigan defeat Hull in the 1985 final. The tradition was that after the anthem, each player's name would be called, and they would peel away from the line-up. But in the 1985 final, Wigan's stand-off, an Australian called Brett Kenny who had signed from Parramatta for one season, just turned from the line-up and walked away, slowly taking off his tracksuit top. He was so laid-back. I remember everyone saying, 'He's not bothered; he couldn't give a shit!' But I look back now and think he was doing exactly the right thing. He was in control of his emotions and not wasting any energy. Anyway, he did give a shit. He cut Hull right open and won the man-of-the-match award by a mile.

I was far too overawed by the occasion to keep my cool like Brett Kenny. When I came on in the fifty-fifth minute to replace Kelvin Skerrett, we were leading 20–12, having recovered from a shaky start. The game was a blur for me. All I remember was that my legs felt like lead. The sheer intensity of the occasion was overwhelming. I had grown up in awe of these finals. Wembley Way, the Twin Towers, the walk onto the pitch before. Standing in the terraces in 1984, I had watched as, on this same pitch, Joe Lydon ran in two length-of-the-field tries – a Wiganer playing for Widnes in a team that also included Colleen's dad. Now here I was in the middle of it all.

To this day, I still haven't played on a better surface. It was like a snooker table. The first time I walked onto the pitch with my suit on, I remember thinking that someone should put a 'keep off the grass' sign up because it was so immaculate. Yet still it felt like I was running in mud. It didn't help that the temperature on the pitch was almost thirty degrees. I did everything I could to get into the game, make an early hit, get my hands on the ball, but I am not sure if I made any difference. When Phil Clarke made a break and his offload put me in space, I took off inside the right-hand touchline. But although I was able to put Martin Offiah away with an inside pass for what looked like a try, the touch judge ruled that John Devereux had just pulled me into touch. No matter, the scoreline remained the same as we won the Challenge Cup for the sixth successive season. And my legs started working properly again after the final whistle!

And so, at the age of just seventeen years and eleven months, I got to climb the famous thirty-nine steps at Wembley and become the youngest-ever Challenge Cup winner. My teammate Shaun Edwards had held the record since that 1985 final against Hull, when he was eighteen and a half. Less than twenty-four hours after being sick in a toilet because of nerves, Dean Bell lifted the Challenge Cup in front of a crowd of 78,348. For his efforts, he was awarded the Lance Todd trophy for the man of the match. In the mayhem, I managed to find my parents and grandad and showed them my medal.

The celebrations were something else. There was a big dinner for the squad and families at the Grosvenor House Hotel in Hyde Park. Now, black-tie dinners may be a regular occurrence in rugby union, but that certainly isn't the case in rugby league. Cup-final night was the one time of the year we would wear a suit, and that gave the excuse for our partners to get dressed up as well. The function was fantastic. When Dave Whelan, the club president, got up to speak, the boys were egging him on to give us an extra bonus for winning. Even more memorable was the coach journey back to Wigan the following day. I never wanted that journey to end. When we got to the edge of the town, we were transferred onto an open-top bus. The wives and girlfriends sat on the bottom deck, and the lads were upstairs with the trophy, waving to the fans. It was a slow drive to Central Park, where there would be thousands of fans on the pitch and a stage with a band playing. It was unbelievable. Sometimes the smallest details stand out, and for me it was the bacon-and-egg sandwiches. They handed out loads of them on the bus and we threw them down to the fans on the way to the stadium.

Martin Offiah rarely drank, so when he did have a few, he was a bit of a mess. Two of the lads, Neil Cowie and Kelvin Skerrett, picked him up and suddenly you could hear all the wives on the lower deck screaming. No wonder, as suddenly through the window they could see Martin's face as he hung upside down. The crowd were screaming too because everyone thought he was going to be dropped. How he wasn't, I don't know, because of the state Neil and Kelvin were in. It was childish, but these were the sorts of things we used to do, and they were the best memories. Another tradition that I experienced for the first time that year was to wreck the dressing rooms before we went back out onto the stage. And I mean smash them up good and proper. We would absolutely ruin them so that they had to be renovated for the start of next season. The same thing happened year on year, and every year we did get a new and improved dressing room. Martin Dermott, our hooker, had to go to hospital one year because he smashed a tile that held soap under the showers with his elbow. Neil Cowie put his head through the wooden panelling of the dressing room wall and got stuck. With unfortunate timing, the club directors walked down the corridor to see Neil's head sticking out as the players were trying to pull him free. It was madness, and I don't know how those things didn't get out into the public domain. But it happened year on year. The following day was known as 'Mad Monday'. A player would pick a pub in town and we would have to meet up in the morning for another massive session.

* * *

Reality struck two weeks later. I was promoted to the starting line-up for the Premiership Trophy final against St Helens at Old Trafford, but our hopes of finishing the season with the five-trophy Grand Slam were shattered in a 10–4 defeat. It brought to an end a twenty-five-game winning streak in knock-out competitions that had stretched back eighteen months.

The defeat would also bring to an end John Monie's tenure as Wigan head coach. He had led the club to four Challenge Cups, four league championships and a World Club Challenge triumph. I learned so much from him. He did not tolerate mistakes and was a tough operator behind the smiles. Our success had been founded on our defence. No one wanted to be last to get off the floor. But he was a tactical thinker too and knew how to manage people.

I saw how he made people feel valued. He was happy to listen to anyone's opinion and take their points on board, but then the final decision would be John's. That clarity was key.

Even at the age of sixteen, I knew that I wanted to become a coach one day. From the age of eighteen, I started keeping notes about what I thought worked and what didn't from the top coaches I encountered. I made sure that I would bring John's best traits with me.

* * *

In the same year that John Monie had given me my big break, another legendary figure, Malcolm Reilly, would catapult my career onto the next level. Malcolm had earned himself legendary status as a player who was hard as nails, having enjoyed a stellar career with Castleford and then proved himself in Australia with Manly during the 1970s. By now he was coach of the Great Britain team, and his reputation was such that all the players would run through brick walls for him.

By the autumn of 1993, I would experience at first hand just how special he was.

The selection whirlwind began when I was picked for the Great Britain academy side against a junior New Zealand side. Malcolm's commitment was such that not only did he always attend the academy games, but also would actually train with the players. He would have been in his mid-forties at that point, but he was a fitness fanatic. One day we were doing a bleep test, which involves running between two lines that are fifteen metres apart and challenges you to reach the line before the next bleep. Days before the test, Malcolm pulled his hamstring, but rather than quit, he had an injection to enable him to complete the test. There was no need for it, but he wanted to make sure that the players realized that you needed to tough it out. He wanted to see how tenacious they were too. Even with his injury and at his age, he finished ahead of some of our players in the test.

My parents kept all the communications from the Rugby Football League at the time, including a print-out of the results of a 'Concept II Rowing Ergometer' test over 500 metres for the Great Britain training squad. My time was 1 minute 38 seconds, eleven seconds behind the best time of 1 minute 27 seconds by my Wigan teammate Barrie-Jon Mather. And at the bottom of the list of the players is the name 'Malcolm Reilly (Coach)'. And his time? 1 minute 28 seconds.

A couple of weeks later I was picked for a Great Britain Under-19 side to play against their New Zealand counterparts in Workington, and Malcolm was there again. At the same time the senior Great Britain side was playing a three-Test series against New Zealand and had taken a 2–0 lead. Almost immediately after my game finished, I got wind that

Malcolm wanted to pick me for the senior side for the third Test at Headingley. I was stunned. In just three weeks I had gone from an academy player to becoming, at the age of eighteen, the youngest Test forward to play for Great Britain.

It all happened so quickly, there was barely time to consider the significance of it all. The Great Britain side contained some familiar faces from Wigan – Shaun Edwards, Kelvin Skerrett, Martin Offiah, Gary Connolly, Denis Betts and Phil Clarke – but now I faced the daunting prospect of sharing a dressing room with guys like Jonathan Davies, John Devereux and Paul Newlove, players I had grown up watching as a kid. Shaun Edwards noticed that I had been quiet and withdrawn during an unopposed training session, when I would usually have been always in his ear demanding the ball. Shaun asked if I was OK. 'There's no point making noise when there is no one there, I'll make a noise tomorrow when there's Kiwis in front of me,' I said. I am not sure he was convinced.

Then Malcolm took me to one side in the build-up to the game. 'Just trust yourself to be yourself, Andrew,' he told me. 'That's why you have been picked in the first place.'

The words have never left me. I still use them myself when I speak to players before Test matches. There is always a little bit of doubt because of the size of the occasion. I know that. I have been there myself. But if they are not able to be themselves, what is the point of picking them in the first place? What you want is for the player to express themselves; to be the best version of themselves. That is what is going to help the team. Malcolm would never pigeonhole a player. It helped to know that he just wanted me to go out and play my own game. And in a similar fashion to John Monie at Wigan, Malcolm was brilliant at introducing young players into a stable and experienced side. He took a little bit of the pressure off me by putting me into a good side for the dead-rubber game in the series.

Thankfully we battered them, and I managed to cross for my first international try in the 29–10 victory, with Sonny Nickle putting me over in the corner. But the standard had been an eye-opener for me. The skill level was through the roof. What I would learn, both as a player and now as a coach, is that when you have the best versus the best, it does not always result in a highly entertaining game, because it can become a stalemate. But what I can tell you is that the difference in quality between a club game that finishes 12–6 and an international game that finishes 12–6 is immense, even if it doesn't always come across like that.

* * *

My breakthrough on the international stage helped cement my place in the Wigan side, but I never took my position for granted. No one could afford to, given the ferocious competition within the squad. On the Sunday morning after we had defeated New Zealand, we were expected to attend a training session with Wigan. We had celebrated the victory with a few beers on the Saturday night, and the following morning Shaun Edwards and Martin Offiah failed to turn up. John Dorahy, another Australian, who had replaced John Monie as head coach, was not impressed. The following weekend, Shaun was dropped to the Wigan replacements' bench and Offiah to the A team.

It was a huge call by Dorahy, who had been something of a surprise appointment at Wigan as, unlike Monie, he did not have a track record of success. I think there was also a bit of history between him and Shaun from his playing days: in a game when Dorahy was playing for Hull Kingston

Rovers, he'd caught Shaun with a punch that knocked a front tooth out. There was a friction too within the senior players about Dorahy's eagerness to change our calls, moves and training methods. I think the senior players felt he was changing things for the sake of it, to let them know who was in charge. This was a squad that had already won six Challenge Cups in succession, and I think they couldn't see the reason for the changes.

As a young player, I just kept my head down, but it made for a difficult season. When Dorahy dropped me one weekend, I was so upset that I almost refused to go to Central Park for the game. It was not the fact that I had been dropped, but that he didn't give me any reason except that I was the youngest player. It was as if it was the easy option to drop me because he was having to deal with the senior squad members. I went to Colleen's parents' house after training and Keiron told me to keep my head up and go to the game. I did, even though I didn't agree with Dorahy's decision. For me, age should have nothing to do with it. Years later, I would remember this feeling and make sure that I never made the same mistake when I had to tell a player he was dropped.

Still, there was too much quality in the squad for that to derail us. The club had signed Va'aiga Tuigamala, the giant All Black winger, and although it took time for him to adjust to the rugby league rules and get his fitness up to speed, he would go on to have a massive impact. Inga, as we called him, would touch all our lives. I was in awe of him. It was not easy to adapt from rugby union to rugby league. But he was blessed with great skills and remarkably quick feet and was a powerful beast of a man. I was devastated in 2022 to hear the news of his death at the age of fifty-two.

We had to overcome a fifth-round scare at Hull, eventually

winning 22–21 to remain on course to reach a seventh successive Challenge Cup final. It was a campaign driven by the fear of becoming the side that failed to maintain our winning run. Everyone wanted to get to Wembley again. Dean Bell would say to us, 'Remember how good it feels to put the Wembley blazer on in front of your friends and family.'

That sense of desperation got us over the line at the Boulevard in February 1994. We were trailing 21–18 with just minutes to go when Hull's Daniel Divet tried to pass the ball across his goal line under pressure and Shaun Edwards pounced and put me over in the corner, a score that put us one point ahead. No one would have remembered that if Paul Eastwood had not missed with a last-gasp penalty for Hull.

And so we reached yet another Wembley final. This time I was in the starting team against Leeds, whose line-up included Ellery Hanley. I think we were all surprised, however, when Dorahy left out Jason Robinson from the match-day squad. Neil Cowie wouldn't have been happy to miss out either.

The final is remembered for a stunning, length-of-the-field try by Martin Offiah. Martin broke clear from a pass by Frano Botica just five metres from his line and, having burst clear of a tackle by Leeds prop Neil Harmon, sized up Alan Tait before rounding him on the outside. I was privileged just to have an on-pitch view of the try. It was Martin at his best.

I was fortunate to also cross for my first try at Wembley. Shaun Edwards put up a high ball and when Alan Tait, the Leeds full-back, failed to gather, the ball bounced into my hands, and it was an easy dive under the posts. I wanted to give it a bit of a celebration, but it was at the Leeds supporters' end, and you can't do much celebrating when it's not your fans who are facing you. Still, it was another moment I would treasure. After Martin scored another brilliant try in the second half from a break by Mick Cassidy, we finished up as 26–16 winners. Martin was a worthy winner of the Lance Todd trophy, and a statue of him would later be erected outside Wembley as part of a tribute to rugby league's history at the stadium.

When I am asked about the best moments of my career, I think of winning Wembley finals as a teenager. Those were the best of days. But perhaps the best of them all was about to come, on the other side of the world.

* * *

The coach journey back to Wigan the day after the final became infamous for a falling-out between John Dorahy and the club chairman, Jack Robinson. Despite the off-field issues, John had delivered the silverware that was expected of a Wigan head coach. We were league and Challenge Cup champions. But all was not right. It seems that John had been annoyed that Jack had not asked him to speak at the post-match function when others had been invited to do so. Apparently, they had it out on the journey back to Wigan the next day. To be honest, I knew little about what was going on. It was a matter for the senior players. John had been great to me. Our fixture schedule to the final had been crazy, playing ten games in just thirty-one days, but we had proven that, despite the infighting, on the pitch we were able to dig deep and win things.

I had seen that the squad was not one big happy family. There were times when I turned up for training and the competition was so fierce that it turned nasty. Guys were fighting to be top dogs. But what united us was the absolute desire for respect from each other. No one wanted to be the one who made a mistake. Guys might not go drinking with each other on a Saturday night, but at training and in games, that bond was unbreakable. It is something that stayed with me. You could be the nicest person, someone who put the team first and said all the right things, but what you would be remembered for is what you did on the pitch and the respect that you earned. That's all that mattered.

This was what had made us champions again. But it did not save John. He had won thirty-five out of forty-three games, but within a couple of days of our Wembley triumph, with the season not even over, he was sacked. Even that did not stop us. Graeme West was appointed as caretaker manager, and just eighteen days after John's dismissal we won the Premiership Trophy, beating Castleford at Old Trafford. But the best was yet to come. Just ten days after the end of the season, we headed to Australia for the biggest game of all, the World Club Challenge game against Brisbane Broncos.

At the time Brisbane were the leading side in Australia. They had been top dogs for a number of years in the best league in the world. Even though we had been the dominant club in England, they were massive favourites going into the game. The Broncos side was stacked with Australian superstars, and we were at the end of a long, hard season.

But Graeme knew exactly what to do. As the second-team coach, and an ex-player with a wealth of experience, he understood that after almost fifty games the last thing we needed was more training. Instead, when we arrived on the Gold Coast, he told us that we could have the first four days to do whatever we wanted. The party had started on the flight to Australia. You would not have thought we were preparing for the biggest game of our lives. But it was a stroke of genius, really. It relaxed us and brought us together as a group off the pitch.

Graeme had a common-sense approach in how he trusted

us to get the job done ourselves. I would have run through a brick wall for him. There was the emotional attachment from attending his summer camp and falling in love with rugby league as a ten-year-old, and the time and encouragement he gave to me when I was coming through the second team. He kept playing well into his forties to help nurture the young players. It was a huge boost to me to have him, a guy who had captained New Zealand and Wigan, behind me and telling me that I was going to be good enough to make it.

* * *

Once the partying had stopped, we were able to switch into game mode in an instant, in part because of a sense of fear that if we didn't, we could be humiliated. The coach journey to the ANZ Stadium was eerily quiet. I couldn't work out whether it was a sign we were so up for this game, or whether privately everyone was shitting themselves because of our lack of preparation or the quality of the opposition. We had our injury problems too. Kelvin Skerrett had broken his jaw in the Premiership Trophy final while Andy Platt was also unavailable because of injury. Not a word was spoken. Brisbane had twelve international players turning out for them and their quality was of the highest order. I had video tapes of most of them, from when I was a kid trying to emulate them.

Yet while I was in awe of their team, in the moment I forgot what a quality side we had. Phil Clarke and Jason Robinson were outstanding that night. Barrie-Jon Mather set the tone by scoring a brilliant try, having some balls to ignore the support of Martin Offiah and instead stepping inside to finish himself. Robinson mesmerized the Broncos' defence, dancing around Wendell Sailor, and Shaun Edwards took the man-of-the-match award.

Throughout my career, I never wallowed in the glory of a result. For me it was always about the next game, the next challenge. Yet even as a raw-boned nineteen-year-old, I knew that night was special. Australia were always the standard-bearers in rugby league, so any win against a top Australian side stuck in the memory, along with my first Challenge Cup final and my first Test match. Winning trophies is one thing, but of more importance to me are the memories – the work that you have done together and how you got matches over the line. I try to get that across to my players now as a coach: make memories together. That's what counts.

Before the year was out, I would play against Australia on four occasions during their tour of Great Britain and France. A crowd of over 20,000 turned up at Central Park to see Wigan's game against the Kangaroos on the third leg of their tour and we put up a decent fight, losing 30–20. Great Britain, under Ellery Hanley, edged the first Test at Wembley, 8–4. But the response by the Kangaroos – comfortably winning the second and third Tests – put into context the size of our achievement in defeating the Broncos, who had six players in the Australia squad.

It was a similar story the following year at the 1995 World Cup when I was playing for England. It was the first time in twenty years that England and Wales had competed, rather than Great Britain. We managed to beat Australia 20–16 in the opening game of the pool stages at Wembley. It was a massive result for us – we caught them cold – but we lacked the consistency to back it up. And if you rattled their cage, Australia were not going to lose twice, even if the Super League war had resulted in the ARL, which administered the national team, not picking players who were associated with Super League clubs in Australia. They still had an aura about them and, when we faced them again in the final, they delivered.

The Kangaroos attempted to set the tone in the final by hitting me with a high tackle from the kick-off. The Australians had a strange way of trying to wind me up. They would say things like, 'You're a cat, Farrell!' I didn't know what to make of it. Was I meant to take offence? We would tend to call their players 'dickheads' or something else more traditional.

I was blessed to play in a remarkable era with Wigan and with some legends of the game with Great Britain and England, but ultimately the Australians just had too much class for us when it mattered. It was unbelievably frustrating, but there was a realization within the squad that their players were playing in the stronger league. We had about five top teams going hard at each other, whereas in the Australian league the teams at the bottom of the table could regularly beat the teams at the top. Their wars of attrition produced players who were not only physically tough but also capable of staying mentally strong. For me, the ARL (later the NRL) was the best league of any sport in the world, and still is today.

6. The Captain

Wigan were pretty much untouchable in the 1994–95 season. Graeme West had been handed the job of permanent head coach after leading us to victory over Brisbane Broncos. It was a hugely popular move with the players and fans alike. Our squad had been bolstered with the arrival of Wales rugby union No. 8 Scott Quinnell and Henry Paul, who joined us from Auckland Warriors as part of a swap deal with Andy Platt. And there were remarkable campaigns by Martin Offiah, who scored fifty-three tries, and Frano Botica, who scored over 400 points.

We managed to retain the Challenge Cup again in the 1995 final, defeating Leeds Rhinos at Wembley. I had started the final on the bench, with Mick Cassidy coming into the back row. I guess Graeme thought it was the right balance for the team.

Unfortunately for Mick, he had to come off injured early on, so I got to play most of the game anyway. I rated our 30–10 win against a really good Leeds side as one of our greatest cup-final performances. We also won the league, finishing seven points ahead of Leeds; and then we battered Leeds 69–12 in the Premiership final to take the treble. We also won the Regal Trophy, beating Warrington in the final, meaning that, including our win over Brisbane, Graeme had, remarkably, won five trophies in succession.

The 1995–96 season, the last of winter rugby, was squeezed into the months between August and January in order to facilitate the switch to a summer season in 1996. We finished top of what would be the last championship before the introduction of the Super League, our seventh title in a row.

But it had been a difficult season. I had been troubled by injuries, missing twelve games after undergoing a groin operation. When I was fit again, I couldn't wait for the switch to the summer season. I felt we would see the best rugby in the best conditions and allow the game to become an even better product. What I didn't know was that Graeme had identified me to be the one to lead Wigan into the brave new world.

**

Graeme got straight to the point, as he always did. 'Andy, how would you feel about becoming captain of Wigan?'

It was a daunting prospect. The Wigan squad was still stacked with senior players. Shaun Edwards, Neil Cowie, Terry O'Connor, Kelvin Skerrett, Inga Tuigamala . . . and I was just twenty. I had to turn this on its head to make sense of it.

If Graeme wanted me to do it, I had to ask myself why he felt that way in the first place. I was fortunate in that Graeme had coached and played alongside me in the Wigan second team and he knew what made me tick. I was not the type of player who could pull something majestic out of the hat like Martin Offiah or Jason Robinson, so team dynamics were my forte. I guess that must have chimed with what he wanted in a captain.

'Do you really think I can do it?' I asked him.

'I wouldn't be asking you if I didn't,' he replied.

It was a massive honour. I cast my mind back to those great captains I had experienced. I never got to play with Ellery Hanley, but he was the player I had looked up to most as a kid and he was the ultimate professional in my eyes. Dean

Bell, who took over the Wigan captaincy, was an unbeliev-ably inspirational leader. With Dean, you knew that whatever he was asking you to do, he would 100 per cent do himself, but with bells on. Shaun Edwards (with whom I would share the captaincy in the first half of the year), Phil Clarke and Denis Betts were also great captains.

Even though I was relatively young to be a first-team cap-tain, I had now been part of the first-team squad for four years. I might have kept my head down when I was playing a year above my age group at school, but when I started to get my feet under the table after breaking into the first-team squad, I started to speak up, drive standards or help others.

But first I had to overcome a tough start and stumbling blocks along the way. We lost our proud unbeaten run in the Challenge Cup, losing to a Salford side now coached by Andy Gregory in the fifth round in February 1996, just a month after the old season had finished.

It was the first time Wigan had been knocked out of the tournament since losing to Oldham in February 1987. That there had been a number of our former Wigan teammates in the Salford side – Steve Blakely, Scott Naylor, Sam Panapa and Steve Hampson – made it even harder to take. Hampo had been outstanding. He seemed on a mission to show that Wigan had been wrong to let him go three years earlier, just a few months before he would have qualified for a potentially lucrative testimonial year.

There was little sympathy for the new captain. In a piece for the *Guardian* newspaper years later recalling the fateful day our Invincibles' run came to end, Terry O'Connor pro-vided a sanitized insight into the stick that would have been flying around. The banter was brutal. You couldn't do the same now or people would start crying.

He wrote:

To be honest, I blame Andrew Farrell. His kicking wasn't up to much, his team talk was rubbish, and it didn't inspire me at all. It was all Andrew's fault, and I don't mind saying that. Joking apart, we didn't take Salford lightly. For me it was a big one going back to my old club, but none of us wanted to be in the Wigan team that lost the unbeaten record. But then the game kicked off and they absolutely tore into us – we didn't know what had hit us.

In those early days of captaincy, I learned that while it was important to learn how to do things and how not to do things from previous captains, the most important thing of all was to avoid trying to imitate them. If I did that, I felt I would come across as false. Instead, I had to be myself. I had to take the same approach a few months later when I became the youngest ever captain of the Great Britain team for the tour of Papua New Guinea, Fiji and New Zealand.

Yet when I look back now, I realize that the Wigan environment had shaped my leadership style. The main ingredient of Wigan's success had come from the top, the coaching and training staff, and because the players wanted respect from each other, even if they were not always friends. Standards mattered. The way we trained was far superior to anyone else at the time and it was a hard place to be. If you didn't put the effort in, or made mistakes, you were told, and you had to be hard to take it. If I dropped a ball, missed a tackle or I didn't work hard enough from the inside and the defensive line was broken, I knew I would get a bollocking. It could be brutal, but the consequence was that standards were through the roof, and that's why we won things.

At the start, I guess my captaincy was an extension of that

culture. I wanted to keep pushing and pushing to get people to believe that they were part of something that was bigger than them. Maybe even bigger than the team. I wanted us to lay down a marker that would give us something to be proud of. To do that you needed a strong mindset. And yet I now look back with total embarrassment at some of the things I did as captain. I used to think it was me setting the tone to show the way forward by fighting hard and showing players that I cared so much.

I can remember jumping up and down on the spot like a spoiled child because someone didn't catch the ball and it rolled into touch. I can remember throwing the ball at somebody once because I thought it was the right way to demonstrate passion and commitment.

What was I trying to achieve? Who did I think I was?

At the time, it was my way of trying to bring the best out of everyone. I thought that I needed to act like that to get everyone up to speed. It was what I had been brought up with. Before my time, when rugby league had a five-metre rule to retreat from the ball-in-play instead of ten metres, the game was barbaric. And I chose to play that game because I wanted to.

Even after I had been captain of club and country for several years, I still made mistakes. When Great Britain hosted the Kangaroos in a three-match Ashes series in 2003, I got stuck into Adrian Morley before the first Test in Wigan. Moz was playing for the Roosters in Sydney at the time and was facing a load of his club teammates in the Australian side. Now, he was an unbelievable player, as hard as nails, and in reality there was never any doubt that he was going to give his all against them, or indeed whoever he played against. Never mind his teammates, he would do the same against his brothers, I have no doubt. But that didn't stop me getting in his ear. 'Now, Moz, I don't want you going soft on your Aussie mates,' I told him several times.

As if he would. He was one of the toughest players I ever played with. From the whistle, I kicked the ball long and it was gathered by the Australia prop Robbie Kearns, who started running it back. Adrian hit him in the face with a stiff arm, and within twelve seconds of the start of a Test, he was sent off. How bad of a captain was I? We only just lost the match 22–18, despite being a man down for seventy-nine minutes. But at the time I thought I was doing the right thing.

Now, as a head coach, what I try to teach my captains to do is vastly different from my own experience. I look at some of the players I have coached, such as my son Owen or Johnny Sexton, who experienced a little bit of that era. When they first started, everything was driven by hard work, relentless standards and being as tough as you could, but both the game and society have completely changed. I have no doubt they have changed for the better, and safety is at the forefront now, as it ought to be. Today's young players have also been brought up differently at school, and working with them is an art form. If you want to develop as a captain or a coach, you have to move with the times.

Of course, there has to still be a little bit of an old-school attitude to the art of captaincy, but one of the mantras I use in coaching now is, 'Desperation is like a disease.' If you are desperate, you cannot think straight. How are you going to manage a team, manage a game, manage a game plan . . . or manage yourself if you are too emotionally wound up? Ripping toilet doors from their hinges doesn't work any more.

* * *

My old-school attitudes to captaincy were still in the first flush of youth when Wigan were invited to play Bath, the rugby union club, in two exhibition cross-code challenge matches in May 1996.

Although we had lost to Salford in the Challenge Cup, we were top of the new Super League and were chosen to represent the thirteen-a-side code on the back of our record of silverware: we had won seven consecutive league titles and eight Challenge Cups in a row. Bath had been similarly dominant in rugby union, winning the league six times in the previous eight years and winning four league-and-cup doubles.

The first game was at Manchester City's Maine Road ground, and just to play there was a massive deal for me as a Sky Blues fan. There was a real sense of excitement at the prospect of doing something different. But it was also madness. I know better than anyone now that to get a rugby league team to play union is impossible. What we were capable of would not even resemble a rugby union game plan. But if we had no clue how to play the fifteen-a-side code, the union lads would have been equally clueless when they travelled up the M6 to play the league leg of what was heralded as the 'Battle of the Codes'.

Shaun Edwards led us out, and I remember there was a feeling that we wanted to show Bath that we had been professionals for a bit longer than them. (Rugby union had turned professional the previous year.) There was also a part of me that admired the courage of the Bath players because they risking being shown up massively on a big stage. It would be the same for us, of course, when we played the second leg by their rules at Twickenham.

Bath had beaten Leicester in their Pilkington Cup final at

Twickenham just four days before they played us. Their only preparation was a couple of sessions with Clive Griffiths, a former Wales international in both codes. We battered them. Their defensive line was all over the place. Unless you have played the game, you can have no idea how draining it is to run up ten metres to make a tackle and then immediately retreat ten metres again, only to have to do it all over again. Kevin Yates, the Bath prop, who would later become a teammate of mine at Saracens, told me afterwards that the experience of running the ball back from long kick-offs with thirteen lads chasing him was like throwing himself into a gladiators' amphitheatre. 'It felt like everyone was trying to kill me,' he said.

We led 52–0 at half-time, but the celebratory mood was punctured by Joe Lydon. He had finished playing by then, but he was still at the club and had been brought in as a coach to give us a hand as one of a couple of former players with rugby union experience. As a youngster he had represented England Under-19s at rugby union and had toured Zimbabwe in 1982. It was one of the more surreal team talks I have heard.

'Lads, what are you doing?' asked Joe, as he slammed the dressing room door. 'Calm down and stop embarrassing them. They are going to batter us in a fortnight if we keep doing this to them. We've got to go to Twickenham in a couple of weeks and they can really hurt us down there.'

All we were thinking was, *Be quiet, Joe, let us get on with it*. We won the game 82–6, with Martin Offiah scoring six tries. Fair play to the Bath lads, though; some of them had a real crack, including Mike Catt, who got well stuck into us.

I guess we knew what was coming at Twickenham. But before we had to contend with the arts of fifteen-a-side rugby union, we had a glorious taster session the following weekend when we were invited to take part in the Middlesex Sevens tournament.

There was a brilliant atmosphere in the stadium, though in some ways it was very different from what we were used to. A lot of supporters were out drinking in the car parks during the day and the stadium would empty after each game. But it seems the rugby union supporters were intrigued by us because they would all come back for our games. We had a good squad that day, including Shaun Edwards, Martin Offiah, Jason Robinson, Gary Connolly, Henry Paul, Va'aiga Tuigamala, Scott Quinnell, Kris Radlinski and Shem Tatupu. Inga at least would have played a bit of seven-a-side back in New Zealand. Martin knew what he was doing, having played in the tournament before for Rosslyn Park, and Scott's background was in rugby union. Though we were exposed at times, our fitness and skills got us through. We beat Richmond, Harlequins and Leicester to reach the final against Wasps.

A young Lawrence Dallaglio was in the Wasps side and he had wound us up a bit earlier in the tournament when we were running out to play against Harlequins. Wasps were just coming off the pitch as we ran out and he shouted across to the Harlequins players, 'Come on Quins!' as if to say, 'Make sure you stuff these guys!'

We heard him and there was a unanimous reaction: 'Who the fuck does he think he is?' But I loved it from Lawrence. He was sticking up for his own. It was great.

Wasps stunned us with their start, scoring three tries to take a 15–0 lead as Twickenham echoed with 'Swing Low, Sweet Chariot'. But we managed to score a try by Inga from our first attack of the game and then Offiah cut loose from inside our half and combined with Edwards for a great score. Our conditioning meant that we could take control of the game in the second half, with further tries by Connolly, Offiah, Robinson and Edwards to secure a 38–15 victory.

* * *

As Joe Lydon had predicted, it was a different story in the fifteen-a-side game. We trained against Orrell a couple of times, just to get a basic line-out going. Let's be fair, it wasn't even a basic one. Our scrum was a mess and we didn't have a clue about rucking, never mind the maul. Trying to take a crash course was the worst thing we could have done. We should have just gone into the game and played it like rugby league, using our instincts.

Bath's side contained England internationals Phil de Glanville, Jonathan Callard, Mike Catt and Andy Robinson, and in the first half they scrummed and mauled us to death. I captained the side from the second row, alongside our head coach Graeme West, who pulled the boots back on. Again. We were paired together for no other reason than I was 6ft 4in and he was 6ft 5in. Graeme was forty-one at the time, and it was his first appearance for the first team in five years. But he had played rugby union in his teens growing up in New Zealand, and it was just his character to put his body on the line again for Wigan. At least he had some idea what he was doing. Joe Lydon, our manager, also came out of retirement to play at fly-half, almost two years after knee injuries had brought his playing career to a premature end.

But neither of those guys could save us. Bath were capable of throwing the ball around more than most rugby union teams at the time, but they were also capable of slowing the game down, relying on their set-piece and kicking game to secure territory and grind out points from there.

They had amassed a comfortable 25–0 lead by half-time, so we just decided to throw the ball around and give it a go. It is what we should have done from the start. Craig Murdock scored two tries from our own in-goal, which I think earned us a bit of respect from the crowd, and hopefully a bit of pride for the large number of Wigan supporters who had travelled down for the game, which we ended up losing 44–19. It was a great experience, and I look back now and feel privileged to have been part of a one-off event that brought our two rugby codes together, if only for a few weeks.

After the game, Andy Robinson, who was coming to the end of his playing career, came up to me. 'Andy,' he said, 'fitness-wise that second half was the hardest game of rugby union I have played.' I must have made an impression. A few years later the same Andy Robinson was appointed England head coach and was instrumental in signing me for rugby union.

* * *

If it was a relief to get back to the thirteen-a-side game, our place as the dominant force in rugby league in England was starting to slip. As the game went fully professional with the advent of the Super League, the introduction of a salary cap levelled things up. Wigan had dominated the previous decade because Jack Robinson and Maurice Lindsay went all-out to make it the greatest rugby league club in the history of the game. We regularly fielded a match-day squad made up almost entirely of internationals. Jack and Maurice attracted the best coaches too and established a brilliant youth development programme that tapped into the town's deep pool of talent.

But for the Super League to flourish, it needed to become more competitive from top to bottom – something the

NRL had achieved in Australia – and the new salary rules helped to even things out. Despite the financial challenges and the competition from other sports, rugby league is still going strong. For such a northern game in England – it is effectively Yorkshire versus Lancashire – I love the fact that it remains many people's second or third favourite sport up and down the country. But the changes were always going to make it difficult for Wigan to maintain our supremacy.

After all the turmoil between the ARL and the Super League, we were glad just to be playing. The new tournament felt fresh and the game was faster on firm summer pitches. The inclusion of Paris Saint-Germain added a new venue and our trip to Stade Charléty in July was a fantastic experience. Terry O'Connor's parents never missed a game, but they had decided not to travel to that one until his dad had a last-minute change of heart and jumped on a flight from Birmingham, arriving at half-time. That's dedication for you. I thought PSG were a great addition to the league and it was a shame when they were wound up after a couple of seasons. We only lost two games during the campaign, but our early-season defeat at St Helens had been the decisive one as we ultimately finished a point behind them.

The Premiership trophy was a separate tournament that season, with the top four finishers in the league qualifying, and we at least got one over on St Helens in the final at Old Trafford, winning 44–14. Redevelopments at the stadium restricted the capacity to around 36,000, but it was another fantastic atmosphere and it meant a lot to receive the Harry Sunderland Trophy, which was awarded to the player of the match. But what people don't realize is how stressed I was when I walked up to the podium to receive the trophy from Maurice Lindsay, who was now the Super League chief executive, and Dave Whelan.

Wigan is a rugby league town, but my first love was football: here I am (*front row left*) with the team at my primary school, St Paul's, in Goose Green.

With my older sister Catherine and my younger twin brothers Chris and Phil.

I grew up in awe of my parents. I think I was probably just trying to please them when, aged nine, I agreed to go to a rugby league summer camp. But I knew immediately it was the game for me, and my younger brothers got the bug too.

With teammates from my youth club, Orrell St James, on tour in Australia, 1990.

I captained the England Schools Under-16 team against France for matches in Huddersfield (*pictured here*) and Leigh in 1991.

My future wife Colleen's dad, Keiron O'Loughlin (*pictured here with Colleen's mum Lynne and baby Colleen*), played for Wigan for a decade, and when I met him he had recently helped Widnes defeat Wigan in the Challenge Cup final at Wembley. Keiron took me under his wing and was a big influence on my approach to conditioning.

Signing my first professional contract, aged sixteen, with Wigan vice-chairman Jack Robinson and chairman Maurice Lindsay.

A docket for my first pair of Wigan match boots.

When Colleen and I got married,
Owen was big enough to get dressed
up and join the celebration.
It was a grand day.

I attended the 1984 Challenge Cup final at Wembley as a Wigan supporter, aged eight. Nine years later, aged seventeen, I celebrated our Challenge Cup victory as a Wigan player.
[Shaun Botterill/Allsport]

Later, in 1993, I became the youngest forward to play for Great Britain, in the third Test against New Zealand.
[PA Images/Alamy Stock Photo]

Australia set the standards in rugby league, so it was a big deal when Wigan played the Kangaroos in October 1994.

[Clive Brunskill/Allsport]

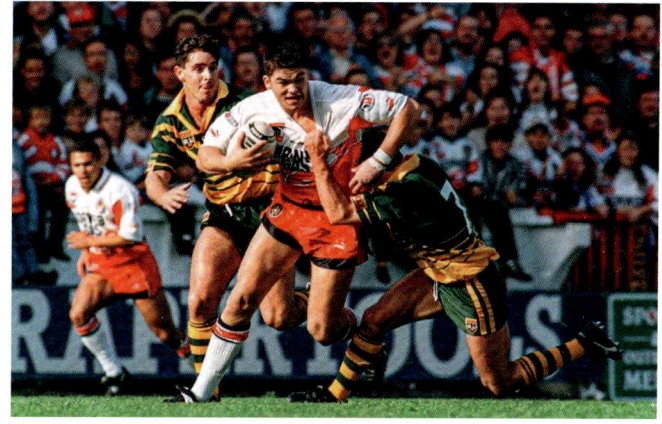

With Owen and teammates in Wigan after winning the 1995 Challenge Cup.

When I played my first Rugby League World Cup, in 1995, I represented England, because the Great Britain rugby league team had been broken up into its constituent nations.

[Allstar Picture Library Ltd/ Alamy Stock Photo]

In 1996, Wigan played a game of rugby union as part of a cross-code series against Bath. You can tell from this photo that I had no experience jumping in a lineout, and we were well beaten, but we made Bath work hard physically, and one of my opponents that day, Andy Robinson, would be the key figure in my switch to rugby union many years later.

[Allstar Picture Library Ltd/Alamy Stock Photo]

It was an honour to captain Wigan to victory in the 1996 Premiership Trophy final at Old Trafford, and to be awarded the Harry Sunderland Trophy as man of the match.

[PA Images/Alamy Stock Photo]

The previous weekend, Maurice had invited Gary Connolly and me along with our wives up for a drink at his penthouse suite at the Midland Hotel in Manchester, where the Super League end-of-season awards were being held. A good night was had and at the end of it Gary and I went into Maurice's bedroom. I can't reveal the exact details, but let's just say we messed up his room a bit. It was just meant to be a bit of fun, but when I woke up the next morning, I was gripped by fear. Oh my God, what had we done?

The anxiety lasted all week. I was preparing for one of the biggest games of my career but kept worrying that Maurice was going to phone us to complain. Before I went up to receive the trophy after the final, I turned to Gary and said, 'Oh shit, Maurice is on the podium.' This was all happening live on Sky Sports.

As I approached Maurice, he looked at me with a smile. 'Thanks very much for the other night, Andrew, that was very kind of you.' It was a brilliant response. Maurice had taken it in the intended spirit, as a joke. As I walked off the podium I turned to Gary and said, 'He knows! He knows!' And we giggled like schoolkids.

* * *

Great Britain's six-week tour to Papua New Guinea, Fiji and New Zealand in the autumn of 1996 was a trip I will never forget. Phil Larder took a squad of thirty-two but there were some notable absentees, including Martin Offiah. Gary Connolly, Lee Jackson and Jason Robinson were not allowed to play because they had contracts with clubs in Australia, while Shaun Edwards, Paul Newlove and Steve McNamara were all sidelined due to injury.

It was the opening game of the tour, against a Papua New

Guinea President's XIII, that will live with me for ever. To even travel to the country was amazing. Rugby league is their national sport, and when a touring side comes over, the whole place goes absolutely crazy.

When we arrived at our hotel, we had hoped to be in time to watch their equivalent of the Challenge Cup final. But we were running a bit late, and we were greeted by hundreds of pick-up trucks, with flashing lights and beeping horns outside.

Security guys in the hotel told us there had been a bit of trouble at the game. It seemed that, with twenty minutes to go, the president of the team that was losing started a fight with the president of the opposition. The scuffle quickly spread to the supporters and rumbled from the stands onto the pitch. The game had to be abandoned. And the supporters outside our hotel? They were from the team who had been winning before the game was abandoned, and they had found out the referee was staying in our hotel. In the middle of the night, one of the lads burst into my room wearing a ghost mask.

The stadium where we were playing our match, in Mount Hagen, was so remote that we had to fly there in eight-seater planes. When we arrived at the ground, I was surprised to see it was empty.

'Where's the crowd?' I asked one of the security guards. He replied, 'You just wait.'

When the game kicked off there was still no sign of any supporters, but within seconds rocks and stones started landing on the pitch. I wasn't playing that day, so I was on the sideline serving as water boy. 'What the hell is this?' I shouted to the touch judge.

The missiles were being thrown over the fence by a crowd

that had gathered outside the stadium. Apparently, this was a regular occurrence. They wanted in but weren't willing to pay and would wait until kick-off before making their presence felt. Suddenly the gates opened, and thousands of fans streamed into the ground. They were baying for blood. Some kept running onto the pitch to get at the referee or touch judge, or just to make a nuisance of themselves. Security guards patrolled the sidelines carrying long sticks, and anyone they caught running onto the pitch would be punished with a couple of whacks to the head.

Despite the distractions and the draining heat of almost forty degrees Celsius, we won the game 34–8. After the final whistle there was a pitch invasion, and we were chased by supporters with sticks. The poor referee was attacked and suffered a broken jaw. The bus that had taken us to the stadium from the airport was driven up to the side of the pitch to rescue us and the journalists from the UK who were covering the tour. We all had to jump in as people were hammering on the side of the bus and rocking it. It was like a scene from a movie: we all just shouted 'Go! Go! Go!' to the driver once we were on board. The bus sped off; then, about 300 yards down the road, someone shouted, 'Where's Dave Hadfield?'

Dave was the rugby league correspondent for the *Independent* newspaper. He was a big fella and obviously hadn't moved sharply enough to make the bus in time. We looked back and there he was, waving desperately at us, surrounded by angry Papuans. We managed to extract him, and by the time we got back to the hotel we were able to have a beer and a laugh at the experience.

The test match against Papua New Guinea in Lae was a gruelling experience, played in debilitating heat, and a few of our players were struggling with illness. PNG had a number of guys playing in Australia and proved they were no longer pushovers. Bobbie Goulding's goal-kicking and our never-say-die spirit edged us home 32–30.

Touring experiences like these created the special memories that have stayed with me most vividly. Shortly after I became head coach of Ireland, I was gutted when our tour to Fiji had to be cancelled because of a Covid outbreak: that would have been proper touring. On tour is when you get to see players' characters, not when they are walking around Ballsbridge!

If only the rest of the 1996 tour had been as memorable as that first game. We easily beat Fiji but then suffered a 3–0 Test series whitewash by New Zealand. We had not been helped by the fatigue caused by the switch to summer rugby that year. Some players had featured in over sixty games in the space of fourteen months, and a number of others either weren't available or had to be sent home early.

* * *

My captaincy was evolving. It had to, as some of the big names left the squad and we struggled for the consistency of the previous decade and had to cope with turbulence and constant change within the coaching team. Another early defeat in the Challenge Cup in February 1997 resulted in Graeme West losing his job as head coach, with Eric Hughes taking charge briefly before John Monie returned for a second spell in charge.

Eric was a brilliant coach to play for: committed, hard-working and honest with the players. He always told you exactly how he saw it, which I respected. Yet we underperformed in the Super League, finishing in fourth place. The league campaign had been interrupted by another new tournament, the World Club Championship, involving teams from the Super League in Australia. I thought it was a fantastic concept, just the type of exposure that the British clubs needed against the Australian clubs. We opened up with an unbelievable performance, defeating the Canterbury Bulldogs 22–18 in Sydney. The win remains one of the highlights of my career. But I think we started to believe our own hype and lost heavily to Brisbane Broncos and Canberra Raiders before qualifying for the quarter-finals after beating Canterbury again at Central Park.

The knock-out stages were held after the completion of the Super League and the last-ever Premiership Trophy, which we had retained, beating St Helens again at Old Trafford. We faced Hunter Mariners, a newly established team. They were well coached by Graham Murray, who went on to coach Leeds Rhinos, and had a decent side – one of their star players, Robbie McCormack, joined us the following season – but I think the difference was their edge. Before the game they had been told that the club would be wound up at the end of the year, as the Australian Super League and ARL were to create a new unified league the following season. With a point to prove, they beat us and went all the way to the final, where they lost to Brisbane in what was their last-ever game.

That was Eric Hughes's last game at Wigan, as the club looked to rekindle past glories by bringing back John Monie. When we reached the Challenge Cup final in May 1998, we were unbeaten in the league, and massive favourites to beat Sheffield Eagles in the Wembley final. It was one of those afternoons when I felt everything was going to be all right. We were back at Wembley with John Monie in charge and the great memories came flooding back. There was no need to be nervous. Except we should have been. Nothing but. Because they were ready. And this time we weren't.

I can remember standing in the tunnel and their players were shouting out numbers to each other. It reminded me of the time the Irish boxer Steve Collins spooked his opponent, Chris Eubank, by telling him that he had been hypnotized not to feel any pain, and beat him in a world title fight in 1995.

Apparently, John Kear's Sheffield players were just calling out numbers of the date of the final, but whether it was bullshit or not, it seemed to spook us. They played like men possessed and were deserved 17–8 winners.

Our response to that huge disappointment set the tone for the rest of the season. The following weekend we faced Sheffield again at Don Valley in the fifth round of the Super League and battered them 36–6. We went on to finish the season at the top of the Super League. For the first time, however, the champions would be determined by a Grand Final playoff series, involving the top five clubs. The innovation met a mixed response from the fans, but I was convinced it was the right way forward. In some previous years, Wigan had wrapped up the title with a few games to go and the end of the season had been an anticlimax. With this new structure, teams had to strive to win a place in the playoffs, and the team that came through the big final at Old Trafford would be worthy champions. I was convinced this would help our players at international level too, as we would have to perform to the highest level when the pressure was really on.

Our 17–4 victory over Leeds in the qualifying semi-final earned us a week off to prepare for the final. Our main motivation was to make up for the crushing disappointment of our Wembley defeat by Sheffield. Leeds, who had finished second in the table, won their preliminary final against St Helens, so we faced them again in the final. We were trailing 4–0 just before half-time when Jason Robinson scored a try with a moment of sheer individual brilliance. I kicked a penalty at the start of the second half, and the game remained tight right until the end, when I managed to land a second penalty. It was one of those pressure moments that I loved.

Winning the inaugural Grand Final was something no one could take away from us. It was the moment, too, when the Challenge Cup lost its place as the centrepiece of the season. I think the competitiveness of the final convinced most fans the new format was here to stay.

Instead of a medal we received a winner's ring, which I thought was a nice touch.

* * *

In some ways, following the start of the Super League, we became more like a football club, and the job of head coach became something of a poisoned chalice. John Monie was sacked the following year after a poor run in the Super League and a fourth-round defeat by Leeds in the Challenge Cup. Andy Goodway replaced him but would only last six months in the job. Goodway would be in charge for the greatest game I played for Wigan. And, without doubt, my most important as captain.

The fate of Central Park as our spiritual home had been sealed when it was sold to Tesco in 1997 for around £12 million. At one stage it looked as though we might have to leave Wigan itself to groundshare with Bolton Wanderers FC. Instead, the following year Dave Whelan took control of our club, which enabled him to press ahead with his plan to build a £30 million stadium at Robin Park, one that would be the new home for the town's rugby and football clubs.

The countdown began to 5 September 1999, which became known as 'Farewell Sunday': our final match at

Central Park. Appropriately, our opponents were our bitter rivals, St Helens. The game sold out months in advance.

Wigan versus St Helens would always have been full to the rafters and with an atmosphere that you wouldn't believe. It didn't matter what was going on for the rest of the season: when it came to derby day, everything was put on hold and the gloves were off. But imagine it being the last-ever game at Central Park. It was a game we just couldn't lose and the pressure that week was unbearable.

I drove past the ground on the Wednesday, our day off. It took me back to when I was a kid sitting with Dad in his car on the way to Grandma's house up in Aspull and him saying to me, 'Heaven's there, Andrew.' The following morning I came into training and called a meeting. I had to make sure that everyone knew how important this game was.

People don't really know unless they are from Wigan or St Helens. At the meeting I tried to explain it to players from outside the area. It was not just about the two professional teams. The rivalry goes all the way down to club games on Sunday mornings or playing for the town age-group sides.

St Helens had a great side that year and went on to win both the Super League and the Grand Final. But arriving at Central Park on the morning of the match, I knew we were going to win. We ran out onto the pitch with each of us accompanied by a Wigan past player, including the legendary Billy Boston and some of my former teammates in Dean Bell, Joe Lydon, Graeme West and Steve Hampson.

The game itself was a blur. Jason Robinson was on fire, creating a try for Denis Betts in front of the Billy Boston Stand and scoring our third try himself. Gary Connolly also touched down, while it was left to Paul Johnson to score Wigan's final try at the old ground. I had the honour of kicking the last penalty as we secured a 28–20 win. Looking back at the game on video, I don't think we actually played very well. But it didn't matter. Against a classy St Helens side, we found a way to win. My overriding emotion was relief.

Afterwards, no one wanted to leave. We stood on the pitch after the final whistle for almost an hour as fans shared the occasion with us, getting photographs taken and match programmes signed. Then Gary Connolly walked us into the directors' bar, with us all still in our kit, and ordered seventeen pints of lager! It was the start of a great night. I took my coat peg from the dressing room and a piece of turf from the pitch. But most precious of all the mementos were my memories. I have a painting of Central Park in my house, and sometimes I look at it and think of all the great times we had together on all those Friday nights and Sunday afternoons.

People often ask me what the highlight of my rugby league playing career was. The first Challenge Cup win at Wembley and beating Brisbane Broncos in Brisbane were both huge for me. But they were nowhere near as satisfying as Wigan versus St Helens in the last game at Central Park. To have finished with a defeat would have been unbearable.

Some people in Wigan at the time would not go to the new stadium because Central Park meant everything to them. It was a special place. For many of us, it really was heaven.

7. The Decision

I am not one to hold regrets. For me, life is always about tomorrow. Yet now, looking back at my playing career, I recognize there were sliding-doors moments that could have changed everything.

Probably the most definitive of them came in 1999. I would never have signed for another rugby league club in England. Not a chance. I would rather have retired. But I had started to think about setting myself a new challenge overseas. People may not realize how close I came to playing the final years of my career in the NRL in Australia, a move that would have almost certainly put my life on a completely different trajectory.

I had always had a burning desire to challenge myself in Australia. As a family, we had been too young to go when I was eighteen and Owen was still a baby. There had been subsequent interest from Australian clubs, but up to this point I had never considered moving because I had been living the dream with Wigan.

Still, I wondered. I had seen teammates I looked up to, like Phil Clarke, take themselves out of their comfort zone and play in Australia. Denis Betts and Andy Platt also signed to play in the NRL with Auckland Warriors. I started to wonder if I should go too.

For me, playing in Australia was the ultimate test. As a young boy, one of my proudest possessions was a VHS tape featuring a compilation of Australian rugby league stars in action. It featured loose forwards like Paul Langmack, the Canterbury-Bankstown Bulldogs lock forward; Ray Price, another lock who played for the Parramatta Eels when John Monie was their coach; and Wayne Pearce of Balmain Tigers. I would watch it over and over. Seeing those players in action made me train harder each week so I could try to mimic them. They were players from what seemed like a different world, and I was spellbound by them.

When players like Brett Kenny, who had also played for Parramatta, arrived at Wigan in 1984 as I started to follow the team, it only added to the intrigue. What had these guys been through and how had they got to this point? It was the same year that *Open Rugby* magazine, which was later renamed *Rugby League World*, created the Golden Boot award. It was the game's equivalent of football's Ballon d'Or, awarded to the greatest player in the world. Imagine what it must feel like to win that!

Wally Lewis, whose nickname was 'The King' and was regarded as one of Australia's greatest ever players, won the first Golden Boot. It went to an Australian every year until 1988, when the great Ellery Hanley won it – but only after he had played for the Sydney club Balmain Tigers during Wigan's off-season. Ellery had proved himself by playing a key role in helping the club reach the grand final of the New South Wales Rugby League. In doing so he achieved what only a handful of British players ever managed to do: earn the respect of the Australians. The influence on me as a boy was profound: to prove you were the best, you had to make it in Australia.

My contract with Wigan was due to expire at the end of the season, and I talked with Colleen about the possibility of moving. It was an agonizing discussion. Few people move out of Wigan, because it is a very family-orientated town; everyone knows each other, everyone looks after each other. We knew how tough it would be for our parents. Gracie was just one at the time and moving so far away with our kids would be like ripping a piece of them away. But Colleen knew what it meant for a rugby league lad from the north of England to go out to Sydney and play for one of their teams. Her dad had almost signed for Parramatta when she was a young girl. Her mum would have been able to work as a nurse in Sydney. But it was trickier for her dad: he was told he would have to live in Australia for twelve months before he could play rugby. They decided against it.

But we decided to go for it.

* * *

I was due to travel to Australia and New Zealand with Great Britain for the Tri-Nations tournament in October. Phil Clarke, my former teammate, had introduced me to an agent in Brisbane called Chris White, who organized for me to speak to a number of Australian clubs after the tournament. To be honest, it was a welcome distraction at the end of an embarrassing tournament for us.

We had lost 42–6 to Australia and 26–4 to New Zealand in the pool matches and our only victory had come against the New Zealand Māori in what was a humiliating curtain-raiser to the final at the Mount Smart stadium in Auckland. Phil Lowe, our manager, missed the game because he had to be rushed to hospital to have his appendix removed, and injuries had forced me to switch from loose forward to stand-off for the game. We won 22–12, but it was simply a warm-up act for the main event. The game was just thirty-five minutes each way, there were no showers in our changing rooms and we did not even stay to watch the final live, instead retreating to our hotel to watch Australia defeat New Zealand 22–20. It was a brilliant game and left us in no doubt about how far off the pace we were.

Most of the squad flew back to the UK, but I stayed on with a few other players. Colleen flew out with Cath Connolly, Gary's wife, and Vikki Forshaw, Mike's wife, so we could look at the clubs together and look at places to live. It was an incredible experience.

The highlight for me was going for lunch at the house of Wayne Bennett, the legendary Australian coach, who was in charge of the Brisbane Broncos at the time. But I think after the four-hour return drive from Sydney to Newcastle to visit the Newcastle Knights, Colleen had had enough. She skipped the next visit to go to a water park with some of the other wives. I didn't blame her. But I was in heaven.

We eventually settled on joining Canterbury-Bankstown Bulldogs. They were a fantastic side with big plans under head coach Steve Folkes. They were offering a significant improvement on my deal at Wigan. After going to a barbecue with some of the lads in Manly at the family home of Tony Mestrov, who had signed for Wigan the previous year, Colleen and I decided we would live in the beachside town of Cronulla.

Then we got news that the offer from Canterbury had to be restructured on slightly less favourable terms. The contract was still good enough to go and live out there and get paid decent wages, and I think we would have still gone ahead – but then, at the last minute, Wigan stepped in and offered a six-year deal worth more than I had expected. I had a long conversation with Maurice Lindsay. I explained to him that my decision to look at a move to Australia was nothing to do with Wigan, it was only about testing myself.

But he wanted me to stay. And Frank Endacott – the New Zealand head coach at the Tri-Nations tournament who had been recruited to be head coach of Wigan – made it clear that I was part of his plans.

'While I'm here, I'll be fighting to keep him,' he said. 'I hear all the rumours about Sydney clubs being after him but that's a decision he'll have to make and I'm sure he'll make the right one. He's a vital cog in the wheel. There's a special way to play Andy Farrell. He's going to be playing a different role with me to what he has in the past, so hopefully, we'll get the best out of him.'

I was not sure what he meant by me having a new role, but seeing Wigan make such a big play to keep me left me feeling torn. After much soul searching, we decided to stay. The things Maurice and Frank had said made it hard to walk away.

From the family point of view, there was a part of us that was relieved to be staying. Later, there would be another reason to think we had made the right decision: within a couple of years the Bulldogs were found guilty of a major breach of the NRL's salary cap and stripped of all their league points.

Still, six months after deciding to stay in Wigan, I couldn't help thinking what might have been. It sat heavy on my heart, not going. I would have loved to test myself in Sydney. But there was no time for regrets. The challenges were about to mount at Wigan. And looking back, the decision to stay took my career in a different direction, and for that I am grateful. I am a big believer in luck. I think every successful person in the world would say that luck plays a big part in their lives. But I also think that when you are faced with those sliding-doors moments, you have to try to use that bit of luck as best you can and run with it.

Would I be where I am now had I joined the Bulldogs? Probably not. I would have tried to make life work in Australia, and almost certainly would not have gone on to play rugby union. And without switching codes, my rugby union coaching career would not have happened. I would love to have played in Australia, but I can have no regrets. Always for tomorrow.

* * *

At Wigan, we found ourselves increasingly usurped by St Helens, Leeds and Bradford. The introduction of salary restrictions in 1999 certainly had an effect in levelling the playing field. The Rugby Football League brought in the 20/20 rule, which limited a club to twenty players earning more than £20,000 per year. This hit us hard because we had needed a big squad in order to be able to compete on all fronts. You started to see Wiganers turning up at clubs throughout the Super League, because we could no longer fit them all in.

We still had fierce competition at age-grade sides in the town, but now other clubs were benefiting from our supply-line of talent. And while we had made good use of converts from rugby union – like Inga Tuigamala, Scott Quinnell and Frano Botica – that source of players had dried up after union went professional. The commercial strength of the international game in rugby union meant the fifteen-a-side clubs were soon able to offer higher salaries than were available at rugby league clubs.

There were other factors in our relative decline. The old-school environment that I had grown up in was no longer working as before. When I had first joined the squad, it was stacked with internationals who were all battling to be top dog and, in the process, ensured that standards were incredibly high. Without as many big names in our squad, that culture was increasingly hard to maintain. The fear of failure lost a bit of its edge.

We had also had a target on our back for over a decade. Every game for the opposition was their biggest game. And that made every game like a cup final. And when you did get knocked down, the question was – how quickly could you get up again? The hardest thing in the world is to be consistent. I may be a Man City fan, but I used to respect how Manchester United dominated English football for so long under Sir Alex Ferguson. Our challenge was to maintain our own standards.

A lack of stability in the coaching set-up didn't help. A bit like Manchester United in the years following Ferguson's departure, it became a tough job for a head coach to maintain the dominance that had been established by Graham Lowe and John Monie. It was a highly pressured role, with a lot of expectation to deliver silverware. That pressure often denied the head coach the time required to rebuild or put his own stamp on the squad.

Frank Endacott is a lovely man, and I enjoyed working with him when he arrived to take charge of the new season in 2000. We had signed Brett Dallas and Steve Renouf from Australia while another Australian, Willie Peters, joined us from Gateshead Thunder and Terry Newton, with whom I had gone to school, was signed from Leeds. Terry was a tough boy and was dying to prove himself for his home club. The foundation of the side was the core of young players I had come up through the club with – Mick Cassidy, Jason Robinson, Kris Radlinski, Denis Betts and Gary Connolly.

As summer rugby became the norm, the Grand Final, which involved a playoff system for the top-ranked clubs at the end of the regular league season, became the premier trophy, overshadowing the Challenge Cup. I guess it is something similar to how the Champions' League final changed the dynamic in football, usurping the FA Cup final. The Challenge Cup was now played in the early months of the season, with the Grand Final replacing it as the end-of-season showpiece. But we still wanted to win the cup, and after we lost to Hull in the quarter-final at the Boulevard it was tough watching the final at home on the television, like the rest of the nation. At least we didn't miss out on smashing up the dressing room: that tradition stopped once we had moved into the new stadium.

We finished top of the Super League table in the regular season. In that season's complicated playoff format, we lost 54–16 to St Helens in the qualifying semi-final, meaning that we had to beat Bradford Bulls to reach the final. We delivered our best performance of the season in winning 40–12 and felt very confident going into the final, against St Helens again, at Old Trafford. But even though we scored the first try and stuck with them for most of the game, Saints were outstanding on the day and took the game away from us in the final twenty minutes.

There was also a frustrating end to the year on the international stage. The World Cup, originally scheduled for 1998, had been delayed for a couple of years because of the impact of the Super League/ARL war in Australia. At the end of 1997 Great Britain had played a three-Test series against an Australian Super League representative side, and even though they were missing their ARL stars they beat us 2–1. The following year our tour of Australia was cancelled. I felt robbed, especially given that even in normal times we only played around three Tests a year

For the 2000 World Cup the Great Britain side was once again split up into England, Scotland and Wales sides, and Ireland made its first World Cup appearance. Splitting British and Irish talent across four nations only weakened our chances of success. Having lost our opening game against Australia, we managed victories over Russia and Fiji and then defeated Ireland in the quarter-final only to crash out in a record 49–6 defeat by New Zealand – who were coached by Frank Endacott – in the semi-finals.

* * *

Frank Endacott's reign at Wigan came to a swift end the following season. Three successive away defeats in the Super League, after we'd been knocked out of the Challenge Cup by St Helens, prompted Maurice Lindsay to act. I was sad to see Frank go. He was loved by all the players and was just about one of the nicest blokes you could meet. Frank respected the skills of the players and put a lot of effort into the psychological side of our preparations, trusting the players to perform with his man management. But there were echoes of how we had started the season a couple of years earlier when John Monie was sacked. The Wigan board, who were not known for their patience, brought in Stuart Raper, a young coach who arrived with his own ideas and was keen to put his own structures in place, and he had an instant impact on the remainder of the season.

Terry Newton, God rest his soul, was outstanding for us that season. Terry's dad was an ice-cream man, and a tough guy. So was Terry. He had been a few years below me at school and had joined Leeds from Orrell St James, so I knew how dedicated he was. He was an unbelievably hard trainer.

If we had a set of ten shuttle runs, he would go hard at it from the first one. He never held back on anything. He was hard as nails too. A fierce and uncompromising player, people underestimated how skilful he was and accurate on the pitch. And behind his hard-man image, he had a mischievous side and a heart of gold too. He would look after players who came from tough backgrounds. We were all devastated when he tragically passed away in 2010.

I still have close mates from Wigan with whom I will have a bond for the rest of my life. Terry should have been one of them. His death really shaped my views on giving players a purpose in life after they finish playing. It does not matter how much money you have, when your playing career finishes, you need to have a plan – something to make your life fulfilling and get you out of bed every morning. When I later joined Saracens, I found that the club excelled at making the players do something else while they were still playing, like studying for qualifications or gaining work experience. Mick Kearney, Ireland's former team manager, has been brilliant at this with the Ireland squad.

Terry's contribution to our 2001 season is a treasured memory. Simon Haughton and Mick Cassidy also had great seasons, as did my close friends Terry O'Connor and Gary Connolly. Gary was probably the best player I played with. He was different from me in that he was unbelievably fit and dedicated but gave the impression that he was laid-back and not at all as bothered. In truth, he was very bothered. He was so accurate in what he did. He wasn't that big, but he had fight in him. I used to ask him why he gave the impression of just wanting to enjoy life. His answer was simple, 'Anyone can think what they want as long as I know.'

I guess my relationship with Terry O'Connor, who now

does commentary with Sky Sports, started off as a love–hate one, and on the pitch it was probably more hate than love! We used to fight every week during games. We would give each other a shove if we didn't agree with what the other one had done. It was mainly me who did the disagreeing, to be fair. If he took a ball into a tackle that I wanted to play, just to get his stats up, I would give him a mouthful. And he would tell me where to go. But ultimately, we had huge respect for one another and because of that we became best mates. After I switched to rugby union I might not see Terry or Gary for two or three years, but whenever we met up it always seemed like it was only yesterday that we had last seen each other.

Brian Carney, the Dubliner who had joined us from Hull at the end of the 2000 season, was another who brought a sense of hilarity to the squad. I was extremely serious about the game, but I came to learn that it was so important to have a laugh as well. If you are too serious it becomes draining. Being a good rugby player is also about adding to the environment and how you make other people feel. You have to enjoy your downtime and not be scared of it because you think you should be doing something else. For a coach, it is important to recognize when to leave the players alone and let them have their own space so that they can become better mates.

It all made for an enjoyable season. But for all the good things we achieved, it was another season that finished without silverware. We finished second to Bradford in the league table on points difference. Then, having qualified for the final with a 44–10 victory over St Helens, for a second year in succession we were outplayed in it, losing 37–6 to Bradford at Old Trafford. It was an incredible letdown. We had played some fantastic rugby but once again we had nothing to show for our hard work.

Successive defeats in the Grand Final were seized upon by our critics, with some labelling us as chokers. When we lost three of our first six Super League games at the start of the 2002 season the pressure began to mount on Stuart, so it was special when we ended our barren spell by beating St Helens 21–12 at Murrayfield in the Challenge Cup final. It was a brilliant occasion. Kris Radlinski won the Lance Todd trophy despite the fact that he had been in hospital for much of the previous week on an intravenous drip because of an infected toe and could barely walk on the morning of the match until our club doctors drained the pus from it and gave him a painkilling injection. I filmed these treatments using a camcorder at the team hotel.

It was great to get my hands on the trophy again in what was my testimonial year. I am so glad I was able to cherish the moment. The move to our new stadium may have brought to an end our post-Challenge Cup tradition of smashing up the dressing room, but we managed to mark the celebrations with everyone getting their heads shaved! It would be the last trophy I would lift in the colours of Wigan.

Stuart set us the target of winning the double, but we had already lost too much ground in the Super League. We finished in third place and lost to eventual champions St Helens in the elimination semi-final in October.

The international season was bookended by humiliation and elation. In the middle of the Super League campaign, Great Britain had travelled to Sydney for a one-off game against Australia. Our head coach, David Waite, had unsuccessfully lobbied for us to be released a week early to prepare for the game and we crashed to a record 64–10 defeat.

The Australian captain, Andrew Johns, afterwards joked that he didn't need a shower because he hadn't got dirty. I came in for the brunt of criticism, along with David Waite. We had only had six days to prepare for the game, but I was not prepared to use that as an excuse. 'We just got beat by a team that blew us away,' I said in the post-match interview.

Yet we managed to restore some credibility with our performances in the Test series against New Zealand at the end of the season. We lost the first Test 30–16 at Ewood Park in Blackburn, drew the second 14–14 at the McAlpine Stadium in Huddersfield and then levelled the series with a cracking performance in a 16–10 win at the JJB Stadium. It was our first win over New Zealand since my debut for Great Britain nine years earlier, and a reminder of what we could achieve when we got to spend a bit of time playing together.

Any hope of continuity with Wigan looked forlorn, however. Midway through the 2003 season, after a defeat by Widnes that left us seven points behind Super League leaders Leeds, Raper was sacked and replaced by assistant coach Mike Gregory for the rest of the season.

It was a challenging time to be captain. I was so desperate for us to maintain the high standards that I had experienced when I first came into the squad as a fourteen-year-old, but at times it felt more like managing decline. With good coaching and continuity, you can keep building. If you keep changing the coach, then you are always starting again. As players you try to take responsibility, but it is tough. I have always stuck to the principle that all you can do is stay true to yourself. You know the truth and, if you are a good person, it all tends to work out. If you are a bullshitter, it usually catches up with you somewhere down the line. There are plenty of people about whom I wonder, 'When is it ever going to catch up with them?'

It works the other way, too. When you get dropped, in the moment you can't alter someone's opinion or gut thought. But if you are good enough, it works itself out. It might take an element of patience, but that is life. It doesn't always go your way. If you are good, or deserve something, it will come around. The cream rises to the top. And if it doesn't, it is because you are not the cream.

Despite the fresh disruption, I was proud that we still managed to find a way through to the Grand Final, defeating Warrington, St Helens and Leeds in the playoffs after finishing in third place. We lost our third final in four years, going down 25–12 against Bradford, but given what we had been through it was a fantastic effort. We might have come up short in three finals, but the reality is that we were still consistently putting ourselves in contention for silverware, a consistency that most clubs would envy.

After Jonny Wilkinson had landed his drop-goal against the Wallabies to win the rugby union World Cup for England in Sydney, we enjoyed arguably our most competitive series against Australia. We played three home Tests in what was known as the Ashes series, and although we lost all three, the combined margin of our defeats was just eleven points. Our performance in the first Test was particularly gutsy, given that it was the game that Adrian Morley was sent off in the first minute after I had wound him up too much before kick-off. If we had won that game, it might have been a different story. But we had at least stood up to them.

It came at a personal cost, however. To that point I had been blessed to have avoided serious injury, but the miles on the clock were starting to catch up with me. At the end of the Ashes series, I had to undergo surgery to clear up a knee problem and was out for four months, missing the early rounds of the Challenge Cup and the opening weeks of the new Super League season.

I had what is known as a chondral surface problem in my left knee. The chondral surface is the articular cartilage that covers the ends of the thighbone and shinbone, allowing them to move smoothly against each other. Well, I had a big hole in my chondral surface. The following year, I discovered I had a similar problem in my right knee as well. The injury required an operation called microfracture knee surgery, a new procedure at the time. It involved using a small pointed tool to punch holes in the area around the damage to create bleeding, which prompted the formation of a replica surface that imitated cartilage.

As it was a new operation, the rehabilitation process was something of a learning experience. At least by the time I had to have my right knee done a few months later, I knew what to expect. But it would only be the start of my injury nightmares.

8. The End

'Andy Farrell is a wanker, is a wanker!' The crowd at Knowsley Road seemed unanimous in their view.

I can't remember when the chanting first started. But it reached its zenith on Friday, 9 April 2004, during a game that is now remembered as the Good Friday Brawl. I didn't know it then, but I had embarked on my final lap as a rugby league player.

Our 21–21 draw with St Helens at Knowsley Road was a brilliant game in front of a full house. St Helens had been flying, going into the game off the back of seven successive wins, while we had been stuttering, losing three of seven. But none of that mattered in the derby game.

I thought my late drop-goal had snatched victory for us, only for Sean Long, my former teammate at Wigan, to reply with one of his own. Yet a rollercoaster game decided by two left-footed drop-goals is still remembered to this day not for the on-field play, but an all-in scuffle that culminated with Paul Sculthorpe and me having a pop at each other. Altercations in derby games were common, particularly when there were no cameras at the ground. But with the game being broadcast live, this fight became infamous. It seems like every year someone replays it on social media.

Mike Stephenson, one of the Sky Sports commentators, got particularly excited as it all kicked off. Stevo could hardly contain himself: 'They're swinging them right and left, they're all coming in, the touch judge is getting involved. This is unbelievable! Farrell has lost total control, they all have. I knew it was going to explode!'

The truth is that it was handbags, not even a proper fight. There were plenty more misses than punches that connected. It was true that Scully and I were big rivals. Scully was a key player for St Helens as they began to dominate the start of the 2000s in the manner that we had done in the late 1980s and 1990s. But we were also mates who had shared rooms when playing for Great Britain. I'd like to think there was mutual respect between us.

The scuffle became a bigger deal because it looked like it was an issue between Paul and me, but it was actually nothing to do with us. It had all started when Terry Newton and Jon Wilkin had a go at each other. The only reason that I got involved was because of what happened to one of our young players, Stephen Wild, who was blindsided by a punch from behind by the St Helens player Dom Fe'aunati. In my mind, there is nothing worse than that. My reaction was all directed at Fe'aunati, and Scully got involved to protect his teammate.

Colleen's brother Sean, who we had once babysat, came into the fight after me. He had made his debut a couple of years earlier, at the age of just seventeen. His first start came in a victory against Warrington, when he was called up to replace me because of an injury. We were so proud of him, and it was the start of a fantastic career for Wigan. From that moment I felt a sense of responsibility to help him out because he would have been a skinny kid at the time. But he was a hell of a player, skilful and tough as well. He would have been influenced by seeing at first hand everything his dad had experienced, as well as watching as his brother Kevin, who had played rugby at a professional level for St Helens and Halifax.

When I retired from rugby league, Sean not only took over my No. 13 jersey but also the captaincy. It meant the No. 13 jersey would stay in the family until he retired in 2020, after a glittering career that included ten trophies. But on that infamous afternoon he was just a kid in a man's world, something I remembered only too well.

When it had all settled down, with me directing a few choice words at Fe'aunati, the referee sent Newton and Wilkin to the sin bin. Fe'aunati later received a three-match ban for his role in the brawl and I was fined £500 after being found guilty of misconduct at a disciplinary hearing. But I escaped a ban as my previous disciplinary record had been unblemished. As for Sculthorpe, he was cleared of any offence.

Some of the abuse I received from opposition crowds was horrible, but I used to see it as a sign that I must have been doing OK if people were slagging me off. But not everyone saw it that way. At one game at Salford, their crowd made up a song about me that horrified my mum. To the tune of the Christmas song 'Winter Wonderland', they sang, 'There's only one Andy Farrell, one Andy Farrell . . . with a packet of sweets and a great big smile, Farrell is a Wigan paedophile.' It went on for the full eighty minutes. Flippin' heck. In a sick way, it was a sign of respect that they were singing about me, but my mum was furious.

After the game she demanded to see the Salford chairman to make a complaint. She walked into the chairman's suite and said that what was happening was disgusting. All the chairman could say was, 'Well, I didn't make the song up.'

At grounds like Featherstone and Hull FC, sometimes fans would spit at us when we ran out. It was the same at Widnes. They had a long tunnel that came out onto the pitch behind the posts. In order to stop missiles hitting the opposition players as they ran out, a cage was put over it. But that didn't stop the spit raining down on us. The crowd were right on top of you at Widnes: they used to sit on the perimeter walls. On one occasion, we had conceded a try and were gathered behind the posts. Their fans were behind us, jeering. I had my back to them as I was speaking to the players when suddenly I felt a thud on the back of my head and then felt a trickle running down my neck. I reached my hand around to discover I had been hit by an egg. When I turned round, the crowd just started laughing. There was nothing I could do, so I turned back and started talking to the lads again, with bits of egg still dripping down the back of my head. Next thing, I felt another thud as another egg struck my head. I'd had enough and turned to a policeman nearby and shouted, 'Are you going to do anything?' The answer was no, and the crowd erupted into laughter again.

At least I didn't have it as bad as poor Neil Cowie, our prop forward. Once when we got off the coach at St Helens, a group of fans were waiting for us and started giving us dog's abuse. A woman ran from the crowd that was effing and blinding at us and threw a full pint of beer over Neil. This was before we had even got into the changing room! Neil was absolutely drenched. He must have been fuming but he couldn't do anything about it.

The most vociferous chanting always came from St Helens. Once, when I was injured, I was asked to be a pundit for one of their games at Knowsley Road against Warrington. But to access the gantry I had to walk through the middle of the stand and all the St Helens fans saw me. Once they knew I was up in the gantry, they began chanting their favourite 'Andy Farrell is a wanker' song again and again, all through the first half. The BBC producers were concerned because the viewers at home could hear the chanting live over the commentary on TV. With a 3 p.m. kick-off, it was well before the watershed! The producer approached me apologetically and said he thought it would be best if I left at half-time. It brought my TV career to a swift end, but not without the humiliating experience of having to climb back down the steps from the gantry into the stand, where I was jeered at all the way out of the stadium.

On another occasion I went to Old Trafford to see St Helens play in a Super League Grand Final. A woman spotted me walking around the bottom of the stand and started shouting in my face that I was an ugly bastard, I was shit, I was this, I was that . . . It was a long walk around the stadium to my seat, and she shouted her abuse in my face the whole way, while her husband walked beside her.

This was the world we had been brought up in. When I first came over to rugby union, they used to say, 'You wait until you go to Gloucester and play in front of the Shed. It's brutal. If you drop a pass they shout, "Ee-aw, ee-aw!"' I thought to myself, *If that is as bad as it gets, I'll be happy enough.*

But I came to understand that the booing, the chanting, the eggs – it was all banter that actually masked a degree of respect. I dealt with it by reckoning that if they weren't chanting your name, then maybe it was because you were not worth singing about. And I am glad I didn't play in the era of mobile phones and social media. Many years later, it would be very different for Owen.

Sadly, too, he was subjected to abuse as a young boy simply because he was my son. Owen had taken to rugby league even more quickly than I had. Having spent so much time with me at training, when he got to year five he was already playing a year up on the Wigan town team, and when he was eight he also joined Wigan St Patrick's rugby league club.

He loved the game, but at times it was hard for him because of my profile. Once when he was playing for Wigan St Pat's against Blackbrook, a scuffle broke out and one of the parents ran onto the field and pushed Owen to the ground. I was playing for Wigan at the time so I wasn't at the match. His granddad Keiron was there, but he didn't see the incident – and I am glad he didn't, because that would not have ended well.

It was hard to take. Owen was just eleven years old. I was able to get a phone number for the parent afterwards. I told him it wasn't right, that you don't do that to kids.

On another occasion, I was training at Wigan and Owen was playing in a game around the corner from the stadium. Colleen phoned me in a bit of a state.

'You need to get here now; there is a fella on the sideline who is absolutely abusing Owen,' she said.

I remember screeching out of the car park to drive over to Wigan St Jude's, where the game was being played. Even as I got out of the car I could hear this guy screaming at Owen. 'He's rubbish,' he shouted. It was disgusting. You would get arrested nowadays. That was the world that was rugby league at the time.

It would have been tough for Owen as a kid, because he loved the game that much but he shouldn't have had to go through all that. Some kids might have thought to them-selves, *This is not worth it.* But it obviously was worth it to him. It is right that people now have a sense of how it was for Owen, because it was brutal and it would have shaped him to a degree.

There was a moment in his childhood when he might have

chosen football over rugby. He loved football. Much to my disappointment, he chose to support Manchester United, not City. He played for his school team, and one of the dads asked if he would like to play for a club team as well. The problem was that it would clash with his rugby league commitments at the weekend. He told Colleen he didn't know what to do, and his indecision went on for days. It seemed he had opted for football, only at the last minute to decide to stick with rugby.

He eventually ended up being offered a scholarship from Wigan, which meant he was part of a select group of players who received specialist coaching. But he continued to play football for his school. One day out of the blue, when Owen was around twelve, his PE teacher at St John Fisher, Jonathan Hill, suggested that he should play in goal after he deputized in a five-a-side tournament when his regular keeper fell ill. Jon had previously been a professional footballer and also worked as an academy coach at Manchester United. He suggested that Owen should come up to United's training ground at Carrington for a trial. He said to Colleen that he didn't usually ask kids from the school because he didn't want to get their hopes up only for them to be heartbroken down the line. But he thought Owen had the right attributes.

'His character suits being a goalkeeper,' he said. 'He is tall, he is loud and bossy and is a good footballer as well.'

Owen was asked to attend training twice a week in the evenings, which meant a nightmare drive for Colleen as I would have been training myself. I could at least pick him up so Colleen could get back to look after Gracie and Elleshia. Alex Ferguson was the manager then and there were high standards at the academy. The kids were not allowed any fancy boots, only black ones, and they had to call the staff 'sir' and hold doors open for their elders. If they were sick or not able to attend, the boys had to make the phone call themselves, rather than their parents doing it for them. It was tough for Owen when we later moved south and he had to give up playing there.

* * *

By the 2004 season, the Super League salary cap had been reduced to no more than 50 per cent of a club's income, up to a maximum of £1.8 million. Just two seasons previously, our spending was closer to £2.8 million so there was a real squeeze on the squad and its depth.

When we picked up a lot of injuries during pre-season, including to two of our props, our coach Mike Gregory began to look for alternatives. 'I'll do it,' I said. No bother.

In rugby league, the middle of the pitch tends to be occupied by props or one or two tight forwards. When I was playing at loose forward, I often tried to get down the middle because there I was attacking big men. If I switched to prop, I could attack them for the entire game. As the game goes on, they are the guys who tire the quickest, so you are able to use a bit of footwork and handling to get around them. Because I was an eighty-minute player, I was probably playing against tired lads for the last twenty minutes of each half. So I found my niche. I worked out how to target tired defenders and I was able to have more of an influence than I did playing out wide.

We were up against it that year. We might have had a real go at St Helens in the Good Friday Brawl, but it could not prevent them from going on to win the Challenge Cup that year. They beat us 32–16 in the final, which was held at the Millennium Stadium in Cardiff while the new Wembley was under construction. Still, it was a special moment in my career to have been led out onto the field by the Wigan legend Billy Boston.

By the time of the final my old teammate Denis Betts had taken charge of the side after Mike Gregory had to fly to Texas to receive treatment for a form of motor neurone disease. We were devastated for Mike. The former Great Britain captain had been one of my heroes growing up, a Wiganer who had forged a brilliant career at Warrington, where he had captained the side. I can still remember him scoring a famous try for Great Britain against Australia in Sydney, when he ran in from the half-way line without passing to Martin Offiah, who was on his shoulder. It would have been some achievement because Martin would have been screaming for the ball the whole way! Knowing Martin as I do now, I was delighted about that. Mike was an icon of British rugby league, and I have no doubt it was a dream for him to come back to his home town and become coach. He had done brilliantly well to come through as first-team coach so quickly. He was tough as teak and never complained when he started to become unwell, and got on with his job until he couldn't any more. Tragically he passed away in 2007 at the age of just forty-three. I felt so sorry for his family and the game lost an icon just as he was making his way as a promising coach. Seeing what happened to him and Terry Newton left me thinking that life really is short, and that we should never take things for granted.

Denis was brilliant at picking up the pieces. He had been very supportive of Mike and was the right man to take over. I tried to lead from the front. I received a bit of publicity after our victory against Leeds in June, because I finished the match looking like the Lone Ranger, with brown strapping covering my face from ear to ear. The trouble started when I collided with my teammate Danny Sculthorpe, Paul's younger brother, in the first half. I wasn't sure if I was going to be able to continue. But after some treatment I was able to return after half-time, only to have to go off again when I was hit in the face with a high tackle by the Leeds player Matt Diskin. Bugger that! I was determined to get back out again, even if I looked ridiculous. The bandage was to keep the cotton buds up my nose, as they kept falling out. It was worth it as we held on for a 26–22 win against a brilliant Leeds side, but I hated the attention. I didn't think I had done anything special. That was the game we were brought up playing. I had seen what others had played through; I just wish they had fixed my nose up a bit better!

Nowadays a player involved in a collision like that would go off for a head-injury assessment. Back in the day, you never came off for concussion. If you admitted it, you were seen as a bit soft. If you were dazed or were seeing stars, you kept quiet about it and played on. Going back another ten years, it would have been an even tougher world.

On several occasions after taking a knock to my head while playing under floodlights, I would see three balls because of the glare of the lights. I would try to catch the ball in the middle.

Knowing what we know now, based on lots of research into concussion, it is right that we look after players better than we used to. We have to keep on doing the right thing.

Now that I know more of the facts, I regret a few occasions when I stayed on the pitch. But back then there was a feeling that your character was being judged if you came off.

When John Monie was Wigan head coach, he would tell us, 'No one comes off the field unless you have a broken leg.'

Hardly anyone ever played a game 100 per cent fit. Many times I played at 75 per cent. A coach would say, 'Look, I know you are nowhere near fully fit, but I would rather you play on and be half the version of yourself because you can still help the team.'

Back then we didn't worry about the next ten years – it was all about the next ten minutes. We had no awareness of the dangers of brain damage or disease. These days, players can find themselves in a cycle of fear, not knowing whether they are all right or not. Some of the specialists who work with the Ireland team now have been able to put the minds of our players at rest massively. What we need more of are specialists in the field who back themselves to give accurate information.

The players now wear gum shields that use GPS technology to measure the force of impacts. Sometimes you see a player become concussed with just a glancing blow and you wonder how he was knocked out. On other occasions you see a player take what looks like a horrendous impact and still be OK. A bang to the face and one to the side of the head are two completely different things, while a bang to the chest can cause whiplash, which is different again.

I have had brain scans, and I feel lucky in the sense that I don't worry about the possible effects of previous head injuries. Yes, my memory is terrible, but it always has been. I reckon that is because I always look to the future.

* * *

We finished the regular season in fifth place, twelve points behind Leeds. After two playoff victories, we were well beaten by Leeds at Headingley.

I did not know it then, but it would prove to be my last appearance for Wigan.

The focus quickly moved on to the end-of-season Tri-Nations tournament, with Great Britain facing Australia and New Zealand in the UK. In a new round-robin format, the teams played each other twice each before the top two teams contested the final. We lost 12–8 to Australia in our opener at the City of Manchester stadium, but then beat New Zealand 22–12 in Huddersfield and then Australia 24–12 at the JJB Stadium. It took a superb second-half display to defeat New Zealand 26–24 and qualify for the final.

The NRL clubs made me laugh when some of their officials raised doubts about the future of the Tri-Nations series by claiming that the tournament took too much out of their players and would affect their domestic form.

'Their players want to try being in an English side and play thirty-odd games a year and then play five Tests on the bounce without a rest,' I told the BBC.

Then, in the week of the final, the most remarkable thing happened. My memories as the boy who had devoured those rugby league magazines detailing the heroics of the Australian Golden Boot winners all those years ago were rekindled as I was informed that I had been nominated for the award, along with Australia captain Darren Lockyer, the 2003 winner, and the Kangaroos prop Shane Webcke. I was stunned. A few weeks earlier I had received the Man of Steel award, for the second time, having also won it in 1996. To outsiders, that might sound like an award for the toughest or hardest player, but it is given to the player or personality who makes the biggest impact on the season, as judged by their fellow professionals. That is the ultimate sign of respect and was a huge honour for me. But the Golden Boot? Wow!

It was something I had dreamed about as a kid but never thought would happen. I attended the awards ceremony in Leeds and was stunned when the announcement was made that I had won.

There were some in Australia who questioned the decision. Apart from Ellery Hanley, all the previous winners had been from the Australian league, and I had not played there. I had been voted the best player in the world despite playing out of position, because I had seen an opportunity to do something different and have more of an influence on games by using my skillset and experience in a different area of the field. To make it even more special, it was presented to me by Ellery, my childhood hero, who had been the first British player to win it.

'It means a lot, coming from you,' I said. As for the trophy itself, it was unbelievably disappointing. Back in the day, when I was a kid reading the rugby league magazine, I would see photographs of it being presented and then look out for it on television. Back then it was definitely a 'golden' boot. It might have been gold-plated, but it was definitively golden. The thing they gave me, though, was a pale imitation: it looked like someone had bought a boot from a sports shop and sprayed it with gold paint. Still, however hilarious it looked, it meant the world to me.

Perhaps my award gave extra inspiration to Lockyer and Webcke, because on the following Saturday we were simply blown away by Australia in the Tri-Nations final at Elland Road. It was my thirty-fourth cap for Great Britain. I hadn't missed a game since making my debut eleven years earlier and had captained the side for the previous twenty-nine. But I have never experienced anything like the physical intensity the Aussies brought to the game. They led 38–0 at half-time, eventually winning 44–4. I looked in a state of disbelief at the end, searching for answers but only finding despair. I was so disappointed that I initially refused to do the captain's post-match interview. I had been left on my own to front up as everyone else had left. Colleen had to persuade me to do it.

I finished the year starting to wonder if I had achieved everything that I could in the game. Was it time for a fresh challenge? My body was starting to let me down, and I knew that with this amount of miles on the clock, I might not have many years left.

I later received notification that I had been awarded the Order of the British Empire for services to rugby league in the Queen's New Year Honours List. It was a huge accolade for me and my family, but perhaps it was also a sign. At the age of just twenty-nine, after 370 appearances for Wigan, eleven for England and thirty-four for Great Britain, I had played my last game of rugby league.

9. The Switch

The phone call, when it came, was from Andy Robinson. The same Andy Robinson who had eight years earlier praised Wigan's attempt at playing rugby union in the cross-code challenge against Bath at Twickenham. The same Andy Robinson who was now head coach of the England rugby union team.

He called my agent, Andrew Clarke, and got straight to the point. He wanted to inquire if I would be interested in playing rugby union for England. He explained that the RFU were proposing to pay a transfer fee to Wigan and to contribute to my salary at a Premiership club to bring me into swift consideration for the national team.

I think I probably surprised myself in the swiftness of my response when Andrew called about Robinson's proposal. 'I like the idea of that,' I said.

Like much of my rugby, my decision was instinctive. I don't remember giving it too much thought at the time. It just felt like the right thing to do. Looking back now, I guess there must have been part of me that felt happy with what I had achieved in rugby league. This was not a thought that I expressed outwardly to myself or at home, but if there had been anything that I was still chasing in rugby league, I wouldn't have stopped. I guess not going to Australia had also left me subconsciously looking to try something different. And this opportunity was certainly different.

I still had two years left on my Wigan contract, but if

anyone could make it happen with our chairman Maurice Lindsay, it was Andrew, even if he was relatively new to his role as a rugby agent. He was the brother of my former teammate Phil Clarke, who was among the players who had taken me under their wing when I first started out at Wigan.

The Clarke brothers were among the few people I knew in professional rugby who had been to university. Andrew had studied sports science at Leeds Beckett University and then completed a Master's at Liverpool University that focused on the analysis and preparation of rugby league players. As a strength-and-conditioning coach, he went on to work for the RFU and the IRFU as well as having senior roles at Manchester United and Liverpool.

In my early days with Wigan, when I used to do extra pre-season training with Phil Clarke and Denis Betts after training with the club, it was Andrew Clarke who used to bring us to a little shed at Orrell rugby union club. At times I would come out of that shed barely able to walk, the training was that hard. One day I was complaining about the agent that I had when I had first started with Wigan. I guess as a young player I had expected I might have got a free pair of boots as part of a sponsorship deal. That would have made me feel like a million dollars. But I didn't hear much from my agent once my contract with Wigan was signed. To be fair, I am not sure there were as many commercial opportunities as there are now. But as Andrew was already running his own business, he offered to start making some calls on my behalf and I decided to let him represent me. More and more players started to go with him. He found a niche because you didn't have to have a contract with him. He would just act for you, and you were never tied down. He ended up doing a few things for Owen.

Critically, by the time of Andy Robinson's approach, Andrew had a pretty good relationship with Maurice Lindsay, as he had already been involved in a number of contracts that, he said, 'had not pissed him off too much'. But he still expected the worst when he went to Wigan to broach the possibility that I might break my contract and switch to rugby union. However, Maurice surprised him with his openness to the idea, provided Wigan was paid a suitable fee.

I think the fact that I had turned down the chance to go to Australia four years earlier was a factor in Maurice's attitude. He knew how much I had given to the club. He also recognized when there was a deal to be done.

My body was starting to catch up with me and I knew that time was no longer my friend in terms of playing at the top level. After my groin operation in 1996, I played in every game for Wigan for three seasons and since then I had only missed a handful. That might sound ridiculous in today's context, but it never bothered me. I just loved playing. Back then squads were not as big and the attitude to injuries was so different. When I started playing for Wigan, we had a physio called Dennis Wright. He was hugely experienced, having started out with the generation of players before the game went fully professional, and he was a no-bullshit character. He had seen it all and was brilliant at physiotherapy. I look at how often players go for scans nowadays and wonder how much the insurance bill must be for clubs. But there was none of that when I played. Back then you believed what the physio told you, and if he had been brought up in the era when players constantly played without being fully fit, then you probably weren't going to miss many games.

Nowadays, squads are so much bigger that it is very easy to say a player needs another week to recover from an injury. We didn't have another week. Wigan would play fifty-two games a season back then, which would seem incredible to the modern-day player. You can't play fifty-two games without getting injured, but everyone would play on, even if they were only functioning at 60 per cent. It is just the way it was.

Players would often suffer injuries to their AC joint, where the two bones meet in the shoulder. A grade-one injury involves the ligaments in the joint being stretched but not torn, while grade two is a separation that involves a slight tear. If you had one of these injuries, you would simply have a painkiller injection before the game each week to get you through the eighty minutes. It sounds mad now, but you would keep having the painkiller injections hoping that the injury became grade three, which is when the ligaments snap. The good thing about that is that while the shoulder becomes weaker, the pain goes away completely once you have an injection. You might not be able to move your shoulder all week, but come the game you could have the injection and get through the eighty minutes pain-free. Those days are long gone and rightly so.

By the time I got to my late twenties, I started to understand my injuries and it became part of professionalism to look after your rehabilitation and be disciplined in every aspect of that. Later I would see this get to the point where players were becoming so professional at looking after their bodies that it got in the way of the rugby. In my view, the main hub of a squad's environment should always be the dressing room or the gym, with the energy coming from the strength-and-conditioning guy, who wasn't just an expert in his field but also in charge of the buzz, the energy, getting people up after a game when bodies are sore and tired. However, for a couple of teams I have been involved with, the physio room became the hub. Individually and collectively as a team, you are on a downward spiral if that is the case. If players are striving too much to understand the injury side of things, that can become a distraction. The sort of naivety that I used to play with is not necessarily a bad thing. I was able to play without any psychological baggage, at least until I entered the twilight of my career.

* * *

Of course, there are some injuries that just stop you in your tracks. During the defeat by Australia in the Tri-Nations final in November 2004, my right knee had started to give me trouble. After six weeks of rest, it was no better. I had hoped to play through the pain, but it kept flaring up after training and when I flew back from a pre-season training camp in Florida in January 2005, I had to undergo surgery. It was the same chondral surface problem that had affected my left knee at the start of the previous year. I faced another four-month lay-off and would miss the opening two rounds of the Challenge Cup as well as the first three months of the Super League. Thankfully, my knee trouble did not seem to put off the RFU.

I later read that the move to target rugby league players had initially come from England's World Cup-winning coach Sir Clive Woodward, who had asked two of his coaches – Phil Larder, a former Great Britain rugby league coach, and my former teammate Joe Lydon – to identify talent after England had lost all three Tests on their 2004 tour of New Zealand and Australia. Larder and Lydon agreed they should each list the first three names that would be written on the Great Britain rugby league team sheet, and both named Paul Sculthorpe, Kris Radlinski and myself.

Clive stepped down as England head coach a couple of

months later, but the idea did not go away after Andy Robinson took over. 'Farrell surprised us, and Wigan surprised us, by saying it might be on,' Larder told the *Guardian*.

It would have been a huge call for Robinson, who was new to the job as head coach. What he was trying to do would be far more complicated than a simple club-to-club transaction. You can only imagine the politics that would have been involved in various RFU committees to get that over the line. It would have taken big balls from Andy to do that, and thankfully for me he took that risk.

We met up and he talked it all through with me. He was very persuasive, outlining why he felt my skillset would be suited to England and why my leadership and experience would add something to the team. Maybe that game against Bath had impressed him and he was looking for something a bit different. That was exactly what he was going to get.

I was looking forward to learning how rugby union worked. I had watched the big international games, and I loved the complexity of it. But my only first-hand experience had been the cross-code game against Bath and the Middlesex Sevens.

Andy's initial thought was that I could play centre, given my distribution and kicking skills and ability to get over the gain line. Playing in the back row, either at No. 8 or as a blindside flanker, made more sense to me, at least on paper. I had played almost my entire career as a loose forward in rugby league and I didn't think I had the speed to play centre. Either way, I knew it was going to be a massive challenge to adapt to a new role in rugby union, and that is what excited me. I knew it was going to be tough, but I had no idea just how tough.

* * *

There was a fair bit of back and forth with Maurice Lindsay for several months before a transfer fee of £200,000 was eventually agreed, with Wigan to receive an extra £50,000 if I was capped by England.

I went down with Andrew to visit the England staff at the Pennyhill Park hotel in Bagshot in Surrey, which has been their training base since 2003. The RFU put us up in a fantastic suite. 'Bloody hell, Faz, this is the life,' said Andrew.

The medical was an experience in itself. I was still on crutches after my knee operation. The following morning, we had to drive to a hospital in Chelsea, where I had several scans. Then I was told I had to go to another hospital in a different part of London to have exactly the same scans again. This was in the days before satnav, and next thing we found ourselves driving past Harrods. 'We are like the northern equivalent of Del Boy and Rodney from *Only Fools and Horses* driving through London,' Andrew said, laughing. I passed all the medicals, even though I could barely walk.

With that sorted, I needed to sign with a club. Andrew and I hit the road, with visits to Leicester Tigers, Northampton Saints and then Saracens. Andrew would later tease me that after each visit, I told him that was the club for me. We spoke with Pat Howard at Leicester, and I was impressed by the set-up. It would have been very easy for me to slot into the well-oiled machine they had there. And the environment would have been familiar in a number of ways: they were a massive club that was used to winning everything, rugby was like a religion in the town, and it was only an hour and fifteen minutes down the road from Wigan. But it would have been too easy. I got a similar feeling at Northampton, where I had a good chat with Budge Pountney and Paul Grayson. No, if I was going to do this, I wanted to take myself completely out of my comfort zone. Saracens are based in north London, and moving to the capital would be like moving to Timbuktu, a bigger cultural challenge than signing for a rugby league club in Sydney.

We had a great meeting with Nigel Wray, the Saracens owner at the time, and Steve Diamond, who was the head coach. First impressions were good. Nigel spoke about what the club were going to do to look after me and my family, and I felt I was being brought into a family-orientated community organization that wanted to get better. It helped that the club's chief executive, Mark Sinderberry, was an Australian who knew his rugby league. Saracens were struggling at the time, and it would take a few years to build something, but it was the opportunity to make a difference that attracted me. If I really wanted to take myself out of my comfort zone, then I knew Saracens was the right club. I believe that every experience, good or bad, can be put to use.

A good friend of mine, Mike Forshaw, had joined the club a few years earlier. I had played with Mike for several years in the Wigan A team and Colleen and his wife Vikki became great friends. It was a massive move for him, too, but after a year with Saracens Mike went back to rugby league, joining Bradford Bulls and playing his best rugby there. I believe he was better for his experience of trying something different, even if it hadn't worked out for him. I often tell people to be careful what they wish for when considering a big move because the grass is not always greener. But what is important is that when you make the decision, you really go for it. If it doesn't work out, then at least you know you have tried it. Mike made the best of it.

You need something happening, be it good, bad or ugly, to keep improving yourself. I hoped that by moving the family out of our comfort zone, Colleen and I were setting a good example to our kids down the line. The easier option would have been to stay put. We had a great life in Wigan. I was playing for the only rugby league team that I'd ever wanted to play for and had great family support for our kids. Owen was thirteen and loving his rugby league and doing his goal-keeping at Manchester United's academy, and the girls were nine and six. It would be a wrench to move them. I can still remember going to see my mum and dad to tell them the news, in the living room of our family home. It was particularly hard on my mum. Her life was centred around going to all the Wigan games and being part of the wider family of the squad: the players and their parents and families. It was a huge part of her life, as much as it was mine. I didn't think of that at the time. My dad remained involved in the game as a scout, but the end of my career in rugby league in Wigan was probably like a death in the family for my mum.

* * *

My three-year deal at Saracens was an improvement on what I was earning at Wigan, and if I was capped by England there would be match fees on top of that. But it was never about the money. It never has been. The deal was announced in March 2005 at the Vicarage Road stadium, where Saracens were groundsharing at the time with Watford FC. Andy Robinson told the press that I'd be training with the England squad in preparation for the Churchill Cup in Canada in June, and that he hoped I'd be part of the squad's development 'as we approach the Rugby World Cup'.

Afterwards a few of us went to a beautiful old pub. Andrew decided to pick up the tab and got a shock when he was handed a hefty bill.

'Bloody hell, Faz, a pub tea in Wigan would have cost around £20 a head,' he complained.

'Just think of all the money you're making out of the agent's fees,' I replied.

I'd hoped that Wigan supporters would understand my reasoning in switching codes, but some felt I had betrayed rugby league. Many years later my dad told me he had painted over a placard that had been stuck up on a 40mph speed limit sign not far from my parents' house which said something like 'Andy Farrell, traitor to Wigan for taking rugby union money'. There was a bit of a hullabaloo, but the most incisive and prescient words came from Ray French, the legendary commentator, who himself had switched codes in the opposite direction, having played rugby union for England before moving to St Helens and Widnes and being capped for Great Britain.

French pointed out the potential difficulties in an interview with the *Manchester Evening News*:

> People have talked about him playing in the next World Cup, so you are expecting Andy to learn the intricacies of backrow play in an entirely different code? With the possible exception of scrum-half, backrow is the most difficult to play in union if you have come from the thirteen-a-side code. He will have to learn the art of rucking, mauling, scrummaging and line-outs, and it is staggering for anyone to expect him to be playing at international level in eighteen months' time. If Andy wants to give it a try, then that's fine, but I have to question the reasoning and sanity of people at the RFU.

The trip to Buckingham Palace, to receive my OBE came as a welcome distraction. I don't know who nominated me or how it came about. All I know is that I was the one who was privileged to have played rugby league, not the other way round. It was almost an embarrassment for me to receive it. I was allowed only three guests, so Colleen, Owen and my mum came with me to the palace. It was an amazing experience. I was following in the footsteps of some legendary rugby league players – Malcolm Reilly and Shaun Edwards – who had received an OBE.

I remember Her Majesty saying something like what a tough sport rugby league was, and how I managed to play it was beyond her. I just remember thinking what a tough job she did. The ceremony went on for four hours, yet she still managed to say a few personal words to each recipient. It would be so easy just to say congratulations and move on to the next one, but she made an individual comment to each person and that attention to detail made everyone feel special. It was very impressive.

Afterwards, we decided to go for a nice meal together on our way back to Wigan. We looked for somewhere relatively close to the M1 just outside London, and settled on a French restaurant called the Bean Tree in Harpenden. It was beautiful, overlooking a common. A couple of months later, having signed for Saracens, I was house hunting in St Albans. It all felt very familiar. I asked an estate agent if there was a small town or village nearby with a green. 'You are looking for Harpenden,' he replied. It was just five miles away, up the road. It was too big a coincidence. Harpenden would become the location of our new family home.

If only the switch to rugby union could have been so easy.

10. The Humiliation

'Just chop it off,' I said. I don't think the surgeon knew what to make of me. But I was serious. 'I don't care, I'll deal without it,' I added. To me it felt like the best solution. The only solution.

Who knew a toe could generate so much pain? Apparently, the smaller the size of a joint that is inflamed, the more painful it is. Forget running, I could barely walk. It didn't make any sense to me. None at all. It was not just the searing pain, which was so acute I could not put any pressure on my foot. No, the emotional angst was worse, a horrible mix of overwhelming guilt and embarrassment. I had barely missed a game in the previous eight Super League seasons. Now, after all the publicity that accompanied my decision to have a crack at rugby union, and the considerable investment in me by the RFU and Saracens, the big shot from league couldn't play because of a sore toe. I could just imagine what they were all saying, especially those who doubted I could ever make it in rugby union.

When Steve Diamond had first introduced me to the Saracens squad, I had not been more nervous since the day I finally dared to move into the first-team dressing room at Wigan. All I could think about was what the other players were thinking. To break the ice, one of them urged me to sing a song, and then someone started humming the tune to 'Money, Money, Money'. Very good, lads. The only way I knew to answer them was on the pitch.

No, doctor, just get rid of it.

During a pre-season training game, someone had accidentally trodden on my foot and a stud had gone straight through the joint of my second toe. The pain was excruciating, but given the circumstances my first reaction was not to say anything. I had only just returned to training following my rehabilitation after the knee surgery and I didn't want to make a fuss. Andy Robinson had initially hoped to involve me in the England Saxons side that took part in the Churchill Cup competition in Canada against the USA, Canada and Argentina in June, but I had been nowhere near ready. My focus instead had been to get in shape for the start of the new season with Saracens and immerse myself in the intricacies of switching codes and the cultural challenges of a new sport and a new way of life. But now I could barely walk.

The first few weeks of the move had already been tricky, far more challenging than I had expected. Colleen had stayed in Wigan with the kids until they had finished their term at school. Then, as they knew no one in Harpenden at the time, we decided to let them have their last summer at home.

I stayed with Matt Cairns, the Saracens hooker, for the first five or six weeks. He was a northern lad, from Liverpool, which helped. I made an effort to mix with the players at barbecues and got back to Wigan when I could at weekends. But if I am being honest, it was a lonely time. Everything was so different. Moving to Australia would have been less of a cultural challenge for me. The people at Canterbury-Bankstown Bulldogs were working class, and I would have had less to prove. For some southerners, the north begins at Watford Gap, whereas for a Wiganer, the south probably starts at

Manchester. I was trying to put on a brave face to the family by saying that everything was great. It was far from that.

The best thing about the move is that with time it changed my perspective entirely. Accent, upbringing, class – none of that determines whether or not you are a good person. People are people. Now, if I hear a posh accent, I don't judge the person at all. I'm sad to say that I would have done so back then.

There would have been a bit of jealousy towards me, too, from some of the players. I got that; I'm not stupid. Would I have liked it if someone from rugby union had been parachuted into rugby league for big money with the view to fast-tracking them into the Great Britain side? I get it. But some people were assholes with it, and there was no need for that.

Colleen and I went on holiday to Barcelona to try to clear my head. 'I'm going to get my toe chopped off,' I told her as we attempted a walk down to the beach. 'Don't be stupid, Andrew, you won't be able to wear flipflops if you do that,' she replied with a laugh.

I had been due to make my Saracens debut in a friendly against Bedford. Instead I missed the first three rounds of the Premiership before the full extent of the injury was recognized. It was initially thought to be a deep bone bruising, but then I saw a specialist in London who did a lot of work with foot injuries sustained by ballerinas. After an exploratory procedure he told me I needed an operation. Remarkably, it was another chondral surface injury. The cartilage had been almost completely ripped off, so every time my toe bent, there was just bone rubbing against bone.

That's when I told him I didn't care, that he should just chop it off. In the end he did chop it off at the joint, but only to repair it. He was a genius and just backed himself to do it. I was knocked out for several hours with general anaesthetic while he worked his magic. I was amazed at the fine detail of the operation. There was some cartilage left on the bottom part of the joint, so he turned it round, chopped a bit off to make the gap better and then screwed it back on. I keep thinking that one day the screw is going to work itself loose and who knows what will happen then, but so far so good. It doesn't bend and it sticks up a bit but I have never had a problem with it since. And I can still wear flipflops.

The operation meant a further two months on the sidelines. Eyebrows had been raised when Andy Robinson had named me in a forty-five-man squad for the Tests against Australia, New Zealand and Samoa in November, even though I had not yet played a competitive game of rugby union. But at least people knew now that I hadn't been making the whole thing up.

* * *

Colleen and the kids had come down to join me in Harpenden just before the start of the new school term. The girls settled happily in a nearby prep school called Beechwood Park. Elleshia and Gracie have always been great at bringing some normality to the family. They didn't care if their dad was a rugby player or coach, or later when Owen became well known. I love the way they brought us back down to earth by being oblivious to our trials and tribulations. They are both fiercely loyal, but don't suffer fools. To them I am just Dad.

Once I bought Elleshia to training with me. While I was doing weights, she caught her hand in a pulley on one of the machines and it hurt her fingers – understandably, she didn't want to come back! Gracie was always too shy to come. When we took them to watch games, they would dress up as Disney princesses or other characters.

They both tried various sports, but they never wanted to be front and centre. Now they are older, I love the fact that they still want to be around their mum and dad. I am told there will come a time when Colleen and I can do something on our own, but apparently not yet!

Of all of us, Owen was the one most against the move south, as any thirteen-year-old would be. We had to bring him down from Wigan kicking and screaming.

I could understand how he felt. He had signed scholarship forms with Wigan and was making decent progress. When he was playing for Wigan St Pat's, Wigan Warriors used to pick the top twelve players from the league, and they could train at Wigan on Tuesday and Thursday evenings. He had been in that group for a couple of years. The Man United thing was also still going on, and you had to live in the Manchester area to remain part of the United academy. Taking him away from all of that, as well as his friends at St John Fisher school, was turning his life on its head. We knew it was a huge wrench for him, but we felt it was the right thing to do in the long run.

One day, before we had moved, we drove down to Harpenden and I saw a group of schoolkids wearing green tweed blazers. 'Look how posh the school uniforms are down here,' I said. Later, when we were talking about what schools Owen could go to, I asked someone which school had the posh green uniform. 'That's St George's,' came the reply. I didn't know how to tell Owen that that was where he had got a place. He would join his future England teammate George Ford at the school, and Maro Itoje would also go there a few years later. He ended up loving it, but it was a tough baptism.

'I hate it; it's itchy and horrible,' he told his mum when he first put the blazer on. Colleen was heartbroken when she had to drop him off at school the first time. He must have felt that he stood out in those early days, with his strong Wigan accent and his uncomfortable new uniform.

Rugby league was almost non-existent in the area. Owen played for North London, because Lancashire would no longer pick him after the move. He was devastated to play against the old enemy, Yorkshire, with a team that did not really know league. I could see him getting disheartened, standing behind the posts on his own and clearly thinking to himself, *This isn't right.*

We said he could travel back to Wigan at the weekends and stay with his grandparents; that way, he could keep playing rugby league for Wigan St Pat's. The club had won the National Cup at Under-14 level before we left, and when Owen was picked for the Under-16 side he travelled back for that. But it would be his last game of rugby league. Within a couple of weeks he had joined Harpenden Rugby Club. On the third weekend we asked if he was going back up to Wigan and he said no, he was going for a sleepover at one of his new friends' house. That was that. He had done what kids do: adapted. Harpenden was a great community club.

With his skillset from rugby league, Owen quickly adapted to union, and before long he won a place in the Saracens academy. In his early years, Owen was influenced by my kicking style and mimicked me almost exactly. But as he started to find his own way of doing things, I didn't try to influence him. I only intervened if I saw something that was interfering with the basics of goal-kicking. Now if you look at Owen, he kicks completely differently from the way I did, and that is obviously for the better. Things progress and techniques improve.

There were times too when Owen had to deal with the flak that comes with having a high-profile father. In one game for St George's, a player from the opposition was constantly telling him 'Your dad is rubbish' and so on. I could see Owen getting worked up and it got to the stage where he started chasing the lad around the pitch. Just as my mum had done for me, this time Colleen ran onto the pitch and chased after Owen to try to calm him down. Then she turned to the referee. 'You need to send one or both of them off before this gets out of hand,' she told him. And off they both went.

* * *

Just before Christmas, Colleen and I were driving to Dunstable, a town around ten miles north-west of Harpenden, to attend a carol concert. I pulled up at some traffic lights only for the car behind me to run into the back of us. It was a pretty hefty shunt, and I started to feel unwell during the concert. By the time the concert finished, my back was killing me. I was practically bent double as I tried to walk back to the car. Back home, now in agony, I phoned the Saracens club doctor. The pain was so debilitating that the following morning I had to ask Colleen to drive me to the club. It was so painful that I couldn't sit up on the seat, so I had to get into the boot of our people carrier. I just about managed to slump in like a big sack of potatoes. When we got to the club, Colleen had to run in to fetch the physios to help get me out of the car.

They took me to the house of the Saracens head of sports

medicine, Dr Roslyn Carbon. I had an epidural injection on the spot, but it didn't even touch the sides of the pain. People who have had a bad back will know that sitting in some positions is better than others, but I couldn't get relief in any position.

It was the last thing I needed. After a few weeks back training following my toe injury, I was due to make my debut for Saracens in the Heineken Cup match against Ulster at Vicarage Road the following weekend. But within twenty-four hours I was under the knife again. I had burst a disc in my spine, the L4/L5. The operation meant that I faced at least another three months on the sidelines, casting doubt as to whether I would be able to play for Saracens at all that season, let alone for England.

I was in a complete mess. Yet the mental challenge for Colleen was worse than it was for me. Far worse. The whole drama had a massive effect on our family. It could have broken us. We were four hours away from our families and friends, with three kids and little support. Mum did get the train down to see us when she could, but Colleen was the only one I could offload on. I was in disarray, having to go to work every day and put on a brave face the whole time and not show any sign of weakness. When I got home the only person I could tell how I was really feeling was the one person who knew me properly. She would have to listen to me telling her that my career was over and that the move to union was not going to work. She carried a huge burden during that time, and getting through it made us unbelievably strong.

After around ten weeks I was able to return to training again. Someone threw me a low pass, and when I reached down to take it the back went again. The pass hadn't been that bad! This time they could not operate – it was too soon after the last one – so it was just a matter of taking the time to let it heal. I felt so sorry for the club. I phoned Nigel Wray and said, 'Listen, I've just moved down to Harpenden and it is extortionate here. But I will play for nothing. When I finish playing, I will give you the money back.' The guilt weighed so heavily on me, but Nigel was brilliant and told me not to worry. I made the offer to him several times, but he always replied that he had no regrets about signing me.

Others were less generous. We went to the end-of-season rugby dinner and during the awards, Nigel got up and said some warm words about me and I got a round of applause. That was embarrassing enough, and it was clear that some people weren't happy about the attention I had received. It takes all sorts. It was nice to have the support of Alex Sanderson, a northern lad who had just had to retire himself because of a back injury. What people didn't know was that no one was more embarrassed about the situation than I was.

* * *

When my son Gabriel was thirteen, he fractured his shoulder just before the start of the Leinster Schools Junior Challenge Cup competition. He was devastated, and I sat down with him to explain that it was just part of the journey. Some-times you have to deal with setbacks and the key to success is how you respond to them. And then I started to share with him the journey that I had been through. I had barely missed a game for seven seasons, I told him. Then I was out for four months with one knee injury, then four months with the other one, then a toe injury, then a recurring back injury – all happening at a time when I was trying to start a new career in rugby union. 'I wasn't able to play for eighteen months,' I told Gabriel. 'You couldn't make it up.'

The reason I missed so few games in rugby league was because I had always looked after myself. I loved the extra bits: being vigilant and trying to keep myself healthy, and finding ways to reduce the risk of injuries. But I think it was probably inevitable that all that rugby was going to catch up with me.

My string of injuries only aggravated my sense of alarm that I had no chance of making it in rugby union. I had studied the Six Nations games from the previous season to learn from players in the back row and inside centre, and Steve Diamond prepared a DVD for me on things I should be working on. But no matter how many questions I asked, or how many videos I watched, I needed to be playing rugby. Time was against me, never mind my body.

You see players come through now aged twenty-two or twenty-three in rugby union and that is regarded as young. I started with Wigan at sixteen, so by thirty I had already played a career's worth of rugby league before I went to rugby union, and by then my body was starting to fall apart. On top of that, I was trying to perform in a game in which I didn't even know the laws.

All of my instincts had been forged in rugby league. When you have no clue how line-outs work, or any feel for a maul or a scrum, or the dark arts of the breakdown, then you are not able to play on your instinct: it is all about survival. If you are so far out of your comfort zone, it is hard to get the best out of yourself, no matter what you do.

The situation was not helped by the fact there was a bit of a club versus country debate about which position I should play. Steve Diamond was sacked as the club's director of rugby while I was still recuperating from my back injury. Eddie Jones briefly took charge as a caretaker before Alan Gaffney was appointed in May 2006. Alan took the view that I was best suited to the back row, whereas Andy Robinson wanted me to play centre.

I could understand Andy's point of view. Centre was certainly easier to learn. But I just wasn't a centre in rugby union. I wasn't quick enough.

When I see my son Gabriel playing rugby union, I can predict he is going to enjoy playing as a loose forward or hooker down the line, because he has decent hands, loves to get stuck in and is keen to understand the connection between the forwards and backs. But he has been learning the game since he was five years old. I reckon if I had my time playing rugby union as a junior, or even changed codes as a twenty-one-year-old, No. 6 or No. 8 would have been ideal for me. But I had no chance starting at the age of thirty.

My kicking ability counted for nothing, either. I couldn't understand it. I had done nothing but kick a rugby ball every day since I was ten years old. Throughout my career I had averaged over 80 per cent success rate, and even when I was missing I never let anyone take the ball off me. I saw that as a sign of weakness. I would say the same to Owen. It makes you a better kicker in the long run. It is the same with kicking to touch. Anyone can kick the ball out twenty metres. But now that I am a coach, I always urge my kickers to go for it: have the balls to kick a penalty to touch to the five-metre line. It makes such a huge difference for your forwards if you are attempting to score a try from the line-out maul. None of that mattered for me any more at Saracens, nor later with England. It was never considered for a moment that I should kick. Sure, blindside forwards don't kick. Centres didn't kick for goal either. At Saracens, our fly-half Glen Jackson was our goal-kicker. He was an excellent kicker, but the fact I wasn't even on their radar baffled me.

I finally made my first appearance for Saracens in September 2006 in a Guinness A League match against Harlequins in front of a crowd of around 1,000 at Imber Court in Surrey. My name on the team sheet, at blindside flanker, was enough to attract significant media attention including several TV crews, as well as the presence of England coaches. Nigel Wray even made the trip, to finally see some return on his investment, as did my former teammate Phil Clarke.

'I was there when he made his debut for Wigan's second team,' Clarke told BBC Sport. 'And I was there when he made his Great Britain debut in 1993, so there was no way I was going to miss this.' Fair play, Clarkey.

For the record, I scored a try, finishing off an exchange with my former housemate Matt Cairns, but we lost the game 30–12. The match reports rather generously talked about how I had lifted well in the line-out and made good decisions at the breakdown. I don't think too many people noticed the moment when I realized how out of my depth I was. It was at a defensive scrum. Our loosehead prop was Nick Lloyd, who had played a fair few games for the first team and was a good lad. He was obviously aware that I didn't really know what I was doing in the back row.

'Andy, whatever you do, keep pushing on me during the scrums, keep the weight on me,' he told me. Well, the first scrum of the game was about twenty metres from our own line. I remembered what Nick had asked for and, as if to prove a point, I gave absolutely everything to pushing. Yet before I looked up, their No. 8 had broken down my channel and scored under the posts. I just didn't have a clue about looking through the scrum, seeing that the ball was out and the break was coming. It was humiliating. I knew then that it was going to be downhill as far as playing No. 6 was concerned.

When I had first started training with Saracens, I was shocked at the skill levels of the tight five forwards. I learned that ball-handling skills were only part of it. The amount of skill it takes to become a world-class tighthead prop is unbelievable. The scrum is his bread and butter. It is the same with line-outs and the incredible detail that goes into the breakdown. The contest for the ball – scrum, line-out, breakdown – is critical in rugby union, and the skills involved in all of these contests are extremely specialized, as I was now learning to my cost.

I think fans of both codes love competition and fighting for the ball. When I was growing up there was nothing more exciting than Nicky Kiss, the former Wigan hooker, ripping the ball out of a tackle and running off with it, and scrums in rugby league were proper scrums in those days. There was competition. The most exciting part of the game – in either rugby league or rugby union – is when a team wins turnover ball. I don't think we have enough of that in modern-day rugby league.

As I made my debut for Saracens, I knew I could pass, carry the ball, kick and defend. But what use would I be as a forward on a wet and windy afternoon?

I made my senior debut off the bench in Saracens' victory over Newcastle the following week, coming on as a replacement in the back row when the game was already won.

After just two games, I knew that Andy Robinson had been right. If I was going to play this game at all, it was going to have to be at centre, even if I knew I no longer had the pace.

The final cruel twist to this whole saga was that Andy, the one guy who had the balls to back me in the first place, had already been sacked by the time I finally made my debut for England at rugby union.

11. The Chariot

I had made just three starts for Saracens at inside centre when Bob Dwyer, Australia's 1991 World Cup-winning coach, said he expected me to be involved with England in the 2007 Six Nations Championship. His comments came after I had played in a World XV side that he coached in a one-off game against South Africa. We lost 32–7 at the Walkers Stadium in Leicester but Dwyer seemed impressed. 'If they have an extended England squad then I would have him straight away,' he said in a press conference after the game.

Having gone through eighteen months injured, and still making my way in the new code, suddenly everything was moving very quickly. Brian Ashton had replaced Andy Robinson as England head coach after the 2006 autumn Test series. Andy is a great bloke, and I couldn't help feeling bad that I had not been able to make any impact at all when he was in charge, after he put so much faith in me.

From my perspective, it helped at least that Brian Ashton was from Leigh, a town in the borough of Wigan. He might have spent his career in rugby union, but he appreciated his league as well. He named me in the Six Nations training squad in January 2007.

'I've been watching him for fifteen years,' Ashton said at the Six Nations launch in London. He went on:

I used to be a season-ticket holder at Wigan. Andy may only have had a handful of union games but, in fact, in terms of what I'm looking for in the inside backs position, he's been playing like that all his life in rugby league. He's got a wide skillset, with his handling, kicking, running and defensive abilities. He's got good game understanding and also really strong leadership qualities, which are important to that position in itself but also to the team as a whole.

They were kind words from Brian, but I was not stupid; there was a 'fast-tracking' element to all of this. Given the RFU's financial commitment, I can imagine Brian was under pressure to involve me as quickly as possible now that I was fit and playing for my club. If I was to play a meaningful role in the World Cup later that year in France, it made sense to blood me in the Six Nations.

It is true that my understanding of the game was improving. The switch to centre had taken away the set-piece responsibilities, and one of the few benefits of spending so much time away from the action was that it had given me the opportunity to study rugby union in depth. I devoured everything I could get my hands on. The note-taking that I had started as an eighteen-year-old continued. I had made a vow to myself that while I couldn't play, I would boost my knowledge by watching videos, reading, and talking to coaches and players. I wanted to know everything. I might not have the skills to play the game instinctively, but I wanted to know my stuff.

It was an eye-opening experience. I made it my business to understand the scrum, how it works. I found it fascinating to learn how complicated scrummaging is and how it keeps evolving. It was the same with line-outs. It takes a vast amount of work for a rugby union side to become like a well-oiled machine. I say to my players now that no one cares if you have six months of preparation or three training sessions: the supporters want a big performance either way. When you come into an international camp, the amount of work these lads do to be a cohesive team in three or four sessions is phenomenal to watch.

By switching codes, I also gained a better understanding of how rugby union people view rugby league. Guys would ask why does the dummy half, the player who picks the ball up after a play-the-ball following a tackle, just run straight into the defence when there is space out wide? The reason is that rugby league is a war of attrition. It's not all about trying to score every time you have the ball; it's also about wearing down the opposing defence. The ball is turned over once the defensive team has made six tackles, and people talk of the need for the attacking team to 'complete your set of six'. After each tackle, the defence has to retreat ten metres and then run up to meet the ball-carrying again. Back and forth, back and forth: it is draining. If you lose the ball on tackle two, then you have missed out on a chance to wear the defence down, and you are losing the war of attrition. It is all about who breaks first. Sometimes you're targeting a specific opposition player. Take someone like Paul Sculthorpe at St Helens. He was a brilliant player and, out of complete respect, one of our tactics would have been to run at him all afternoon to make him tackle again and again. In one game we played against him, I think he made over fifty tackles. When you are making tackle after tackle, by the end you are no longer superhuman. That is the war of attrition. It can test your mettle like you wouldn't believe. Sometimes it feels like you are drowning.

I remember watching some games of rugby union when

Jason Robinson was at Bath, and Robbie Paul and Gary Connolly were at Harlequins. I can remember seeing Robbie doing some fitness work after one match because he didn't feel like he had done anything during the game.

Of course, both codes require huge levels of physicality and bravery; they just take somewhat different forms. When you see a player in rugby league taking the ball from a back-line at kick-off and sprinting towards a big defensive line coming forward, it looks barbaric. In rugby union, I saw the bravery that is required for a player to put his head over the ball at a breakdown when he knows he is going to get absolutely smashed. I started playing at the end of the era when, as a forward, if you hadn't ripped someone's shirt with your 21mm studs at a ruck then you hadn't had a good game. And the physicality needed in scrums, mauls and pick-and-go drives equalled anything in rugby league.

Getting to understand and learning to love the nuts and bolts of rugby union meant that when the England squad met up for a training week ahead of our opening game against Scotland at Twickenham, I was at least able to do so feeling like I could be in full voice, even if I knew I was far from the best version of myself as a player. I was heading towards the end of my career and had a lot going on with my body injury-wise. To be honest, even if I'd been playing rugby league, I'm not sure how well I could have applied myself. But at least when I was playing for Great Britain in rugby league, I knew I had earned the right and was comfortable in my own skin. As a newcomer to union, I never felt comfortable in the England squad: there was never a sense of belonging.

When Brian told me I would be starting against Scotland, there was also a familiar face in the side. He had managed to persuade Jason Robinson, my old teammate at Wigan, to return fifteen months after he had retired from the international stage. Jonny Wilkinson was also back, having been through his own injury hell. It shows the respect he commanded that he went straight into the starting XV having played just forty-odd minutes for his club the previous weekend after five months on the sidelines and over three years since his last England cap. I was picked to play at inside centre, although I was encouraged by Brian to step up as first receiver when I could. It brought me closer to the action and also helped to stop the Scottish defence from drifting because they weren't sure if I could carry the ball or not.

As I stood for the anthems, I sucked in the atmosphere of Twickenham. I am not sure I could say that the dark times I had been through since making the switch felt worthwhile in the moment, but the experience of the build-up was everything I had hoped for. The Six Nations is special. I had watched many games when I had been a league player, and the atmosphere was like a Challenge Cup final back in the day when they were absolutely humming. Fans felt so lucky to get a ticket to Twickenham and there was such an intense atmosphere. The rivalries in the Six Nations are fierce – every game was massive. It was like a cup final, every week. It still is.

My parents were in the crowd. It was their first visit to Twickenham and they loved the atmosphere, but sadly Colleen was absent as she was in America attending a friend's wedding. I had played in many Test matches for Great Britain in rugby league, and big cup finals at Wembley and Old Trafford, but despite all that experience I could not help feeling nervous. I knew there were a lot of eyes on me, to see how I would perform. But I was masking the feeling that I never felt comfortable in my own skin as a rugby union player. I wondered myself if I was good enough or if I had earned the right to be there. There was never any of that doubt when I played rugby league for Great Britain.

We won comfortably in the end. Jonny Wilkinson stole the headlines by scoring twenty-seven points – a record in a Calcutta Cup fixture – in a 42–20 win. I managed to get my hands on the ball a few times, helping to create one of two tries scored by Jason. My only frustration was that at centre I was a good distance away from being able to pick out tired forwards.

We backed it up with a relatively straightforward victory over Italy at Twickenham before we headed to Dublin for one of the most extraordinary games in the history of the Six Nations.

With Lansdowne Road under redevelopment, the Gaelic Athletic Association had made the historic decision to allow rugby and football to be played at Croke Park, their 83,000-capacity stadium in north Dublin. The stadium is regarded as a sacred place, given that fourteen people had been killed and many wounded there in 1920 during Ireland's war of independence after British forces opened fire on crowds watching a GAA match.

Brian Ashton had asked Conor O'Shea, who had played for him when he was head coach of Ireland in the 1990s, to give us a sense of what to expect. He arrived at our team hotel in Bath to give us a history lesson. Conor's father had won the GAA's All-Ireland football final playing for Kerry at the stadium on three occasions in the 1950s. Two weeks earlier Ireland had lost in the last minute to France in the first game of rugby to be played at Croke Park. Before then 'foreign' sports such as rugby and football had been banned. Conor told us that it would be more than just another game for Ireland. We knew this was a game Ireland would feel they simply could not lose.

We had also heard about how England had travelled to Dublin to play against Ireland in 1973 at the height of the Troubles after both Wales and Scotland had refused to go there the previous year. John Pullin's side had spoken about their fears of the threat of violence when they arrived but the warmth of the reception from Ireland supporters was overwhelming.

The situation in 2007 may have been vastly different, but lots of things were going through our heads when we travelled. We drove from the airport to the Intercontinental Hotel in Ballsbridge under armed guard. I didn't know whether our team bus would be bricked or worse – all sorts of things ran through my mind. It is ridiculous to think about now, because you could have heard a pin drop during 'God Save the Queen'.

It was an unbelievable honour to be involved in that game. I don't say that lightly, because we were not just beaten but took a real hiding. Ireland had built it up in the right way. They didn't just play the occasion but allowed themselves to play their best rugby. I had a sense of the pressure they had been under to perform. I had felt similar pressure when we had played our last game at Central Park against St Helens, and in big Tests against Australia. Performing when the pressure is at its most overwhelming is something I have always been fascinated by. One of their standout moments was Ronan O'Gara's kick pass to Shane Horgan to score in the corner. In the build-up Denis Leamy, the Ireland No. 8, had picked the ball up from the base of a five-metre scrum. We had got a bit of a shunt on and I shot out of the line to tackle him. He went low, and although I was able to bring him down, by the time I was on my feet again Horgan was collecting ROG's crossfield kick above his head like a Gaelic footballer. We probably missed a bit of experience on the day, leaders who could stand up to the pressure and take the game to Ireland. But my abiding memory is that the pressure brought the best out of that Ireland team. It was one of the greatest examples I have seen of a team nailing it when they had to, even if it was tough for me to take at the time.

Winning matters to me: I have been competitive all my life. But what I regard as the crème de la crème is performing when it really matters. That day I saw grit, mentality and a togetherness from Ireland. Not only did they not lose the game, they destroyed us.

It would also be my last experience of the Six Nations as a player. My back flared up again and I was ruled out of our final two games – a victory over France and then a defeat by Wales – that ended our outside hopes of winning the title.

* * *

When I was picked to play at centre for England's World Cup warm-up match against Wales, I was asked about my fitness. It was a common theme by now. I had been picked for the two-Test tour of South Africa in May and June, but was struck by a stomach virus that had swept through the squad and missed both games.

Looking after my body was taking up more and more of my time. Some days my back was so bad I had to walk down the stairs backwards. When I was a kid, I would just stretch my calves for a couple of minutes and then

I was off. Now it was taking me almost an hour to warm up. When you have to spend so much time on your body, something else has to give. Yet having had the summer to prepare for the 2007 World Cup in France, I felt in decent enough shape.

'I would think it was 2004 when I was last fully fit,' I told reporters ahead of the Wales game that would be one of the final trials before the World Cup squad was announced. 'I have had six weeks of really intense training, three or four sessions a day. Six months ago, I wouldn't have been able to have done that.'

I loved the tournament from start to finish. Every player has an opinion on what went on in France. Afterwards there were reports of a player revolt after our heavy defeat in the pool stages by the Springboks.

Few people know there had actually been a mini-revolt *before* the South Africa game.

I had been named on the bench for the opening game against the USA, with Mike Catt and Jamie Noon starting in the midfield and Olly Barkley at fly-half because Jonny Wilkinson was struggling with an ankle injury. When Barkley picked up an injury, I trained at fly-half for one of the sessions. Brian had clearly decided to have a look at playing me there against the Springboks. I guess the decision was based on what had been seen in camp over the previous three months. It was a ballsy thought from Brian.

I am always a believer that to do something worthwhile in life, you need an opportunity, and to do something extra special, you need a big opportunity, one that you are scared of taking, one that makes you say to yourself, *Really? Can I do this?* They are the opportunities that make you concentrate so much that you can make them pay. I was up for playing out-half against the Springboks – but it didn't happen. During the week of the game, Mike Catt got a sniff of what was happening and went to Brian to ask him what he was thinking. He had a good relationship with Brian. There were a few discussions behind the scenes, and Catty ended up playing 10, and I played 12.

It didn't bother me. If someone asks you to do something, then I always think you should just go ahead and try to do your best. But looking back, and considering that we lost the game 36–0, I knew what the story would have been afterwards if I had played fly-half. I had at least been nominated as goal-kicker, but never got a shot. The closest we came to scoring was a long-range drop-goal attempt by Catty.

The manner of our defeat caused a bit of upset. There were some meetings afterwards about how we should play. I think that some players didn't get what it was that Brian was trying to achieve. Back then the relationship between coach and player would have been, 'Do as I tell you.' But Brian did not want to dictate the whole time. Instead he was allowing us to contribute to working out what was best for the team.

The experience of losing to South Africa had a galvanizing effect on us as a squad. Rarely does a team win a trophy without having to overcome a period of adversity. Brian Ashton's England squad found a way to get over it. For all the talk of the conflict that went on behind the scenes in 2007, that is what usually happens. It was the same at Wigan: for all those trophies that we won, there was all sorts of shit going on behind the scenes. People seem to want sport to be a fairytale, and it is never that.

I was dropped to the bench for the next game, a 44–22

win against Samoa, as Jonny Wilkinson returned at fly-half. Then I scored my first and only try for England, coming off the bench in the 36–20 victory over Tonga as we clinched a place in the quarter-final against Australia in Marseille. After the tough start, I felt I was playing myself into the tournament, and I was selected at centre again for the quarter-final. It would have been my biggest game in rugby union. But it wasn't to be: I pulled my calf chasing a kick in training just hours after the team had been named. It probably summed up my rugby union career. It was Catty who took my place, and with a memorable scrummaging performance we shocked the Wallabies to win 12–10. Then we beat France in the semi-finals before losing a very tight final to South Africa. If the TMO hadn't ruled that Mark Cueto's foot was in touch before he touched down early in the second half, it might have been different.

I would have loved to be on the pitch at the business end of the tournament, but it was still a privilege to be involved at all, and I have a lot to thank Brian Ashton for. You can look back at all the tough times, but I prefer to recall the memories I made along the way, and I cherish having had the opportunity to witness at first hand what it takes for a squad in rugby union to go to the World Cup. The whole journey was an amazing one.

After the tournament I had a conversation with Brian, and we agreed: I couldn't perform at international level any more. Should I have made the change to union earlier? The injuries came at a bad time for me, when I was trying to learn a new code under so much scrutiny. There were times when I got back from training feeling completely hopeless, and brought nothing but stress and worry into the house. It was awful for Colleen, who had done so much to facilitate my move. But I wouldn't change anything. Being able to go through all those dark times made me stronger as a person, and us stronger as a couple. And as the door began to close on my playing career, another big opportunity was about to present itself.

12. The Relief

Eddie Jones, who was widely praised for his role as a technical advisor to the Springboks during their World Cup-winning campaign in France, came back to Saracens at the start of 2008, initially to assist Alan Gaffney by heading up recruitment for the following season. He quickly made his mark by securing the high-profile signatures of Steve Borthwick, who at the time was England captain, Wales No. 8 Michael Owen, and Springbok flanker Wikus van Heerden.

Within a few months he had taken complete control, with the club announcing that Gaffney would be joining Leinster as backs coach at the end of the season. It had been a tough campaign for Gaffs. We had failed to deliver on our potential in the Premiership, eventually finishing in eighth place, but had rallied to reach the semi-finals of the Heineken Cup after a surprise victory over Ospreys in the quarter-finals. The Welsh region, who were stacked with internationals, had been heavy favourites after giving us a real beating in the Anglo-Welsh Cup semi-final a couple of weeks earlier. But we beat them 19–10 at Vicarage Road, when Richard Hill displayed his incredible warrior spirit by leading from the front despite limping around the pitch in what was his fifteenth and final season at the club.

My season was already over by then: I ruptured my AC joint in the first half against Ospreys. No painkilling injection could mask this injury. My shoulder ended up half-way down my chest and I had to have an operation to pull it back into place. I faced another three months on the sidelines.

I was already seriously starting to doubt whether I could keep playing on for another season when Eddie called me into his office during pre-season training. He told me he wanted me to be co-captain with Steve Borthwick. As an avid Australian sports fan, he knew me from my rugby league days, and we shared a working-class background. He loved to talk rugby, and he started to encourage me to think about coaching too. One day he asked me to go for a coffee with him at Saracens' training base, which then was at the University of Hertfordshire. It gave me the opportunity to pick his brains.

'What would be the best piece of advice you would give to anyone considering going into coaching?' I asked him.

'You've got to know a lot about a lot,' he said.

'To be a head coach?' I replied. 'Yeah, but even as an assistant coach,' he added. 'You need to know how it all comes together.'

Eddie's point chimed with me. Whether playing rugby league or union, I had always wanted to know as much as I could about attack and defence. If you understand defence, it gives you an insight into attack. If I was going to move into coaching at some stage, I never wanted to be pigeonholed.

'The best piece of advice I was given was by Bob Dwyer, who said you need to have a coach's eye for everything in the moment,' Eddie added.

I probed him more about the 'coach's eye'. 'Everyone has laptops now and they try to go back and work out why something has happened,' he said. 'Coaches need to be able to see the game in real time, and be able to understand why things are happening, rather than just rely on video.'

His final point seemed the most daunting one. 'Andy, you

need to be able to build a team in seven days, even though some people need or want six months. Otherwise, you are overcomplicating things.'

I went home that night and wrote up everything in my beloved PDA palmtop computer that had replaced my old notepads.

* * *

It seemed that Owen had caught Eddie's eye during our pre-season training. Owen was just sixteen at the time and had just returned from an England Under-18 tour of Argentina. We were due to play the Australian side Western Force in a pre-season friendly at Old Albanians and Eddie spoke to me after training. 'Andy, I wasn't going to play you in this one,' he said. 'But I am thinking about playing Owen. Do you want to play with him?'

I didn't hesitate. 'Shit, that would be brilliant,' I replied.

'OK then, I will put you both on the bench and you can both come on together.'

If Eddie thought Owen was ready, that was good enough for me. He had earned the right.

Owen and I had always competed against each other. At the start, I never let him win at anything, just as my dad had been with me. Even if we were playing tiddlywinks, I would want to win. I knew how much I had benefited from tough love from the senior players at Wigan when I had first come into the squad. They were never soft on any of us.

Owen relished the journey, every step of the way. I can remember taking him along to a pre-season training session the year that I signed for Saracens. The academy players were training too, and Owen immediately made an impact, not afraid to start barking orders even though he was only thirteen at the time. When he was interviewed ahead of his debut against Western Force he said he didn't stop talking when he was on the field because he had watched me do the same for all those years. I insisted that he got that from his mother, not me!

As a senior player and co-captain it was my duty to show the young players what it took to make it and help drive them on. I would do the same for Owen, but as a fellow professional, not as my son. There was no point in a club having star players if they were out of reach to the next generation coming through. By now it had reached the stage when Owen was starting to keep me on my toes. Yeah, he was ready. And as a father, I was simply bursting with pride.

We had both been named on the bench against Western Force, but when the time came to go on together, Owen was nowhere to be seen. The flag was already up for us to go on so in the end I had to run on by myself. It turned out Owen had been on the toilet. He must have been literally shitting himself. Within two minutes, my injury jinx had struck again as I fractured and dislocated my thumb. As Owen appeared on the touchline having relieved himself, his role was now as my replacement and we were only on the pitch together as he ran on and I trudged off, cursing my luck again. We had been named in the same squad, had changed together in the same dressing room, but I am not sure it can really be said that we played together, which, looking back now, is a shame.

Two weeks later Owen became the youngest player to make his competitive debut in professional rugby union in England when he came off the bench in the Anglo-Welsh match against Scarlets at Vicarage Road. It was just eleven days after his seventeenth birthday. What took you so long, Owen? Only joking, son.

With me out injured again, this time Colleen and I could watch together as proud parents. It was left to me to bring him back down to earth after the game. 'He's still got to do his homework tonight and go to school in the morning,' was my blunt assessment when asked by reporters how he had done. But having been there myself, I knew how much hard work he had put in and just how tough it was to break into the men's game while still a schoolboy.

'It's hard for these young players,' I added. 'They have gone from being the top in their peer group to a really harsh environment and playing professional rugby is not easy. It is a test of character. Owen is really serious about his rugby and, yes, it was magnificent to see him play in the first team.'

* * *

While Owen's playing career was taking off, mine was slowly grinding to a halt. If I play golf nowadays, I can barely walk the next day. But that doesn't matter. What mattered then was that I was finding it harder and harder to back up train-ing days, never mind matches. Some days I was in such pain I would have to slide down the stairs on my backside. At Wigan, I couldn't wait to get off to training in the morning. Now, I dreaded it. I was in survival mode.

While I appreciated the culture change that Eddie was driving at Saracens, he knocked the stuffing out of me by deciding to drop me to the bench for a Premiership match. What hit me the hardest was that he didn't tell me himself. Eventually, after I had asked, he left it to one of his assistant coaches to deliver the news. I had been playing professional sport for over fifteen years and had not been used to that. It absolutely killed me.

From Eddie's point of view, it might just have been because

he wanted to give someone else a chance, or whatever. But I received no explanation of why I'd been dropped, or what I needed to work on. And I needed to know. Looking back, it affected me more than it should have, and I took it home with me. But it would also shape my mindset later as a coach. When you don't get an explanation, it is harder to accept or to put right what is wrong. I know what the players are going through and what it means to them, and I never underestimate that when I'm selecting a side.

Eddie appeared to have been left somewhat in the dark himself when a new South African consortium invested in Saracens. We were still struggling in the Premiership when Edward Griffiths replaced Mark Sinderberry as chief executive. And with a major overhaul to the squad looming, Eddie stepped down in February 2009, with Brendan Venter taking over as director of rugby. It was a brutal time. There were rumours of a major cull of the squad.

I still had a year left on my contract, but was concerned that I would be at the top of their list of players to get rid of. I could just imagine Brendan saying, 'He is on decent wages, and we are not getting value for money because he is not playing much.' And he would have been right. I had a young family and a mortgage. But I needed to retire. I felt desperate. I just couldn't keep going, but had no idea what the solution was.

The pivotal moment came at a vineyard in Cape Town. I was on a short holiday there with Colleen and the kids when Dominic Silvester, who was a major shareholder at Saracens at the time and later became club owner, rang to ask if I would meet Brendan for lunch.

Brendan had been in the World Cup-winning South Africa side in 1995 and forged a reputation as a physical player with

London Irish. He was a straight talker. 'I know you have a year left on your contract,' he said, 'but I think you should finish playing and instead come on board as one of our assistant coaches.'

The relief was overwhelming. I could almost feel the stress that I had been carrying around with me for more than a year evaporate in the Cape Town sunshine as we sipped our coffees. In my state of relief, everything felt possible. Ever since I was eighteen, I had wanted eventually to become a coach, and here was an opportunity to move into the next stage of my career. Yet as we talked, a sense of fear arose too. I had spent my whole career as a player, working my way up the ladder. When I went into coaching, I knew I would have to start all over again at the bottom. It was a daunting prospect. I knew I would also have to deal with coaching players who had been my teammates, and that would bring its own challenges. But I knew this was something I had always wanted to do and I was prepared to work as hard at it as I had done making my way as a player.

There was not much negotiation about my new contract. Brendan told me the salary, which was around a third of what I was currently on. 'If you can't live on that then there is something wrong with your lives,' he added.

Colleen and I were sitting there thinking, *How does he know what we can afford?* I guess Brendan was valuing things from a South African perspective, and when you converted pounds into rand it was a different story.

Brendan smiled and we shook hands. And in the moment, I realized that it had all been worth it. All the hard work in attempting to transition from rugby league to union, all the dark times that I had gone through with my injuries, of feeling trapped and unable to show the best version of myself and ultimately reaching the point when I was getting up every morning knowing that I couldn't do it any more. It had been a big old cloud, but what a silver lining.

When I later heard the stories of what was happening with some of the other players, I felt even more fortunate. Each member of the squad was called into two-minute meetings with Brendan and Edward Griffiths, and told either that they were still part of the squad or that their services were no longer required. It was as brutal as that. A total of fifteen players, including former All Blacks forward Chris Jack, were sent packing. You can only imagine the shit that was flying around.

I announced my retirement from playing in April, with no doubts or regrets. After our final game at Vicarage Road, a narrow defeat by eventual champions Leicester, I was given a jersey by the club. It was half Wigan, half Saracens, and a record of all the games I had played for Saracens (28) and England (8) in rugby union and Wigan (370), England (11) and Great Britain (34) in rugby league. There were other more worthy players who were also getting a send-off, such as Kris Chesney, a club stalwart who was joining Toulon. He had been at Saracens his entire career and it should have all been about him. I felt a bit of a fraud even getting a mention at the end.

If I had been given a send-off at Wigan, it would have brought a tear to my eye because I had had a career and loads of memories of what I had achieved at the club. There is nothing better than being at your home-town club and looking back at the success that you enjoyed. The feeling of sadness at Saracens was very different. I felt helpless that I had been unable to pay back what Nigel Wray and Dominic Silvester and the rest of the board had invested in me. They had treated me brilliantly, but there hadn't been much pay-back. At least I felt now I had an opportunity to start making amends as a coach. I couldn't wait.

* * *

Brendan proved to be the perfect man for the moment. He had to completely rebuild the squad. It was as if the old Saracens suddenly didn't exist. As part of the group of coaches, I had to play my part in getting a completely new-look squad together for the start of the season.

What Brendan and Edward Griffiths achieved in such a short span of time was phenomenal. Edward was a genius in terms of how he built the club back up again from nothing, with the backing of Nigel Wray and Dominic Silvester. He and Brendan turned the club around within two years. I think they saw themselves as disruptors, taking on the established order of English rugby, and they gave the squad a purpose and an identity that it hadn't had before. It was all underpinned by two key tenets: working hard for each other and caring for one another. Before they arrived, Saracens had a reputation for being underachievers. It took real leadership to come in and start from scratch. I don't think they were given the credit they deserved. People forget they brought in a group of largely unknown players and made them into big names, with a squad that was not as deep as the big clubs at the time.

Internally, the culture was positive, caring and supportive, a world very different from the one I had forged my career in. Yet outwardly Edward created this narrative that it was us against the world. It is what good teams do: everyone hates us, let's circle the wagons. Brendan was just as committed to the philosophy, and got the players on board as well. As lovely a man as he is, he also has an unbelievably competitive edge. He sold this vision to the players: that we were going to strip everything back and play a structured kicking game based on where we were on the pitch, giving the opposition possession but putting them under ferocious pressure. The less possession you had, the fewer mistakes you made.

He had assembled a fantastic group of coaches. Mark McCall joined from Castres as backs and attack coach. Smally, as he is known, also acted as Brendan's sounding board. Paul Gustard and Alex Sanderson, who had also retired early and had been coaching for a couple of years, had learned a fierce work ethic from working under Eddie. They more than survived that because of their capabilities, and Brendan trusted them both. They were way ahead of me, fantastic guys to learn from.

Within a couple of months Mark turned to Brendan and said that I should be coaching the backs. There is nothing precious about Mark; he does what is best for the team. Before long I was in charge of the attack too. Mark remained Brendan's right-hand man and was effectively the senior coach – heading up what was a young coaching team and acting as the go-between with Brendan.

It was brilliant for me to be under that kind of pressure. It was like a fast-track coaching academy. And I had so much to learn. I would speak to other coaches and our players and absorb as much information as I could.

What I wrestled with the most was presentation. It is all very well having ideas, but they are worth nothing unless you can get your message across to the players. Striking the right tone was something I would struggle with for several years. Guzzy and Alex would come up with these brilliant presentations, using all sorts of props, video footage and powerful messages, and I felt under pressure to mimic them. If I had a presentation on a Thursday afternoon, I would spend all week preparing for it.

I understand now that I should have been spending less time on presentations and more time on what matters most: the sessions, the tactics, the plan. I should have let the main thing be the main thing. In my naivety as a new coach I was missing the point. It is a piece of advice I pass down to new up-and-coming coaches nowadays.

On reflection, I should have known better. As a player, I can remember sitting there feeling uncomfortable if a coach was trying to be something he was not. Rugby players are not rocket scientists; they want their coaches to be real. You get a lot of buzzwords thrown around, but to me, being authentic, being yourself, is all that matters. If you are being yourself, the players can relate to that, and they feel more comfortable in joining in and airing an opinion. But it took a long time for me to realize that, because I felt that being my best was about how to deliver the message, rather than the message itself.

As backs coach, I was only allowed to work on two moves. Two. All Brendan wanted us to do was to get over the gain line, get the defence going backwards around the corner, and then we would beat them on the outside. There was no intricacy about it. How on earth was I going to sell this as the backs coach? Even if you were limited to two moves, you could have three or four variations of each, but Brendan wanted me to keep it as simple as possible so that the backs were free to concentrate on other aspects of the game. I had to convince two of my former teammates, Justin Marshall, the former All Blacks scrum-half, and Glen Jackson, our star fly-half, that this was the right approach. They felt that we needed more moves.

One morning when I arrived to training at Old Albanians, Brendan called me into his office. I knew what was coming.

'Faz, we have got a problem with some of the senior players,' he said. 'We are going to have to pull the boots on ourselves to prove a point.'

It was a moment to forget the high-tech presentations that had been devouring my time and return to an old-school live demonstration. We held a training session with two back-lines going at each other, with Brendan and me playing as centres on opposing sides, each tasked with running one of the moves to get over the gain line. 'Let's show them that this works,' he added.

I was first up. I had to get over the gain line from a scrum play. I knew that Brendan was going to come for me because that is the only way he knew. I loved that about him. He might have been in his early forties by then, but he flew up at me. My job was to try to find a 'soft' shoulder (when a tack-ler overcommits in one direction and the ball-carrier steps inside), but Brendan doesn't have any soft shoulders and there was an almighty collision. I did my job, though, and Brendan bounced straight on his feet. 'That's brilliant, Faz; you see, it worked!'

Next it was Brendan's turn. When Brendan was carrying, he used to have what he called his 'sword': an extended fore-arm that he used to fend off the tackler in contact. I knew it was coming, and once again we crashed into each other in another big collision. In a second Brendan was back on his feet. 'You see, guys, that is how it is done,' he said.

Brendan's point was not tactical. His point was that he wanted to make sure everyone was on the same page. Sara-cens in the past had been used to signing big names who collectively had underperformed. Many of the new squad were not household names but suited the way he wanted to play. Brendan wanted us to stand for intensity, hard work and fighting spirit, and believed that we could achieve that with a simple game plan: get over the gain line, create quick ball and then let the defence deal with us.

By getting me to run at him and then tackle him, he was saying to the players that it did not matter if you had twenty-five backline plays: you had to stand for something.

What he didn't know was that in the process he had suffered a deep gash to his forehead, and blood started spilling down his face. I wasn't in much better shape: I had taken a finger in my eye. The players looked on in silence, not knowing what to make of us both. We went back into the office after the morning session. 'Thanks, Faz, that was good. I think we made our point,' he said. Blood was still pouring out of him, but he seemed more concerned about me. Brendan was a doctor by profession. 'Your eye looks pretty bad; you should go to the hospital.' I went off to get it checked and missed the afternoon session. It turned out I had been lucky to escape more serious damage. A big chunk had been taken out of my eyeball, just a millimetre away from my pupil and I had to wear an eye patch for a couple of days.

Whether our bloody demonstration was successful in getting the point across to the players, I don't know. But what I do know is that they did buy into it and we were pretty successful with it. And I reckon Brendan would still be up for doing the same again, all these years later. It showed me what you could achieve as a team if everyone bought in. Teams need an identity to succeed, and that's what was so powerful for the club in those couple of seasons under Brendan. It might have been a limited game plan, and might not have won over many neutrals, but we won our first eight league games and, after a draw against Worcester, were top of the league at Christmas.

We ended up finishing the season in third place and reached the playoff final at Twickenham by defeating Northampton at Franklin's Gardens in the semi-finals – a fixture that had extra edge following our failed attempt to sign their Tonga prop Soane Tonga'uiha.

Brendan couldn't attend the final as he was serving a ten-week ban for making what an RFU disciplinary panel described as 'inappropriate gestures and comments' to spectators during our win at Leicester in May, so Smally was in charge. It was tough for Brendan, but it added to the narrative of us against the world. In just a matter of months he had established a group of players who would do anything for each other. During the last third of the season, he had also allowed us to broaden our attacking game. Meanwhile, Edward was stoking up our fans, calling on them to assemble at Twickenham to 'give the players a welcome to the stadium like no other they will have experienced'.

We gave the final against Leicester one hell of a go, losing 33–27 in what was described as the greatest Premiership final ever played. It had been an extraordinary first season in coaching for me, witnessing Brendan reconstruct a side from nothing, give the players an identity and a cause to believe in, and come within a couple of minutes of being crowned champions of England. Despite the disappointment of defeat, as we travelled back to St Albans I knew that the experience would strengthen this group.

* * *

Andy Clarke, my agent, knew Stuart Lancaster from the days when they shared a house together while at Leeds Metropolitan University. Still, it was something of a surprise when

Andy said that Stuart had been in touch to ask if I wanted to become part of the coaching team for the England Saxons, which was the name for the 'A' team back then. Stuart was the Rugby Football Union's head of elite player development and was putting together a coaching team for the Churchill Cup in the United States in June.

It was even more of a surprise when I learned that he wanted me to be his defence coach. I had been learning my trade coaching attack, backs and skills at Saracens, but I had never done the defence. I guess there was a perception that rugby league players who had switched codes were ready-made defence coaches.

Phil Larder had led the way when Sir Clive Woodward hired him to be defence coach for the senior England squad in 1997, a key appointment that culminated in their World Cup win in 2003. Phil put structures into their defence, founded on the marker defence in rugby league, where two players stand at the front of the play-the-ball while the rest of the defenders have to retreat ten metres. It was Phil who used that system to construct the 'pillar' defence at the ruck in union, where a defender would guard each side of the breakdown; and he had his defenders push up and out, forcing the attacking team towards the touchline.

Before Phil's time, I can remember watching England rugby union games on TV and asking: 'Where is the defensive system?' Rugby union defences, even at the highest level, were really unstructured in those days. The organizational principles imported from rugby league made a big impact on rugby union defences. John Muggleton, the former Parramatta Eels forward, had done something similar with the Wallabies, and their defence won them the 1999 World Cup, conceding just one try in the whole tournament.

Suddenly everyone in rugby union wanted a defence coach from rugby league. Shaun Edwards was hired by Wasps and Dave Ellis was hired by Gloucester. And now I was about to join the list, even though I was still a rookie coach who had only ever experienced the club environment at Saracens.

I didn't hesitate. 'No problem, I'll do it,' I told Stuart. I saw it as a massive opportunity, and another chance to take myself completely out of my comfort zone. Eddie had told me that I had to know a lot about a lot, and this was a chance to fast-track my knowledge as a defence coach. I knew I had to live the experience. Feel it. The more severe the challenge, the greater the possibility for learning. Switching to rugby union and the transition to club coaching had tested me like I could not have imagined. Now I was being plunged into the world of international coaching, with no preparation time. It was too good an opportunity to turn down.

I had cut my teeth in games against Ireland A and Italy A in January and February, but I knew the real step up would come with the Churchill Cup in the summer. The day after our defeat in the Premiership final, I was facing the prospect of having to build a defence in just seven days, with Eddie Jones's words ringing in my ears. We beat Russia and USA in the pool stages and then, in the searing heat of New Jersey, defeated Canada 38–18 in the final.

I was just thirty-five and had just completed my first full season in coaching. I loved the thrill of the international stage. I was starting to find my own way.

13. The Tears

When Owen was released by Saracens to play for Bedford Blues in the Championship, the second tier of English rugby, it reminded me of those Friday-night matches playing for the Wigan second team in the Alliance League. As an academy player, you can do as much training and skills work as you like, but nothing fast-tracks a young player as quickly as playing against men.

When you are a youngster facing men in their late twenties, there is not just a physical challenge but also a mental one. A young player has to quickly find his voice within his own side and prepare to be a target for the opposition. Getting roughed-up every now and again and finding a way to get through it can be priceless.

Bedford had already been a proving ground for the likes of Tom Youngs, Dan Cole, Mouritz Botha and Karl Dickson, and Owen loved his time there. He was able to play four games for the club at the start of the 2010/11 season before our fly-half Derick Hougaard ruptured his Achilles tendon. Our resources were pretty thin at 10, so Brendan decided to recall Owen. It was a huge endorsement. Brendan felt Owen was ready to step up and would be able to execute his game plan. My job as backs coach was to help him. He and I both knew this was business. There were no guarantees.

The club signed former Wales and Lions back Gavin Henson, who was released from his Ospreys contract having been on unpaid leave for eighteen months, but he did not make his debut until Boxing Day because he was competing in the BBC show *Strictly Come Dancing*. It was a bit of a left-field decision to bring him in, but I loved him as a player. I had played against him at the back end of my rugby union career, and he was far better than me: tough, strong and skilful. He used to take some stick about his appearance, with his fake tan and flamboyant hairstyles, but he just didn't care. He was one of the game's characters.

While Gav was away dancing, Owen made his first Premiership start against Bath at the Rec in November, drafted into the side at the last minute when Alex Goode and Brad Barritt both failed late fitness tests. At the time Colleen was pregnant with Gabriel. The timing was not lost on me: she had been pregnant with Owen when I had made my senior debut with Wigan. She was beside herself with nerves about Owen. I had to ring her three times on the way to the game to make sure everything was OK and to tell her not to get too hyped up. It was another reminder to me of just how hard it is to be a player's parent. It was easier for me because I was coaching. As soon as I got to the training ground at eight o'clock in the morning I was his coach, and when I got home in the evening I was his father again. It was that simple. And it was made simpler by the fact that neither of us knew any different.

It was Mark McCall's job to tell Owen he was starting against Bath – he found out the same way as everyone else in the team meeting. I could tell Owen was nervous, but having so little time to think about it was a blessing. Just get on with it, son, you'll be all right. A penalty in the first half helped settle his nerves, and although we went 13–3 behind, two tries in ten minutes, both converted by Owen, turned the game on its head. He was up and running, and would go on to start at fly-half in all but one of our remaining games that season.

By then my own role had changed. Brendan had to return to South Africa for family reasons and Mark stepped in as director of rugby, while my roles and responsibilities were broadened. Brendan returned every three or four months as a consultant, which allowed him to come back in with fresh eyes and monitor what was working well and what needed to improve.

With Brad Barritt emerging as our rock at inside centre, Gavin found himself on the bench and it surprised everyone in February when he asked to be released by the club to sign for Toulon. At the end of one training session before he left, I lined him up with all the backs and asked him to name them. He could only name one. Dan Vickers, our kicking coach, would have kicked the ball back to Gav every day, but Gav didn't know his name either. It was hilarious. He wasn't being rude; it was just the way he was.

After our defeat by Sale at the start of January, we went on a run of ten successive league victories all the way to the final at Twickenham again. If in the previous season we had caught teams by surprise, this season we benefited from playing with greater cohesion. Four penalties by Owen were enough to edge out Gloucester 12–10 in the semi-finals and book our place in the final against Leicester again.

Watching nineteen-year-old Owen walk out in front of 80,000 supporters at Twickenham brought back memories of my Challenge Cup finals. It was another fantastic occasion. He did all right as well, landing six kicks out of six in our 22–18 victory. I reckon he probably got as much satisfaction out of making a big tackle on Toby Flood, who was the England fly-half at the time. Owen had been playing at inside centre during the previous year and had put a lot of work into his defence. It was the first Premiership title for Saracens, and a special moment for Nigel Wray and Dominic Silvester.

'Owen was very, very good,' said Ben Youngs, the Leicester scrum-half, after the game. 'He looked very relaxed, and I think he was the calmest guy on the pitch. He has had a great season, and I am sure that in the next couple of years you will see him in a Test match.'

* * *

The following season, Saracens had made a decent start to the defence of our title when the phone rang. It was Stuart again. England had endured a difficult World Cup campaign in New Zealand, losing in the quarter-final to France, and there had been off-field controversies too. Martin Johnson had lost his job as head coach and Stuart had been asked by the RFU to take charge on an interim basis for the Six Nations. I must have done an OK job with the Saxons because now he wanted me to do defence for the senior England team. Bloody hell!

It was a dark afternoon in December. My initial instinct was to turn him down. I had a job to do at Saracens. I had enjoyed coaching the Saxons in the summer, but I didn't feel I could step away for three or four months in the middle of the season. It wouldn't be fair on the club that had given me my big break in coaching. And I was loving life at Saracens. It was such a change from my struggles there as a player. I was among a great group of young coaches who were thriving in a brilliant environment under Mark. It couldn't have been a tighter group and I was in no hurry to go anywhere. Yet Mark and Edward Griffiths, our chief executive, both thought I should do it. They felt it was a great opportunity for

coaching development. So it was agreed that I would effectively go out on loan to England for two months. I remained
with Saracens until the end of January and would only miss
four Premiership games during the Six Nations.

The whirlwind of events included a press conference at
Twickenham, when I walked out with my fellow assistant
Graham Rowntree and Stuart in brand-new England track-
suits to face the media. It was surreal. Just four years earlier
my England playing career had come to an end. Now I was
an international rugby union defence coach. Inevitably, the
questions addressed to me turned to the prospect of Owen
making it into the squad. Stuart was intent on making a fresh
start and had told a number of senior players that he would
not be requiring them for the new campaign.

I was happy to address it. 'I want England to win, and
if Owen is playing well enough, he will be considered like
everyone else,' I said. 'My vision is to be part of this exciting
group that is going to set a culture that will drive the players to fight for one another, enjoy each other's company and
play with a smile on their faces. I have done that before with
Stuart and with a lot of hard work we can do the same.'

Owen made England's Six Nations squad, and when it
came to our first selection meeting, Stuart decided to start him
at inside centre for the opening round. Our opponents were
Scotland, the team I had made my debut against five years
earlier. Yet I didn't have time to dwell on the coincidence. I
was quickly finding out just how hectic it can be to get a squad
together for the start of the Six Nations with only five or six
sessions to get up and running and no time for any sentimen-
tal stuff. The night I knew Owen had been selected, when I
got back to my hotel room in our training base at Pennyhill
Park, my mind did drift for a few moments. I was bursting

From my earliest days playing football, I always knew I could strike a ball. In rugby league, unlike rugby union, there was no assumption that the goal-kicker had to be a back.
[Clive Brunskill/Allsport]

By 1998, Wigan's days of dominance were numbered, but we beat Leeds to win the inaugural Super League Grand Final. It was immediately clear that the Challenge Cup was no longer the only big piece of silverware.
[Mike Hewitt /Allsport]

Wigan's Central Park ground was a truly special place. My father called it 'heaven', and I agreed. When the Australian club Manly came to Central Park, I sat for hours on a wall at the front of the old terrace shown in the photo on the left in order to make sure of a good view. And I used to be one of the kids looking down into the tunnel when the Wigan players walked out.

[Allstar Picture Library Ltd/Alamy Stock Photo]

Australia dominated the international game throughout my rugby league career, and we never really caught up with them, but we gave them a tight home Ashes series in 2003, losing the three Tests by a combined eleven points.
[PA Images/Alamy Stock Photo]

It was a huge honour to be awarded an OBE in 2005, following in the footsteps of two rugby league legends, Malcolm Reilly and Sean Edwards, and to go to Buckingham Palace with my mother Carol, Colleen and a thirteen-year-old Owen.
[PA Images/Alamy Stock Photo]

Left: Because of injuries, I made no impact in my first eighteen months in rugby union, and I felt bad that I had not been able to repay the faith that Andy Robinson and Saracens had shown in me. But when Brian Ashton took over as England coach, he named me in the training squad for the 2007 Six Nations and gave me his backing.
[Paul Ellis/AFP via Getty Images]

Below: Jason Robinson's move from Wigan to rugby union was far more successful than mine. Brian Ashton coaxed him out of retirement in 2007, and it was great to celebrate yet another of his tries when I made my Six Nations debut against Scotland.
[John D McHugh/AFP via Getty Images]

Ireland's performance against England at Croke Park in 2007 was one of the greatest examples I ever saw of a team nailing it when they had to. There had been speculation about how 'God Save the Queen' would be received, but you could have heard a pin drop.

[Shaun Botterill/Getty Images]

My first – and, as it turned out, only – try for England came in the group stage of the 2007 World Cup. I felt I was playing my way into form, but I was injured in training before the quarter-final and missed the rest of the tournament.

[David Rogers/Getty Images]

I was surprised when Eddie Jones asked me to be co-captain of Saracens in 2008, because I'd played so little rugby for the club. He and I had some great conversations that influenced the way I thought about coaching.
[Warren Little/Getty Images]

Eddie picked both me and a sixteen-year-old Owen on the bench for a pre-season friendly against Western Force, and his plan was to bring us on together. But Owen – already looking a bit queasy here – was on the toilet when the call came. So I went on without him, immediately got injured, and was replaced by him. We never did get to play together.
[Steve Mitchell/Digital Sports]

By 2011, I was a coach at Saracens and Owen, at nineteen, was a key figure in our victory in the Premiership final against Leicester.
[Mike Hewitt/Getty Images]

It was a pleasant surprise when Warren Gatland (*right*) asked me to join his coaching ticket for the British and Irish Lions tour of Australia in 2013, along with Rob Howley and Graham Rowntree.

[David Rogers/Getty Images]

There were some similarities between Sam Burgess and me, and after he switched to rugby union I worked with him in England's preparations for the 2015 World Cup. He took flak after starting in the group game that we lost to Wales, but he'd played well and England were ahead when he was brought off.

[David Rogers/Getty Images]

England's chances of progressing ended with our heavy defeat to Australia. The faces of myself, Stuart Lancaster and Graham Rowntree tell the story.

[David Rogers/Getty Images]

with pride, like any dad would be, and I thought of all those times we'd spent together, kicking the ball back and forth at Wigan, seeing him rise through the ranks first in rugby league and then rugby union. I knew he had earned the right.

I didn't feel the need to address the father/son relationship with the squad. I would never mention Owen in selection meetings, and the final call has to come from the head coach anyway. If I was guilty of anything, it was of being extra hard on Owen. We both preferred it that way. He didn't want his teammates to think that ours was anything but a 100 per cent professional relationship. We barely talked when we were in camp together.

Nathan Cleary plays for Penrith Panthers in the NRL, where his father Ivan is the head coach. It is obvious that Nathan is not only the best player in Penrith but also the whole of the NRL, so that is never going to cause a problem. But it can be really tough when you have responsibility as head coach and your kid is trying to come through and it is your job to help him. It was so much easier for me because Owen's career had already taken off without me having to make any big decisions, and because I was never his head coach. We also knew no other way. Our approach was just to be as professional as we could.

It was a new era in every sense of the word for England. Owen was one of seven players making their debuts at Murrayfield, while Chris Robshaw was appointed captain for what was just his second cap. It was a brave move by Stuart. He could have chosen to be much more conservative in his selection if his sole intention had been to secure the job on a full-time basis. But having been overseeing the England development pathways, he had better insight than most about the new generation of talent coming through. He felt a new start was the best for English rugby, given that we were at the beginning of a World Cup cycle.

His courage paid off. We returned from Murrayfield with a 13–6 victory, with Owen converting a try by Charlie Hodgson and also landing two penalties. We were unlucky to lose to Wales at Twickenham after David Strettle was certain he had scored a try in the final minute as we were trailing 19–12. But the television match official ruled 'no try' because the footage was inconclusive. Wales would go on to secure the Grand Slam, but our strong finish to the campaign, a thrilling 24–22 victory over France in Paris and a thumping 30–9 win over Ireland at Twickenham, convinced the RFU that Stuart should get the job on a permanent basis. He had earned it.

I had loved my first taste of coaching in the Six Nations, but thought nothing more of it as I returned to Saracens at the end of March. We had a title to defend, and Harlequins and Leicester were proving major threats. But my world was about to be turned on its head. Again.

* * *

I am not used to seeing grown men cry. But now Edward Griffiths was sitting in my kitchen in Harpenden in tears. It was tough to see him upset. I hadn't cried myself since the day when I was dropped by Haydn Walker for rolling that coin. What was I meant to do?

The drama had begun a few weeks earlier. After being confirmed as the permanent England coach, Stuart had been in touch again to offer me a job. Within a couple of days Edward was in talks with the RFU, having ruled out any possibility of a job share similar to the one that Shaun Edwards had with Wasps and Wales.

It sent me into a spin. I loved working at Saracens, and I was only in my third season as a coach there. But the thrill of coaching at international level was undeniable. I still had two years left on my contract with Saracens, and if I left that would have to be sorted out with the RFU. But that was never going to be the issue. It was about doing the right thing. I knew it was a special environment at Saracens. They treated people the right way. Dominic Silvester had been there for me in a big way when I had my car crash, and again when my playing career came to an end and I was offered the coaching position. It is remarkable to me that someone who is so successful in business in his own right, and so busy, is able to give people like me so much of his time. My playing career at Saracens had led to some of my darkest days, but now I was fully engaged in the club's coaching project.

And yet my gut instinct was telling me that this offer to go to England might be a life-changing opportunity. Mark McCall was hugely supportive. He didn't want me to go, but he understood my dilemma. Would the grass be greener with England? I would never know without trying. I talked it over with Colleen. A week passed and I decided to stay. I told the press that 'the job [at Saracens] isn't anywhere near half done and I have decided I want to help finish the job'.

And then I changed my mind. England's summer tour of South Africa was the type of trip I had yearned for when I'd played rugby league for Great Britain, only for the Super League/ARL war to disrupt our schedule. And if I took the England job, I would be involved in the 2015 World Cup campaign.

I told Edward and Mark that I had changed my mind. The club agreed that I could leave, and a fee was negotiated with the RFU. It was too late to join up with the tour in South Africa, so I decided to fly out to Australia to pick the brains of some NRL head coaches. Some contracts include a specific sum to cover the costs of a coaching development plan, but sometimes I would just do it myself. I always like speaking to coaches from other sports and comparing ideas: sometimes it can just trigger something.

One day before I left, Edward knocked at my front door. He wanted one last conversation with me. Sitting in my kitchen, he told me he had huge ambitions for Saracens and a vision of how the club would keep developing. He desperately wanted me to be part of it and he offered to match what England were going to be paying me. I guess his tears reflected how deeply he cared about Saracens. His emotional outpouring wasn't for effect, it was just him being himself. We have laughed about it since, but at the time it was incredibly difficult.

I told him I would sleep on it. I tossed and turned all night, but in the morning, after another chat with Colleen, I knew my decision was final. I rang Edward and told him how much I appreciated his offer, but that I was going to stick to my guns.

14. The Speech

In less than two years I had gone from rookie club coach to England's defence and backs coach. And it would not take long to find out just how green the grass really was.

I quickly discovered how short the honeymoon period for a new international coaching team can be. During the autumn campaign of 2012, we beat Fiji comfortably but then came unstuck against Australia and South Africa. The defeat by the Springboks had ended in a bit of controversy when, very late in the game, Chris Robshaw opted to kick a penalty to the posts rather than go to the corner when we were trailing by four points. Owen, who had come off the bench for Toby Flood, kicked it, but there was not enough time to win back possession from the restart and our defeat was met by boos from some sections of the crowd.

With New Zealand up next the pressure was on. The All Blacks were world champions and were unbeaten in their previous twenty games. Given that our starting XV had a combined total of just over 200 caps, few people gave us a chance. It was my first experience of facing the All Blacks. We could have seen it as a daunting challenge, but in my eyes it was a special opportunity.

Their side was stacked with stars such as Richie McCaw, Kieran Read, Dan Carter and Ma'a Nonu, and coached by Steve Hansen. In contrast, we were rookies. We knew it was going to be unbelievably tough, but I felt it was also going to be a brilliant opportunity for us to learn about ourselves.

Somehow the guys found a way to win, showing what is possible when a team has their backs to the wall and are desperate. Our 38–21 victory was written up as one of England's greatest victories. It was a big moment for Owen, too. He had deputized for Toby Flood in the previous two games, but Stuart brought him into the starting XV and the pressure did not bother him. It is not often that everything clicks against New Zealand, but on that occasion we were dominant. A lot of our players grew up that night.

* * *

That was just my ninth game with England, so it came as a huge surprise when my phone rang and Warren Gatland asked me to be part of his coaching team for the British and Irish Lions tour of Australia the following summer.

I had read the speculation that my name was under consideration but not thought much of it. Shaun Edwards, my former teammate at Wigan, was Gatland's defence coach at Wales and had been part of Ian McGeechan's coaching team for the Lions tour of South Africa in 2009.

I assumed that Shaun would be Lions defence coach this time. When Gatland asked me to do it, I knew I had massive shoes to fill. A lot of the media questioning at the announcement of the coaching ticket centred on Gatland's decision not to go with Shaun. Gats didn't dodge the question:

> Obviously, Shaun was disappointed. It was an agonizing decision to make. But when I looked at the set-up, I wanted continuity from 2009 and the experience that was gained there, but also a bit of freshness. Andy comes hugely recommended, he is very well thought of. But that is taking nothing away from Shaun. He is a world-class coach and has been

very successful in the role he has. It was a tough decision, but I have made that call and it is something I have to live by.

No pressure then, Gats!

Even when my world had been completely dominated by rugby league, I had been aware of the significance of Lions tours. Just like the Olympics or World Cups, they come around every four years and everyone loves them. I couldn't believe I was going to be part of a tour now myself.

After the whirlwind of the announcement, I had to quickly swap the red shirt of the Lions back to the white of England to prepare for the Six Nations. We went into the championship with a real sense that we could build on our second-place finish from the previous season following our performance over the All Blacks. Victories over Scotland at Twickenham, Ireland in Dublin, and France and Italy at Twickenham backed that up. In the final week, we headed to Cardiff in the hunt for England's first Grand Slam since 2003.

Wales could still win the title if they beat us by seven points or more. Gats, who was on sabbatical from coaching Wales ahead of the Lions tour, was licking his lips, stating before the game that it was the perfect test for players to seize the moment and put their hands up for Lions selection.

We had agreed to Wales's request for the roof at the stadium to be closed. To be honest, I have always found it a nonsense that they need the agreement of the opposition to close it. It is their stadium, they should be able to do what they want. I mean, there is a roof over the stadium in Dunedin and it doesn't come off – so what choice have you got there?

Wales had a surprise waiting for us anyway. We had trained all week for a dry-ball game and conditions were perfect at the stadium as we ran through our moves at the captain's run on the day before the game. But when we ran out for our warm-up before kick-off, the pitch was saturated. As I bent down to touch the grass, I looked over at Rob Howley, the Wales assistant coach, and thought to myself, *You bastards!* He saw me looking and just started laughing. But I had no beef with it, really. You see it happening in football, when a visiting team arrives at a stadium wanting to play a high-tempo game but finds the pitch is sodden. While we had spent the week throwing the ball around for a wide and open game, I have no doubt that Wales prepared for a wet-ball game, playing for territory and possession. We quickly found ourselves stuck in our own half, defending multiple phases of pick-and-go drives.

We also had to cope with a six-day turnaround, but the biggest factor was that Wales produced the type of performance that Ireland had at Croke Park in 2007. We got battered, 30–3, and Wales won the title.

Gats had seen the Wales players put their hands up, and when he announced his Lions squad the following month, fifteen Wales players had made it compared with ten from England.

* * *

I had watched Lions tours before, and the *Living with the Lions* video, but being at the heart of it was more special than I could have imagined. It was the kind of touring experience I had yearned for as a player. Midweek matches, constantly on the move, and little time to prepare or review games – there were simply not enough hours in the day, and the players were pushed to limits that they would never experience with their national sides.

We had flown to Hong Kong for a pre-tour match against

the Barbarians and faced extreme weather conditions, with humidity often above 90 per cent and temperatures above thirty degrees. The evening kick-off time brought no relief. We had huge water fans set up at the side of the pitch and the game was stopped twice for water breaks. I don't know how the players managed to catch the ball because it was so slippery, never mind draw a breath. By the time I had walked from the changing room to the coaches' box, I was saturated with sweat.

But I was living the dream, being part of an old-fashioned tour. When something is put in front of you, and you are told 'this is what you have to do', you just do it. You don't even think about it. It is remarkable what the mind and body can adapt to. Everyone wants a seven-day turnaround these days, but I loved the unique challenge of the Lions, with games every three or four days. It reminded me of the best of days with Wigan, when we were going after five trophies.

It felt like we were in a good place after the tour matches, but the Tests were a huge step up in intensity. It took a slice of luck to get us over the line in the first Test in Brisbane, with Kurtley Beale missing a potentially match-winning penalty for the Wallabies with the last kick of the game. Owen made the bench, but didn't get on. Gats raised it with me when we reviewed the game. In retrospect he felt we should have brought Owen on and told me not to be afraid to speak up if I thought we needed to make a change. But Rob Howley was the backs and attack coach, and he might not have thought it was the right thing to do. I didn't think it was my place to suggest making changes. Gats was the head coach.

Seven days later in Melbourne, we narrowly missed the chance to win the series, this time with a missed kick of our own. With five minutes to go we were leading 15–9, thanks to five penalties by Leigh Halfpenny, before Adam Ashley-Cooper had gone over for the only try of the game, with Christian Leali'ifano's conversion putting the Wallabies in front. There was still time for one final shot at goal, but Leigh's long-range penalty attempt fell just short.

We travelled to Noosa, a resort town on southern Queensland's Sunshine Coast, for a few days' R&R after Melbourne. While the players enjoyed a couple of days letting their hair down, the coaching team wrestled over the biggest decision of the tour.

Brian O'Driscoll was a Lions icon, playing on his fourth tour. But the Wallabies had gone hard at him in Melbourne, and with Jamie Roberts fit again after recovering from a hamstring injury, and the young pup Jonathan Davies playing great rugby, we had a choice to make. A collective decision was taken on the Tuesday night for Jamie to return to the side at No. 12, with Jonathan switching to No. 13. Gats felt that Manu Tuilagi would have more impact off the bench, so Brian was left out of the twenty-three.

It caused huge controversy in Ireland, and Gats came under a lot of fire. With the starting XV for the third Test containing ten from Wales, he became an easy target for those who claimed he was favouring his own players.

Everyone in the squad also looked up to Drico. I know he would have backed himself to do the job. But my overriding memory is how he took the news. Being dropped often reveals a player's true character, particularly if they are as highly regarded in the game as Brian. As disappointed as Drico was, and you could see it, he was a proper team man. On that tour I saw other players who were not picked go off and sulk or throw their toys out of the pram.

Drico's attitude was phenomenal. The way he handled

himself showed true greatness. I don't think it is possible to get over the disappointment of something like that in just a few days, but when we got back to training he was on it, helping the team and helping Jonathan Davies as best he could. That is what a true professional does.

* * *

Two days before the third and series-deciding Test, I found myself standing in front of the squad in the team room of our Sydney hotel. The Lions hadn't won a series since the famous tour of South Africa in 1997, and the players were understandably on edge. I was too, although I couldn't show it.

Colleen would tell me that I can be bullish and opinionated, or come across like an alpha male, but the truth is that I dread public speaking. It is why I spent most of the week preparing for the speech I needed to give to set the tone for our defensive effort. I felt I had to deliver a powerful message to the players. Everything was on the line.

I decided to draw upon my own experience representing Great Britain in rugby league to make my point about our defensive mentality for the third Test. The camera crew making the documentary of the tour filmed my speech:

> Last weekend, it was a good effort – good effort as far as D is concerned. A lot of pressure was coming on us, especially on our own line. They kept pounding away and pounding away and it was a gallant effort, boys. That's what I would say to you if I was your club coach or your international coach, but I'm not.
>
> We're your Lions coaches. And a good defence, or good spirit, isn't enough at this level. On D, we cannot allow our emotional energy to dip whatsoever. You know why?

Because there is no tomorrow. There is no tomorrow. We are taking them boys to the fucking hurt arena this weekend. Because our mentality is going to be a different mentality to what the British Lions teams have had over the last sixteen years. Right, a different mentality. Because over the last sixteen years it has been about failure. You shock yourself by taking yourself to another level. Because that is what being a fucking Lion is about. It ain't about anything other than that. It ain't about taking part. It ain't about being here. It is about winning.

'They won't have that,' I added, pointing to the 'Lions Mentality' heading on the whiteboard. 'They won't have that. Make it your point of difference.'

The idea that I had been trying to get across is that I felt the Australians would struggle to hit the same level of emotional intensity that had got them over the line in the second Test. James Horwill, their captain, had been on his knees crying at the end of the game, as if to say they had done it. Well, they hadn't done it. This was a Test series, and it was only 1–1. In my experience of playing for Great Britain in a three-Test series against Australia or New Zealand, when we had managed to get a win before the decider, sometimes the relief was so dramatic and overwhelming that it proved almost impossible to get back up to that emotional state for the third game. You need to be balanced and in control of your emotions.

It is why I was always envious of teams that won games with ease and kept winning, like the All Blacks under Steve Hansen. Winning is tough. But it is even tougher to keep winning, again and again. It takes more than emotion. I always felt it was easier to react to something, such as when you have lost a game or are pissed off about something. It is far more difficult to find consistency at a very high level and be emotionally in control.

I had been awake all night trying to come up with a way to put it all across to the players. I wanted them to know that this was why we were going to win. Because all you are trying to do as a coach before a game is imbue the players with belief. Sometimes when you are in the middle of it, you can't see the reality. It is the coach's job to stand back and paint the picture and tell them the narrative of what is going to happen and why.

I know people have made a big deal about what I said being one of the memorable Lions speeches, but the truth is that I cringe when I look at it now. I am embarrassed because it was not me. I wasn't being authentic.

The hardest thing for a young coach to cope with is the critique that comes from your players. Like a new teacher in front of a classroom, it can be a brutal experience. And in professional rugby, you are not dealing with people of varying ability but with the elite of the game. These players have been coached all their lives and suddenly you are a new coach trying to prove to them that you are half decent. In trying to do that, you can get caught up in bullshit. I remember thinking to myself that I needed to step up to the plate, putting hours of work into planning it and having sleepless nights worrying about it.

If I had a chance to advise myself back then, I would say, 'Stop being so dramatic. Trust yourself and be more natural. You don't need a Herculean speech. The story is a good enough one, the narrative is a good one, but it is not about you and making your presentation stick.' As a coach now, I don't feel I need to force things. What I said that day came from the heart, but today I would trust myself and my experience and be more concise. I would ask myself what I wanted to get out of a speech. How did I want it to start? How did I want it to finish? I would have a theme, but I would let the bits in between be more natural.

The only thing that matters is how your message converts to the field for the players. The simpler the better. It was about using our disappointment, understanding it and getting the players internally to believe that whatever was going on outside was just bullshit, and that we understood the truth of where we were at and what was coming our way. In his speech in the dressing room before the game, Alun-Wyn Jones, our captain for the third Test, rightly corrected me by saying that there was a tomorrow, but that the players now had eighty minutes to decide whether it would be with or without a Lions jersey. He was talking about the legacy the players would leave: history would note whether or not they took a stand for the jersey.

The players' answer was emphatic. After seven weeks together, it all clicked. The 41–16 final score in the third Test in Sydney justified everything. Owen even got on, as one of five England players who came off the bench. The result didn't come as a surprise to me. But this was not about any decisions we had taken as coaches: the players had earned their place in Lions history.

15. The Sack

I first came across Sam Burgess when he was a young kid who had burst onto the rugby league stage with Bradford Bulls. He was one of those players who immediately stood out. He was 6ft 5in and almost nineteen stone, but his real superpower was his confidence. He backed himself and didn't care about the physical or mental challenges of playing professional rugby, or any of the off-field dramas.

I guess there were some similarities between us. He had signed for Bradford when he was fourteen and made his debut for Great Britain as an eighteen-year-old against New Zealand, scoring a try and making a huge hit on Kiwi prop Fuifui Moimoi that went straight onto YouTube. After just three seasons in Yorkshire, aged twenty, he took the plunge and signed for the South Sydney Rabbitohs to test himself in the NRL. To do that you have to be mentally tough. Bloody tough. Trust me.

And yet, like me, I wonder if he knew what he was really letting himself in for when he decided to switch codes to have a crack at playing in the 2015 rugby union World Cup. Stuart had gone to see him in Sydney the month after we got back from the Lions tour to sound him out. The main difference between Sam and me was that he was in the prime of his career at twenty-four, but the conversations were just the same – should he play centre, should he play in the back row? When I moved, the RFU had paid half my salary. By now the sensitivities of the governing body helping out financially for a player who would benefit only one club were such that Bath had to sign him themselves. People thought I had a lot to do with his signing, but that wasn't the case. It was between Stuart and Bath, and ultimately it was Sam's choice to switch.

The deal was announced in the middle of the 2014 Six Nations, although Sam would not join Bath until the end of the NRL season in October. I knew how tough it would be for him to make the transition and learn the intricacies of rugby union in such a short timespan. I also knew that, as I had, he would face people who would object to a rugby league player being fast-tracked into the national squad. But the prospect of having such a brilliant and hard-nosed athlete joining us was hugely exciting and I was happy to be a sounding board for him. I sensed that he wanted a different challenge, as I had. He would have to learn he could no longer play off his instincts. It was my duty to help him. Then it was up to him to prove he was good enough to be selected.

* * *

We were making real strides forward as a squad. After a narrow 26–24 defeat by France in Paris we went on to win our next three games in the Six Nations, including a 13–10 victory over Ireland at Twickenham, and won our first Triple Crown since 2003. The title was to be decided on the final weekend. We smashed Italy 52–11, but the margin was not enough to put us ahead of Ireland on points difference. It meant that Ireland would be champions if they beat France in the final match in Paris; we would be champs if the French won or drew.

We watched the game from our hotel in Rome. We were told we had to be ready for a trophy presentation after the game if we won it. With Drico leading the charge, Ireland held on for a 22–20 win after Jean-Marc Doussain missed a late penalty and then, in the final minute, Damien Chouly had a try disallowed for a forward pass.

It was gutting to watch. As we drowned our sorrows with a few beers, Drico on his 133rd and final game for Ireland was named man of the match and received a standing ovation from the Stade de France crowd. Fair play to him. As one of the true greats of the game, he had earned that moment.

* * *

I loved the decision to make our tour of New Zealand in June 2014 a three-Test series, plus a midweek game against Canterbury Crusaders. It was a tour that would put our players under pressure, and we would discover more about their character. They had to deal with the chaos of many of our first-team players not being available for the first Test in Eden Park because they had played in the Premiership final between Northampton and Saracens the previous weekend. We lost 20–15, a decent performance; and then we lost the second Test even more narrowly, 28–27, in Dunedin. Then we ran out of steam, losing 36–13 in the final Test in Hamilton.

After just six games for Bath, Sam Burgess made his first international appearance for England Saxons against the Ireland Wolfhounds in January 2015. His final act in the NRL had been to help the Rabbitohs win their first NRL Grand Final in forty-three years, playing the full game despite suffering a fractured cheekbone and eye socket in the first minute. It had delayed his Bath debut by a couple of months, and the Saxons game showed he was not quite ready to be in contention for the Six Nations, but Stuart brought him into training ahead of our final match against France as part of a 'continuing education process'.

Once again, we entered the final round of the championship with a chance to win the title. Ireland's defeat by Wales in Cardiff in round four set up a crazy climax to the tournament. Wales, Ireland and England were level on points, and all three teams had a realistic chance of taking the championship on points difference. Wales beat Italy by forty-one points in Rome, setting Ireland the target of having to win by more than twenty points against Scotland at Murrayfield in order to get their noses ahead of the Welsh. Joe Schmidt's side won 40–10, which meant that we had to beat France by more than twenty-six points in the final game at Twickenham.

For a defence coach, the shootout that followed made for hard viewing, but I loved the way our boys went for it. We led 55–35 going into the final minute, still needing a converted try to be champions. We thought it was all over when France turned the ball over and won a penalty. But then Yoann Huget tapped it and ran, keeping our hopes alive, before the French scrum-half Rory Kockott kicked the ball into touch to hand the title to Ireland again. We had scored eighteen tries to Ireland's eight, and Stuart later pointed out that if there had been bonus points at the time, we would have been champions. But they were not the rules at the time, so Ireland were worthy champions.

Still, the way we had carved open France and got Twickenham bouncing that night left us all optimistic that when we returned in September for the start of the World Cup, we would be ready to produce something special. At least, that was the plan.

* * *

The three-month preparation period before the World Cup gave us time to really work with Sam Burgess and integrate him into the squad. He was part of the forty-five-man party that we took to Denver in Colorado for a two-week fitness camp. It was brutal work, training at altitude in temperatures over thirty degrees.

Sam made his England debut in the warm-up match against France at Twickenham. It was clear that he was one of our four best centres. Stuart knew his selection in the World Cup squad was going to be massive news. I had a pretty good sense of what that would feel like for Sam.

He did not make the starting XV for our opener against Fiji, with Stuart opting for a midfield of Brad Barritt and Jonathan Joseph, with George Ford at fly-half. He came on with Owen in the final quarter. It had been a nervy display but thanks to the power of Billy Vunipola we got what we needed, with a four-try bonus point in the 35–11 victory.

We knew the game against Wales would define our pool campaign, and with Jonathan Joseph ruled out with a pectoral injury, Stuart brought Sam in and also promoted Owen and Billy. Everything seemed to be going to plan when we led 22–12 in the second half and seemed in control. But Wales, even with their mounting injuries, found a way to win. It was the kind of backs-against-the-wall performance that we had produced against New Zealand three years earlier.

Trailing 28–25 in the seventy-seventh minute, we won a penalty by the right-hand touchline, just inside the Wales twenty-two. We had a chance to level the game, but the penalty shot would not have been easy from that angle. Chris Robshaw took the decision to kick to the corner – and we lost the line-out. There was no right or wrong decision here. It would have been a mad decision if our line-out wasn't good, but Geoff Parling was a brilliant line-out operator. If we had won the line-out and scored it would have been the best decision ever. That is sport. Put it this way: there were twenty-five other things we could have done better before that to ensure we were not in that position in the first place.

If you want players to take responsibility for their actions during the week, then you have to show trust in that type of decision-making during a match. My philosophy when I was a captain was that if I made a big decision, then I would walk tall towards it and do everything I could to make it work. Indecisiveness by a captain in such situations is the worst scenario for me because then you don't have a fucking clue what you are going to do and it doesn't exude confidence to the rest of the team.

And despite what some people suggested afterwards, it was not Sam Burgess's fault that we lost. Sam played well, and England were ahead when he was brought off. The bottom line? Wales were a bloody good team and deserved to win.

The result put us under tremendous pressure. Lose against Australia and we were gone. It was unthinkable: no host of a World Cup had ever gone out at the pool stage. I know we all felt a huge responsibility not just for the squad but also to the game in England. A home World Cup was a brilliant opportunity to grow the profile of the sport.

Australia had the benefit of having rested their starting XV in their previous win over Uruguay. Jonathan Joseph was fit again and returned to the midfield in place of Sam, while Ben Morgan came in for Billy Vunipola, who was ruled out of the remainder of the tournament with a knee injury. Once we fell behind by two tries in the first half, the writing was on the wall as we caved under the pressure.

I look back now and wonder how things might have been different with a bit more savvy. We were all relatively young and inexperienced coaches. At half-time Graham Rowntree and I showed just how inexperienced we were when we had a go at assistant referee Marius Mitrea in the tunnel. We were losing 17–3 and three scrum penalties had gone against us. Michael Cheika, the Australia head coach, saw us. 'Oi! You can't do that,' he shouted. Cheiks had been warned earlier in the year about speaking to a referee at half-time during a Super Rugby game when he was at the New South Wales Waratahs, and wanted to make sure the incident was highlighted. We would end up being banned from the changing room and tunnel area for our final pool game against Uruguay, but it hardly mattered by then. Australia took complete control of the game after the break, and their 33–13 victory ended our chances of reaching the quarter-finals.

It was the end of our world. The bullshit that followed shone a light on some of the attitudes in English rugby. I was accused of having too much influence in selection, and in championing Sam's inclusion in the squad and then the team to face Wales, and in favouring Owen to start against Wales. It was all nonsense.

It was a massive learning curve for me, just as it had been for me as a player switching codes to rugby union. Now, as an assistant coach, I saw up close the consequences of making a 'controversial' decision. I've since seen people make decisions that are not best for the team, just because the story will not be as sensational. In my opinion, that is not what you are paid to do. You have to make what you think is the right decision for the team.

The game against Uruguay was at Manchester City's stadium. It should have been a thrill for me to be there as a City fan, and also an opportunity to showcase rugby union in the north. It was anything but. Across town, my brother-in-law Sean was captaining Wigan in the Super League final at Old Trafford, which attracted a record crowd of over 73,000 as

Leeds Rhinos edged a thrilling match 22–20. Meanwhile, our ten-try win had something of a funereal air to it. After just sixteen days, we were out of our own tournament.

After the Uruguay game, Stuart said he would not walk away from the job. The RFU launched a review. They were just trying to buy time. It went on far too long, with the powers that be trying to look professional.

It was an eye-opening experience. I didn't see the point in canvassing everyone's opinion weeks after our campaign was already done and dusted. My philosophy is that if anyone has got something to say, then they should say it there and then. Feedback is only useful if it happens in real time, otherwise it is already too late. Time is too precious in international rugby. Holding an inquiry only gave people with an agenda time to say things months later that were far from the truth. Players leaked stuff to the press for their own sakes and everyone forgot what the truth was.

I was more interested in working out why Wales and Australia had coped with the pressure better than us. Instead, the review was conducted like a trial at the high court. It was all about politics. I felt for Stuart. He carried a lot on his shoulders and came under fierce scrutiny.

It is not in my make-up to look back and dwell on things. We lost against two very tough opponents, and it is not as if everyone wasn't giving 100 per cent. Australia went on to reach the final, and Wales might have reached the semis but for their mounting injuries. We were perhaps too desperate to succeed. In the end we probably lacked a bit of experience in coping with the pressure of getting the big games over the line.

Stuart has since said himself that we included too many players in the squad from the start and spent a lot of time trying to whittle it down rather than saying 'this is our squad' at the beginning of our camp and starting to build cohesion. Questions were asked about our fitness training in Denver, but the camp was great. I think Stuart had a point: players didn't know early enough whether it was their team to grab hold of.

I remember feeling a little bit cocooned in our training base at Pennyhill Park. Maybe we were too wrapped up in our own bubble, rather than getting out there and embracing the tournament, making the players feel extra special and forging a connection with the nation. But whether any of these things would have made a difference, I'm not sure.

The assistant coaches – Graham Rowntree, Mike Catt and myself – all got the sack. It was right for the new head coach, Eddie Jones, to start afresh.

The harder the times, the more closely people stick together and remember each other. I worked with some great people with England, people I have massive respect for and who I am still mates with today, including Catty and Graham Rowntree. We had some fantastic times together, not just with the rugby but with our families too. That is the great thing about rugby, the connections that you make for ever.

I pledged to myself that the experience would make me stronger as a coach down the line. I would learn from it. Otherwise, what was the point of it all?

16. The Second Chance

It was Colleen who suggested that I should fly to Sydney to clear my head. She was right, as usual. I needed to get away from all the noise. When you are in the middle of it all, it is very hard to reassess and see where you are at.

Alan Gaffney invited me to stay at his house. He was working at the New South Wales Waratahs at the time, so I spent a few days at the club. Gaff came up through the amateur era at a time when Australia were playing brilliant attacking rugby, and he had a great eye for detail. He is a good man too.

The break offered me the opportunity to do some coaching development training.

As well as the Waratahs, I also spent time with the Sydney Roosters, South Sydney Rabbitohs and other rugby league clubs. With the pressure off, it was an invigorating experience to see others up close in professional environments. Maybe a bit of a break would do me good, I thought. And then the phone rang. Treviso, the Italian club, were interested in talking to me about becoming head coach. Then a few days later, it rang again. It was David Nucifora, the IRFU's high-performance director. Ireland were looking for a new defence coach after Les Kiss had left to become head coach at Ulster. Would I be interested in meeting up?

So much for that break.

I had never been a head coach before, and if the move from Wigan to London had taken me right out of my comfort zone, the prospect of running an organization in a language I knew nothing about was even more extreme. Yet I knew there would be nothing lost in speaking to Treviso. I know that Eddie Jones used to go for every interview under the sun, just out of interest and to test himself. Sometimes he hadn't even *applied* for the job but was just being nosy. I don't think it does you any harm to put yourself in uncomfortable situations. They can often benefit you down the line.

I arranged to have meetings about both jobs at a hotel near Heathrow. David Nucifora was flying over with Joe Schmidt, the Ireland head coach, and they wanted to meet in a 'secret' room, I guess to avoid our meeting becoming public knowledge. My meeting with the people from Treviso finished only about twenty minutes before David and Joe arrived, but luckily they didn't bump into each other.

I later learned that Joe had done his homework on me, having spoken with guys like Johnny Sexton, whom I had worked with on the Lions tour in 2013. Of course he had. He wanted to quiz me on my coaching philosophies and how they compared to his, but one of his first questions was a test of my commitment.

'Andy, if you were offered the job, would you move to Ireland?' Joe asked, straight out.

I replied without any hesitation. 'Yes, of course.'

I know that the great Jack Charlton lived in England when he was manager of the Republic of Ireland football team, but most of his players would have been based in England too. The Ireland rugby team was different. Everyone was based in Ireland. If I was to do the job, I wanted to be there on the ground so that if Joe wanted to meet up for a coffee or a chat outside of camps then I would be available. And I'd want to show the players that I was committed, because I would be asking for commitment from them. It would show the Irish people, too, that I was serious about the job.

We finished the interview, and they offered me the position there and then. Just a few weeks earlier I had been in the middle of a shitshow with England, but I didn't think twice about returning so quickly to the international stage. To be honest, it was a relief that another job had come up so quickly. Not just that, it was an opportunity to grow my career under Joe, who had been hugely successful with Leinster and then an instant success with Ireland, winning the Six Nations in 2014 and 2015. An injury crisis at the World Cup had contributed to their quarter-final exit against Argentina, but I knew I was going into a first-class organization.

The only problem was that I hadn't discussed any of this with Colleen. When I had left the house in Harpenden to drive to Heathrow a few hours earlier, we had not really gone through the implications of my taking the Ireland job if I was offered it. Gabriel had just started school in Harpenden, so Colleen had probably been assuming that, with Luton airport only twenty minutes away from our house, and Dublin just over an hour's flight away, I would be able to commute.

'How did it go?' she asked me when I got home.

'I think it went well,' I replied sheepishly. 'I've been offered the job, but if I take it, we'll be moving to Ireland.'

She thought for a moment. 'Well, then, let's just do it.'

No looking back.

* * *

My gardening leave with the RFU meant that I couldn't work for another team in the Six Nations until the end of the 2016 championship, so I spent the first few months working as a consultant with Munster. They had a relatively new coaching team under Anthony 'Axel' Foley and they had gone through a tricky transition period. I had worked with some of the Munster guys on the Lions tour, and Paul O'Connell suggested that I could add a fresh perspective. It was a different line of work for me, and I loved it. It was a nice way to integrate myself gently into the Irish rugby scene.

I didn't know Axel personally, but I knew from watching him play what a committed player he had been for Munster and Ireland. His passion for Munster was no different as a coach. I remember being struck immediately by how much the club meant to him. I felt privileged to work with him, even for such a short period of time. He invited me back to his home in Killaloe for dinner and I met his wife Olive and their two kids. We spent time in the car together, driving to the province's training base at the University of Limerick, and had fantastic chats about the game. They were precious months. It was eye-opening for me to embrace a new rugby culture, and there was an element of relief in getting away from the rugby politics I had left behind in England.

Like everyone else who knew Axel, I was devastated when I heard of his sudden death in his sleep at the age of just forty-two. Like Mike Gregory, it was such a sad story – a legend lost well before his time.

During my time with Munster, preparing for my Ireland role, I cast my mind back just a few months to when I had faced a really tough press conference after England had lost to Wales and Australia. I had been asked if I had too much influence on team selection. Had I pushed for Owen to start against Wales? Had I pushed for Sam Burgess to start? Once the shit had hit the fan, I guess I knew the story was going to be about the fact that my son was playing. But it felt like people were suggesting that England's exit from the World

Cup had been all my fault. The criticism had hurt. I tried to turn it into a positive, a great learning experience for me. As long as I and the people who were important to me knew the truth, that was all that mattered. But I look back now and realize that it took me a while to get over it all. I had grown up in something of a goldfish bowl in Wigan. I thought I had seen it all, but I hadn't.

Now I knew the story would move on to me coaching *against* my son. I spoke with Owen before I accepted the Ireland job, and he had no problem with me joining one of England's main rivals. He knew I needed a job and that I was ambitious to be a good coach. Anyone involved in rugby would appreciate that it was a great opportunity. Owen knew a lot of the Ireland players from the Lions tour, so that helped too.

It quickly became apparent to me just how different the rugby culture was in Ireland compared with England. There is no jealousy or bullshit. In Ireland, people *champion* their national team. They want to support it and for it to do well. People come up to thank you for what you do, and you can see in their eyes what it means to them. I found it so refreshing.

I was genuinely pleased to see Eddie Jones make an instant impact with the England squad, harnessing the hurt of the World Cup failure. Eddie had enough time to assess everything, talk to people and know exactly what was needed to turn things round. He had a young enough squad that was not breaking up, and Eddie was clever enough to use their disappointment to get the best out of them.

There were a lot of good players in England, many of whom were hurting and with a point to prove. Stuart's teams had come close for four successive campaigns: we had been consistent without being quite good enough. I had learned lessons during my time with England, and there was no point looking back and thinking about the *if onlys*. I was getting on with the next stage of my career.

Ireland had been brilliant for a couple of seasons under Joe, but in 2016 it was England's turn. It didn't surprise me that they went on to win the Grand Slam. It is what tends to happen when a good team has their backs to the wall: you get a reaction. Fair play to Eddie and the players for picking themselves up from the canvas. That my son was part of it was special, and I was delighted for the English lads who had been through a lot, especially Chris Robshaw. He was no longer captain but played some of the best rugby of his career that season.

The end of the championship meant that I could start in my new role as Ireland defence coach. Colleen and the kids remained in Harpenden to finish the school year and give us time to sort out the move. Dominic Silvester invited me to stay in his apartment in Dublin, which enabled me to come over for two or three days a week, getting my foot in the door with the provinces and meeting the players. It meant I could put in long hours to get me up to speed and also start to get things set up for my family to come over at the end of the summer.

Mick Kearney, the Ireland team manager, took me under his wing and gave us a proper tour of Dublin, including advice about house prices, areas to live and schools for Gabriel. He spent a few days showing us around and then summed things up: 'Andy, you are going to live in Booters-town, Gabriel is going to go to St Michael's School and join Lansdowne Rugby Club.' (It just so happened that Lans-downe was *his* club.) We ended up doing none of that! We rented a house in Monkstown, enrolled Gabriel into Willow

Park Junior School, the feeder school to Blackrock College, and he joined Old Belvedere RFC. He was only five years old at the time and we had no idea if he would be interested in rugby. But like his big brother, he took to it pretty quickly.

Moving even further away from our extended families was tough. Elleshia moved to Dublin with us on a placement year with her degree at Leeds Beckett University. Gracie was in the last year of her A levels, so she boarded for a year at Aldenham School in Radlett. I am pretty sure it was unheard of for a girl from Wigan to attend a posh boarding school near London. On the weekends she either went to Harpenden to stay with Owen, who had just bought his first house with his girlfriend Georgie, or flew over to Dublin to stay with us. The following year she went off to university in Manchester. We saw Owen when we could. It took some time to adjust to life in Dublin, but we soon realized what a great place it was to live.

Meanwhile, I was trying to convince Joe that Ireland's defence needed to change.

* * *

Like a new player coming into a squad, all I wanted to do was earn the respect of the other coaches and of the players. The first way for me to do that was to make sure people knew that I was trying to understand what made them tick. And more importantly, what made Joe tick.

When I had served my gardening leave, Joe had been working overtime, taking both the defence and attack. The challenge for me was that my ideas on defence were the opposite of his. The New Zealand way, which Joe had been raised on, was based on watching the man. I wanted us to switch to a defensive system based on watching the ball. It was something that we used to do a lot in rugby league, and when I started coaching at Saracens Brendan Venter thought it was the only way to defend effectively.

By the time I started with Ireland, I wanted to bring in something of a hybrid system that would work only if everything was connected. People assume defensive systems are only about phase defence, but that is just part of it. Your front-line defence might be perfect, but the system will break down unless it is in sync with your backfield. It is the same with defence around the breakdown, the set piece and in transition.

I wanted to bring more intent to our defensive line, in terms of line speed, and to introduce deception.

I wanted our defensive line to be able to adapt to what was in front of them, to present the fly-half or first receiver with a picture that was false. Was one of our wings up in the defensive line, leaving space in the backfield? Or were our wings sitting back and the space was on the edge? I wanted our defence to 'tell lies' to keep the attacking side guessing. At the heart of this theory was my desire to turn defence into attack as quickly as possible. Our target was to get the ball back in just three phases. I didn't want us expending energy by defending for twenty.

My first big test was to get buy-in from Joe. I guess it would have been easier for me to have come in and just refined what was already in place. I think Joe wanted me to bring new ideas and challenge his way of thinking, but my philosophy was so far from his that it would be a major job to convince him to change. But I have never been scared of a challenge.

Any perception of Joe as a control freak is well wide of the mark. It was his team, he wanted it to be successful, and if he thought someone had an idea that would be right for the team, he was prepared to back it. But you had to be on point to convince him.

* * *

It is easy to start something, though some people give up when they are in the middle of it and see it is not always going their way. But for the ones who keep fighting, then eventually things start to fall into place. The research shows that this type of stress – the kind that stimulates you – is brilliant for us.

I remember trying to learn to drive as a kid and thinking, *How in the hell am I going to do this?* Or when I was trying to learn to play the guitar and thinking it was never going to come together. But if you persist, then before you know it you are playing the guitar. The middle part is the key. It is always the hardest part. If you don't push through it, then you are never going to crack anything. When you get to the end part, it is all the more rewarding because of the journey you have been on to get there.

Joe and I would meet in his room at the IRFU offices on Lansdowne Road during the couple of months before we were due to tour South Africa. I made numerous presentations involving hours of footage. He made me work hard. It went on for weeks, and rightly so, because if the head coach didn't believe in a philosophy put forward by his assistant, how could he sell it to the players? Everyone would have to buy into it and understand it.

I made sure I pushed hard at the middle part. And just a couple of days before the squad arrived for our camp at Carton House in Kildare, Joe decided we would go with it.

* * *

I can only guess what Joe was thinking when, just twenty-three minutes into the first Test at Newlands in Cape Town, CJ Stander was shown a red card for a collision in the air with the Springboks fly-half Pat Lambie. It was probably a consequence of me telling CJ to sprint off the line from a five-man line-out and put some pressure on their playmakers. Lambie chipped the ball over the top, and CJ jumped and then collided with him, knocking him out. It was a harsh decision. CJ was unbelievably competitive and tough, but there was not an ounce of dirtiness in him. It was just one of those things. Then, by the thirty-first minute, we were down to thirteen when Robbie Henshaw was shown a yellow card for a high tackle on Elton Jantjies, who had replaced Lambie. Talk about a test of the new defensive system!

Joe had been forced to name a relatively inexperienced side, because of injuries to Johnny Sexton, Rob Kearney, Dave Kearney and Luke Fitzgerald. We had spent a bit of time working with the new system in the build-up to the first Test, which involved reassuring the players when things went wrong. I didn't want them to get downhearted when they were practising something they had never done before and it didn't feel right. The Irish players can take a lot of information on board: they like detail. For this system to work there were around six stages of learning. But the boys were buying into it.

Despite our numerical disadvantage, we produced a brilliant performance and secured a famous 26–20 victory, the first by an Ireland side against the Springboks on South African soil. For me, it was a sweet return to the international stage. The history part didn't bother me. It never does. But I loved the feeling of winning again.

We were a tight coaching group. Simon Easterby took the forwards, Greg Feek was scrum coach and Richie Murphy was skills coach, and the tour was a great bonding experience for me. It was great to get to know the players, too. We came agonizingly close to winning the series in the second Test in Johannesburg. But having raced into a sixteen-point lead in the first half, and leading 26–10 going into the final quarter, the high altitude caught up with us in the end. We might yet have snatched the series in the third Test at Port Elizabeth, despite losing Robbie Henshaw with a knee injury, but Faf de Klerk made two brilliant defensive plays as we sought a late winning try.

It would have been brilliant to win the series, and we were gutted to have lost it at the death, but knowing that we had given it our all and competed at the highest level against a team we had not beaten before on their home soil was satisfying. My overriding feeling was that, with a young squad, we had really attacked the Springboks. We knew we were going in the right direction.

17. The Shift

From the rooftop patio of the Trump Tower hotel in Chicago, we had a bird's eye view of the mass of people gathered along Michigan Avenue. I had never seen anything like it. An estimated five million people were lining the streets for the bus parade to celebrate the Chicago Cubs winning the World Series baseball championship for the first time since 1908. It was said afterwards that it had been the seventh-biggest gathering in the history of mankind.

Someone said that down below, somewhere in the middle of the chaos, were the All Blacks, the team Ireland had never beaten – dating all the way back to the first fixture in 1905. They were best team in the world, on a record winning streak of eighteen Test matches. They were in town to raise the profile of rugby union in the US as part of a deal with their sponsors, AIG, who also sponsored the US team. I have always been a huge admirer of the All Blacks, because they are unbelievably professional, and have managed to stay on top year after year. But maybe, subconsciously, they were not quite as focused on the job in hand as they normally would have been. Perhaps in the back of their minds, they were thinking, *We'll beat Ireland, that's what we do. Let's go and enjoy the spectacle.* There was a feeling that we were there just to make up the numbers. Up on the sixteenth floor of the Trump hotel, we were happy to keep our heads down.

Our preparation had begun the previous Sunday, when we had gathered at Carton House. We had challenged the players to come into camp ready to work after two tough rounds playing for their provinces in Europe. We had to factor in the jet lag, so there was not a lot of physical work done when we arrived, but the message to the players was 'no excuses'.

Joe's narrative for the week was founded on analysis of Ireland's 24–22 defeat by the All Blacks three years earlier. Ireland had raced into a 19–0 lead and still led 22–10 going into the final quarter, only to lose the game in the final minute. Having come so close last time, we knew that we had a good chance if we really went for them. *But we had to keep playing.*

There was a strong emotional factor too, as it was just a few weeks since Anthony Foley's death. It was Greg Feek's wonderful idea that the players would stand in a figure eight – Axel's position had been No. 8 – when the All Blacks performed the haka.

The stadium was so big that to get from the coaches' box back to the changing room, we had to get a lift on a buggy. But after the whistle blew at the end of the first half, there was no sign of the buggy, so Joe and I decided to run back. The run quickly turned into a sprint because we were both so competitive and Joe, a former winger, was quick. By the time we got to the changing room, we were knackered, and the players must have been wondering where we'd been.

We were leading 25–8 after tries by Jordi Murphy, CJ Stander and Conor Murray, and our message was simple: we had to keep going after them. We knew they would come back into the game, and they did. But critically, we didn't try to defend our lead. Even when they started scoring points, we kept playing rugby and attempted to take the game away from them rather than hang on in there. When Scott Barrett scored to reduce our lead to four points with over fifteen minutes to go, many sides would have caved. Once the All Blacks scent blood, there is normally no stopping them. But we kept attacking. With five minutes to go, we got a five-metre scrum but there was no thought of trying to run the clock down. We rightly saw it as a position to go and win the game from: Jamie Heaslip picked up from the base on a 45-degree run and a simple inside ball created the soft shoulder for Robbie Henshaw to score and seal a 40–29 victory.

I believe a good night was had by the players, but I was in bed as soon as possible. I was shattered. My overriding feeling was one of relief.

It is often the way for me after such a high-adrenaline contest. It had been the same when I was playing for Wigan as a kid and we beat the Broncos in Brisbane. You might think it would have led to one of those legendary nights out. A few of the lads partied for a couple of days. But I changed my flight with Neil Cowie and came home the next day because I was exhausted physically and mentally by the whole experience and just wanted to get home and see Colleen and Owen. Often, I get a feeling of anticlimax after great victories and I get to the point in an evening when I think, *Enough is enough, I am out of here.*

It was the same that night in Chicago. As a coach, I also think it is important at times to let the players have time and space to celebrate by themselves. And we had to start preparing for what everyone expected could be a fierce backlash from the All Blacks, when we faced them in Dublin two weeks later.

* * *

People have their own views about whether or not the All Blacks' reaction was over the top. It doesn't matter. In some ways I respected what they did. Great sides always respond.

They came with a plan to beat us up, and it worked. They were raging and you could see it in their performance. The match was brutal. Legally or illegally, they ripped in. We lost Robbie Henshaw, Johnny Sexton and CJ Stander in the first half to injury. They made their point with a 21–9 victory.

But something else was happening. It was also the moment when there was a shift in the All Blacks' mentality. By winning in Chicago, we had provoked that reaction. Ireland were no longer considered a walkover or a guaranteed win for them. We were left to lick our wounds, but we had been given a vital lesson in what it takes to stay at the top.

Anyone can win a one-off game. Winning consistently is a much harder challenge. We also knew that, from that moment on, the games would become harder for us: teams would prepare more intensely. And that was our opportunity to grow. The bar had been raised. We had beaten the Springboks in South Africa and the All Blacks for the first time. We had made history, but there could be no going back to being known as the 'plucky Irish'.

* * *

When Warren Gatland offered me the job of defence coach for the Lions for the 2017 tour of New Zealand, I was more daunted than I had been when accepting the job four years earlier because, while nothing could have prepared me for the workload on the 2013 tour, this time I knew what was coming.

In New Zealand we faced ten games in six weeks, including three Tests against the world champions. It would be as hard as it gets.

I reckon if someone calculated all the hours the coaches, players and backroom staff put in during a Lions tour, an HR department would have a field day. My contract stated that my hours of work would be what was needed to get the job done. But I would never stop to think that if we were getting up at 4 a.m. and working through to 10 p.m., that meant we had put in an eighteen-hour shift. My only thought would be, *What a brilliant day!*

Those of us lucky enough to go on Lions tours don't consider it as 'work'. We just do it, and I love it: everyone mucking in together and working long hours. Without the bonding and team spirit, it would be too hard.

At least I didn't have far to travel when I was unveiled as one of the Lions assistant coaches. The press conference was held at Carton House. We had just finished our autumn campaign with a brilliant performance to beat Australia 27–24, with a late try by Keith Earls ensuring that we bounced back from the New Zealand defeat to finish 2016 with victories over the southern hemisphere 'big three' in the same year for the first time. It was mad to think it had just been a year since I had been let go by England.

Steve Hansen's side had averaged over forty-three points in their six matches during the Rugby Championship. I told the press that if the Lions were going to have any chance of winning the series, that we would have to score at least twenty-eight points in each of the three Tests.

* * *

After the breakthroughs of 2016, the 2017 Six Nations was disappointing. We had lost in Edinburgh and Cardiff, and England had already secured the championship when they came to Dublin on the final weekend in search of back-to-back Grand Slams, and having equalled the All Blacks' record of eighteen successive Test wins by a Tier One nation. The prospect of England winning the Grand Slam at the Aviva

Stadium was tough for Irish supporters, so there was a bit of extra motivation for us. It was also the first time that I faced questions about coaching against Owen, and England.

I get it. I get how weird it seems to people. But that is not our reality. The reality for Owen and me is that rugby is a job. It has never been any different for us. I was his coach for four years at Saracens, and then for four years at England. Now I was coaching against him. But it was always business. Family time was different. When we talk during the week of a game, it is about catching up with each other, never about the game. I was once asked if Owen had a penalty kick to win the World Cup final against Ireland, would I want him to get it or miss it. My answer was simple: 'Miss it.' Every time. He would think exactly the same way. That is why I always say it is so much harder for Colleen, our other children and Owen's grandparents than it is for Owen or me.

The Grand Slam is such a difficult thing to achieve. And Ireland do not lose many games in Dublin. Peter O'Mahony was promoted to the starting XV during the warm-up after Jamie Heaslip suffered a back injury, and he dominated the line-out for us in a 13–9 win. I just love those types of scenarios when the team faces a late setback and has to find a solution. Owen still got to celebrate with his teammates by lifting the Six Nations trophy on the pitch while our lads did a lap of honour.

When it was over, Owen was gracious in defeat. 'Fair play, Dad,' he said. It is always easier to take a defeat if you know it has been a proper battle. Rugby is such a tough sport to play that when you have spilled blood together there is a mutual respect after the final whistle. Everyone knows each other and chats about the game over food and a beer after the event.

A couple of months later, Owen and I would be on the

same side again as the touring party assembled for the daunting mission of trying to become the first Lions side to win a Test series against the All Blacks since 1971.

* * *

When we convened for the first pre-tour training camp at the Vale of Glamorgan, only fourteen players out of the forty-one-man squad were there: the rest were involved in Premiership and PRO12 semi-finals and other playoffs. With both finals taking place on the weekend before our first game against the New Zealand Barbarians in Whangārei, it meant we arrived in Auckland just seventy-two hours before kick-off. The journey involved a flight from London to Melbourne, sleeping in a hotel for three or four hours, and then another flight to Auckland. From there we had to drive up to Whangārei in a fleet of sponsored Land Rovers, stopping along the way for filming and community visits. It was so unfair on the players. On the way to the game, some of them were asleep because of the jet lag.

Against a scratch side that included Gats's son Bryn, we scraped to a 13–7 win. We had hung our players out to dry. But from then on, we just got on with it. The camaraderie was brilliant. There was no moaning, even though we were on the move almost every third day.

The tour games went reasonably well, and we felt in good shape going into the first Test in Auckland. With tour captain Sam Warburton not quite fit enough to start – he had missed six weeks at the end of the season with a knee injury and then suffered an ankle injury – Peter O'Mahony was asked to lead the side. This was a great tribute to the character of a player who had forced his way into the squad with his performance against England. But New Zealand were outstanding in their tactics. They played tight and they played through us. I think they changed the way they played against us because of how Ireland had played against them. Rather than look for space out wide, they played off the scrum-half and through a lot of short-side attacks, which was effective at negating our line speed. They won 30–15 with a fantastic display.

We had our backs to the wall now, one down in a three-Test series. It was in the week building up to the second Test in Wellington when we saw the true character of the squad.

Sam Warburton was fit to return to the starting XV and he led from the front. I thought Sam was a wonderful player: tough and no-nonsense and a great example of how to look after yourself. And what I loved about him is that, in the captain's role, he didn't try to be something he wasn't. By nature, he is rather quiet. He would have grown up watching all the videos of everyone bawling and shouting in Lions dressing rooms, but he was comfortable in his own skin and he trusted people around him to make their voices heard. I have no doubt that when he was thrown into the job as Lions captain as a young kid four years earlier, he would have seen it as a hugely daunting task. But he handled it superbly well because he was just being himself. In 2013 he had the likes of Paul O'Connell and Drico to support him. In New Zealand, he had the likes of Sean O'Brien and Alun-Wyn Jones, who were strong characters.

What I love about Lions tours are the unlikely friendships that are forged between players who you might assume have little in common or even had a bit of hatred towards each other. Players who are completely different and you wouldn't even think would click but end up being best mates at the end of it.

Owen and Johnny Sexton were a great example of that. They had been fierce rivals and competitors who had been trying to get one over each other playing for their clubs and countries. But they had huge respect for each other. Their friendship had started on the tour in 2013, when they had spent so much time together doing kicking practice with Leigh Halfpenny and Neil Jenkins. In New Zealand they started rooming together and the respect – and the rivalry – grew from there. Sometimes those relationships can fizzle out, but to this day they phone each other regularly and help each other out when they can. They are able to confide in each other because of what they have been through together.

For the second Test in Wellington, Gats decided we should start them both, with Johnny coming into the side at fly-half and Owen switching to inside centre, a combination that had been effective off the bench in our victory over the Crusaders. Ben Te'o had started at 12 in the first Test. He was a brilliant player, and his footwork and power were great at getting us over the gain line, but we felt that getting another ball player in would give better balance to the backline.

Having two playmakers with big voices would also improve the communication to the forwards, making sure everyone was on point and working together. It was the same for England when they played George Ford and Owen at 10 and 12. It doesn't have to be 10/12. The second playmaker can be an outside centre, a full-back or even a winger. The problem that Owen faced with England at times when he started at 10 was that he often didn't have a ball player outside him, the way George did when Owen played at 12.

In the end we had to dig as deep as we could to secure the 24–21 victory in the wind and rain at Wellington, even with the All Blacks going down to fourteen men in the first half with Sonny Bill Williams's red card for a high shot on Anthony Watson. That created in-game adversity for the All

Blacks, and they showed their class by going into a nine-point lead in the second half. We held our nerve, however, and with the Lions supporters creating a brilliant atmosphere, we levelled the series with tries by Taulupe Faletau and Conor Murray before Owen landed the decisive penalty.

It had been a monumental contest, but we knew then we would face the very best of the All Blacks in the decider. They are a side that always delivers a response, as Ireland had experienced after Chicago. They don't tend to lose two Tests in a row. We had the task of raising ourselves again. The Lions have tended to struggle in series deciders, as the demands of a long tour catch up with the players. I had experienced the same thing on tour with the Great Britain rugby league side.

On the eve of the game, I spoke to the squad. Sometimes you have to take emotion down, sometimes you have to take it up. We had just come off a bit of a rest in Queenstown, and I wanted to paint a picture of where we needed to be emotionally. It was time to take it up a bit.

'I started off by saying to you, how far can we take this?' I said to them in our team room at the Pullman Hotel in Auckland. 'Well, it's here. This is it. You dream about it, boys. I'm actually trying to ask myself, Faz, what is it that you're after? Honestly, it's something that is unbeatable.

'We're a fire team [this is code for driving through the breakdown], and if we're going for the steal, we have got to be fucking accurate. Performance, everything put together. We haven't done it yet. It'll be too much for them. They can't handle it. We've got fucking winners in this room. I believe tomorrow we become the best team in the world.'

It didn't quite happen. If we are honest, we were pretty fortunate to get away with a 15–15 draw. New Zealand created more try-scoring opportunities, and could have pulled away, but a late penalty by Owen brought us level. Off the restart, with two minutes left in the game, Liam Williams knocked on in the air under pressure from Kieran Read, and Ken Owens was penalized for playing the ball in an offside position. It would have been a very makeable penalty kick to win the game for the All Blacks. Replays showed that Read had been offside at the kick-off, but nobody seemed to notice that at the time. Sam Warburton calmly gathered information from teammates, then spoke to referee Romain Poite. Poite then went to the TMO. Initially he stuck by the penalty call, but as he walked towards the centre of the pitch he changed his mind and ruled that it was accidental offside: a scrum rather than a penalty. We held on, just.

It felt a bit of a flat finish at the time, but looking back now a drawn series in New Zealand, against an All Blacks squad of that quality, is something the players should be proud of.

18. The Offers

The Beast from the East was biting hard. I don't remember ever being so cold. Even the snowflakes seemed to freeze again as they were blown around violently by blasts of wind at Twickenham. It was St Patrick's Day but it felt like midwinter.

The freezing conditions had disrupted our training. But with a Grand Slam on the line against England, the players had barely noticed. There might have been a temptation to ease off, given that we had already secured the Six Nations title with our victory over Scotland in Dublin on the previous weekend. But there had been a relentless focus within the group since we had assembled for our first training camp in Oliva Nova, on the east coast of Spain in January.

Ireland had won the Six Nations title in 2014 and 2015 under Joe, but after landing the historic wins in South Africa and against the All Blacks, the players understandably wanted more. A Grand Slam was something Ireland had achieved only twice, in 1948 and 2009. We had a backbone of experienced players – Rob Kearney, Keith Earls, Johnny Sexton, Conor Murray, Rory Best, Iain Henderson, Peter O'Mahony – and there was a feeling that 2018 was our year.

That mindset came off the back of a clean sweep of wins during the previous autumn campaign, including a record 38–3 victory over South Africa, a game in which Jacob Stockdale announced himself as a potent finisher, scoring on his first home game for Ireland. He was one of a number of highly promising players who had made their debuts in 2017, including Bundee Aki, James Ryan and Andrew Porter. Jacob scored twice in our 28–19 win over Argentina in the final game of the autumn and he continued his remarkable streak into his first Six Nations campaign. In our victories over France, Italy, Wales and Scotland, he had already crossed for six tries.

A recording was made of Eddie Jones, speaking at a corporate event, which was published on social media a couple of days before we travelled to London: 'We've played twenty-three Tests, we've only lost one Test to the scummy Irish,' Eddie said. 'I am still dirty about that game. We'll get that back; we'll get that back, don't worry. We've got them next year at home, we'll get them back.'

It was classic knockabout stuff from Eddie. But we didn't need extra motivation. The prospect of winning a Grand Slam *at Twickenham* was more than enough to drive the players.

As we climbed the steps to the coaches' box at Twickenham, we felt we were in a good place. And then, as we took our seats just before kick-off, a gust of wind blew all three of Simon Easterby's line-out sheets out of his hand and into the air, before they landed, rather unfortunately, in the England coaches' box. *Shit.*

* * *

It had been a pretty dramatic journey to this point, starting on the opening weekend in Paris. When Teddy Thomas scored in the seventy-first minute to put France in front for the first time, our Grand Slam dream looked over before it had begun. Yet what happened next was a major signpost. The players refused to accept defeat. When Iain Henderson claimed a brilliant twenty-two drop-out by Johnny Sexton in the final couple of minutes, and their conditioning and mindset allowed them to put together one of the most remarkable climaxes in the history of the Six Nations. Five minutes and forty-one phases later, Johnny knocked over the drop-goal for a 15–13 win. The patience and detail at the breakdown, across all of those phases, were remarkable. So too the work rate to go and go again to get the field position for the kick. But crucially we also had good fortune on our side. There could easily have been a knock-on just two phases before Johnny pulled the trigger. Or we might have conceded a penalty. I reckon if you go back through every Grand Slam that has been won, there have been moments when the winners rode their luck. It is such a tough thing to win. I have blocked it out now, but I am sure if you go back through our four campaigns with England, when we finished in second place each time, there were moments when the bounce of the ball or a referee's decision went against us. That is just sport.

That night in Paris, we hadn't been at our very best, but we had found a way to win. It was not just hugely satisfying; the manner and the magnitude of the victory generated the momentum that carried us all the way to Twickenham.

We scored eight tries against Italy, but I had to have some words about our defensive display in the post-game review. Our games against Wales had an extra edge around that time, and they made it nervier for us than it should have been, coming back from 27–13 to get within three points of us before Stockdale's intercept try sealed a 37–27 win. We were much more ruthless in the 28–8 win over Scotland in Dublin, and it left England needing to score four tries and win against France in Paris later that night to stop us lifting our third Six Nations title in five years. When England lost, the title was ours.

Having privately set the Grand Slam as our target, there

had been little trouble keeping everyone on point in the final week. The senior players made sure of that. And it showed. If England got to see our line-out pages, it made no difference. We had wanted to take the game away from them from the start, and had almost got the job done by half-time as we led 21–5 with three first-half tries. This was a day when we really *performed*. If you constantly perform close to your best, the winning tends to look after itself more often than not.

Our second try, finished by CJ Stander, was an example of the level the players were operating at. A perfect line-out, and then Tadhg Furlong's little inside pass to Bundee Aki to put him into a gap. Tadhg had received a pass from Johnny, who then ran around him, with the England defence expecting him to receive the pass back. It was classic Joe. He was brilliant at picking the right player who could subtly sell a move, and he knew that no one would expect our big tighthead to be at the centre of such deception. Tadhg, for all his raw power as a scrummager, is also a good footballer. We ran the move several times that week, but executing it to perfection with everything on the line was special.

England, as you would expect, came back at us after half-time, but our lead was such that we had that rare occasion of being able to enjoy the final moments of the game, knowing that we had secured Ireland's third Grand Slam.

We went back to our hotel in Richmond to celebrate with our families and it was a great night. I always love it when you see everyone sticking together rather than dispersing off into the night. The celebrations continued the next day at the terminal as we waited to fly home. I think the fans loved seeing what it meant to us, and I find that the Irish public tend to be very respectful about what is put out on social media compared with what happens in the UK.

I am not sure if anyone recognized me anyway. Before we left London, I had completed one last job: shaving my beard off. I had promised a few lads I would do it if we won the Grand Slam, so off it came.

My son Gabriel *hated* my new look.

'Gabriel, this is the real me,' I said to him, with a chuckle. 'I didn't have the beard when I was born, you know, son.' But he was having none of it. 'Dad, please grow it back straight away,' he told me. I had my orders.

* * *

I was over visiting Owen in Harpenden when the call came from Eddie Jones. He wanted to meet up. He said he would come to see me at Owen's house.

I had only recently returned from Ireland's tour of Australia, which had been another big step forward for us after the Grand Slam win. Like the Lions tour in 2013, it went down to the wire. We had lost the first Test in Brisbane, bringing to an end our twelve-match winning run.

Joe had given Joey Carbery a start at fly-half, to give him some minutes in a good team. It would have been daunting enough for Joey, but it was a fantastic experience for him. Johnny came back in for the second Test and kicked sixteen points as we levelled the series in Melbourne, Ireland's first win against the Wallabies in Australia since 1979. The third Test was the most dramatic and nerve-racking of them all, with Johnny's late penalty just enough to see us home in a 20–16 win, Ireland's first series victory over a southern hemisphere side in thirty-nine years.

But the celebrations that night seemed like a distant memory as Eddie sat in front of me in Owen's house and asked me if I would like to return to England and join his coaching team.

Owen had succeeded Dylan Hartley as England captain and had just returned from their tour of South Africa, where they had lost the series 2–1 but finished on a winning note with a victory in the third Test in Cape Town. Paul Gustard, Eddie's defence coach, was leaving to become head of rugby at Harlequins.

It was then that he told me that the reason he had let me go at the end of 2015 was because of the issue of working with Owen. I told him that everyone who knew the real story knew that there was no issue. But he said he had to deal with the perception that it was a problem and that a fresh start had been better for both of us.

Eddie insisted that enough time had passed from the 2015 World Cup campaign. 'Owen is a more experienced player now, and you are a more experienced coach,' he said.

I asked about Eddie's plans after the 2019 World Cup. There was no way I was going to leave Ireland unless there was a specific commitment that reflected my ambition to one day become a head coach. Eddie hinted that he might be moving on, but there was nothing concrete.

At the same time, I was receiving offers to be head coach back in rugby league, and there were jobs coming up with the Irish provinces too. I went to David Nucifora, the IRFU's performance director, for some advice about what I should do. Nuci told me that Joe had decided to move on after the 2019 World Cup, and he wanted to speak to me about succeeding Joe as Ireland head coach.

It was a no-brainer. From the days when I had first started taking notes as a rookie player with Wigan, I had wanted to be a head coach. Things might have moved more quickly than I had imagined, but the truth is that I had been working towards this moment for a long time. Ireland was a brilliant place to work, with good people and a great system. One of the best things about the set-up is that the head coach reports to the director of high performance, rather than the chief executive.

I have enjoyed good working relationships with Kevin Potts, the IRFU CEO, and his predecessor Philip Browne. Nuci largely dealt with the board on non-coaching matters, which allowed me to get on with the coaching – and made it easier for me to have a positive working relationship with the CEO and the board. Nuci had won the World Cup as a player with Australia in 1991 and had gone on to coach the ACT Brumbies and Auckland Blues. I valued working closely with a person who had such an understanding of the game, and I think this management structure is a part of why Ireland have been able to punch above their weight on the world stage. David Humphreys has since succeeded Nuci and is a great support in the same manner.

I appreciated the interest from England and gave it serious consideration, but when I talked it through with Colleen, it was a simple decision to become Joe's successor with Ireland. We knew there was going to be more scrutiny and pressure in the head-coach role, but her take was, 'Just get on with it.' And she certainly loved living in Ireland.

From player to captain, and then from captain to starting off in coaching, I had always sought progression. Sometimes I would feel a pang of jealousy at people who could say, 'No, this is me, this is good enough, I don't want the hassle.' I admire people who just love doing what they're doing and are happy with their life. Sometimes I wish I could be the same. But I knew it was the right time for me to take the next step.

I hugely appreciated the offer from the IRFU to become

head coach after the World Cup, particularly as I hadn't done it before. Ireland were showing faith in me, and that was enough for me. I didn't want to play people off against each other. To me a deal in any walk of life is where both sides are happy with it. If someone feels that they are feeling ripped off, or having their arm twisted, then there is no point. That is not a deal. Whereas if both sides give a little bit and are happy, then you can work properly together.

When I first started coaching, it was because I wanted to put into practice all the things I had learned from the great coaches I had played under, but I had no idea how it was going to unfold or how I was going to act. You never know until you have lived it and you can't be at your best until you have been through it.

I was fortunate enough to be part of Joe's coaching team and see what it took for Ireland to become one of the best teams in the world. By the autumn of 2018 there was an argument to be made that we were *the* best, following our 16–9 victory over New Zealand in Dublin. It was a ferocious contest, with Jacob Stockdale's twelfth try in fourteen Tests proving decisive. The try – the only one of the match – came from a brilliant line-out move, with Johnny Sexton switching the point of attack by passing the ball inside to Bundee Aki, who then fired a long pass to Jacob, giving him the space to execute his chip and chase perfectly.

The All Blacks remained No. 1 in the world rankings, but Steve Hansen, their coach, declared his hand. 'I said this at the beginning of the week that these are the two best sides in the world playing each other,' said Hansen. 'So as of now they are the number one team in the world.' At the World Rugby awards in Monaco the following week, Ireland were named team of the year, while Joe received the coach of the year award and Johnny was the player of the year. As we headed into a World Cup year, we felt we were perfectly placed. But the biggest challenge – and lesson – of all was to follow.

* * *

Our opening game of the Six Nations at the Aviva Stadium against England has since been identified as the moment that things started to slip for us. We lost 32–20, and although we went on to win our next three games, against Scotland, Italy and France, any hopes of defending our title went as Wales beat us convincingly in the driving rain in Cardiff. People were asking if we had peaked too early ahead of the World Cup.

All I can say is that we didn't think that was the case. Our standards were good and we remained unbelievably thorough in our preparations. But the hardest thing in sport is to stay at the top, because everyone is chasing you. And I don't think we dealt with that as well as we could have done. Suddenly everyone was raising their game by 10 per cent against us. It is always easier to get yourself up for a game when you are chasing someone else. Now we were the ones being chased. The lesson I learned is that when you get into that kind of position you have to go harder, push harder and evolve as a team.

At least our finishing third in the Six Nations had shifted the spotlight from us a little. The night before our opening game of the World Cup against Scotland in Yokohama, I was asked to present the jerseys to the players. It was an honour, and I decided to use the occasion to tell the story of my experience of playing against Ireland at Croke Park in 2007. I wanted to let the lads know how an Irish side is perceived from the outside. That night at Croke Park, Ireland had blown us away because they simply had to win. The words came easily to me because I totally believed in what I was saying and had been waiting for the right moment to get it out.

We knew how important it was to start the tournament well, and it was reflected in the ruthlessness of our performance, winning 27–3. There is no way I am taking any credit for how we played, because that was down to Joe's plan and how the players executed it. But it was a nice five minutes for me to be able to share what I thought beforehand.

We had a couple of injuries, and we rested one or two players going into the Japan game, but that was not the reason for our defeat. Japan were the reason, brilliantly coached by Jamie Joseph and Tony Brown. They had been poor enough in their opener against Russia but had clearly been targeting our game. They caught us with good tactics, playing with nice width and an all-in fifteen-man attacking game that got the best out of their players on the day. They really shocked us by how they played at the breakdown. Whether it was legal or not didn't matter, because the referee allowed it and we weren't expecting it. Japan's attacking plan required quick ruck ball. There was an energy and flair about them but also a real intent to tackle people early or beyond the breakdown to create small holes and stop the flow of our defence. They did a brilliant job, and their 19–12 win gave them control of Pool A. I know everyone remembers the winners, South Africa, but for me Japan stood out as the success story of the tournament, to perform like they did at their own World Cup. They were a great side to watch.

The All Blacks were waiting for us in the quarter-final, having had a two-week break as their final pool game against Italy had been cancelled because of a typhoon. Our preparation again had been good, and there was a real sense within the group that this would be the moment when everything would click again, and we would return to the heights of the previous year. But this time New Zealand had an excuse to get that bit more out of themselves, because of how we had gone against them in 2016 and 2018. They delivered their performance of the tournament, beating us 46–14. The disappointing thing for us is that we felt we had got to the point where we were a lot better than that.

I was gutted for Joe. He deserved so much more in what was his last game in charge of Ireland. It was the end of an era too for guys like our captain Rory Best, who had given so much for the side.

Colleen and Gabriel were coming out to join me for the final two weeks of the tournament, and the next challenge was trying to book accommodation for us all in Tokyo. England had reached the semi-finals after an impressive win over Australia in the quarters, and I would be experiencing the rest of the World Cup solely as a parent.

I hadn't pre-booked because I had been optimistic that Ireland would get through to the semi-final at least. Now hotel prices were through the roof and the cost of flights had trebled. Not only that, but the girls wanted to fly out to join us as well. It cost a fortune, but I loved those two weeks. They helped me get over the pain of our quarter-final defeat, and Colleen and I were now able to enjoy it as parents. Owen got us tickets for the semi-final, and I can tell you that watching a match as a father is far harder than being a coach. When you are coaching, you monitor every player; but as a parent, all you see is your son or daughter. It is agony.

I met up with two mates from Ireland, Bobby O'Brien and Mick McCarthy, who were Gabriel's coaches at Old Belvedere. They were great at taking the piss but did a shit job of bodyguarding me! To be fair to them, they were both supporting England because of Owen. It was Colleen's birthday on the day of the semi-final, which made it extra special. We met up with Bobby and Mick, got the train together and went to the fan zone at the stadium. Like everyone else, I remember not being able to find a toilet.

The game itself was amazing, the way England took it to New Zealand. There was an image of Owen seemingly smirking as he faced the haka. I don't think he was snarling in a cocky way. It would have only been him thinking, *How lucky am I that I am here? Where else would I rather be?* That is the opposite of letting the pressure get to you.

England were super-ready for it. New Zealand would never have been complacent, but it is always hard to back up a huge performance in the World Cup. England won 19–7 and, looking back, it was the most enjoyable day I experienced watching Owen, to see a performance like that against the side everyone was saying was the best in the world.

All the parents were invited in for a quick beer afterwards at the England hotel in Tokyo. I congratulated Eddie on his win and he was great. I recall seeing Gabriel at the end of the night over in a corner chatting away to Eddie. I remember thinking, *What is he saying over there?*

England then discovered how hard it is to back up a huge performance themselves when they lost to South Africa in the final. As ever, my mind was already looking ahead. I knew in a couple of months' time I was going to be in the hot seat.

19. The Clean Slate

Following the World Cup, there was so little time to start preparing for the Six Nations and so much to do. Joe had left behind an outstanding environment. He was the most successful Ireland head coach there had ever been, and he taught Irish rugby how to reach the high standards he set.

Yet I knew I had to make changes, because I had to be myself and do the job my way. One of the first things I learned in coaching is that if you try to be a copycat, you don't come over as sincere and the players can see right through you.

Announcements about my coaching team had already been made before we had travelled to Japan for the World Cup. Mike Catt joined us as attack coach, a role he had been doing with Italy, while I asked Leinster's John Fogarty, or 'Fogs' as everyone knows him, to become scrum coach. Simon Easterby would continue as forwards coach and Richie Murphy as kicking and skills coach.

A key part of putting together a coaching team is cohesion: making sure that everyone is different but that they also complement each other and gel together. Fogs was brilliant in that respect, not just because of his superb scrummaging expertise but as a big character. If we were all the same, it would be boring for everyone else. Fogs is brilliant at his detail, but he also realizes he has a role in bringing energy to the group. His personality makes it easier for other guys to be themselves.

Simon is incredibly hard-working and detailed and cares deeply about his job. At first he continued doing line-outs, but he wanted a fresh challenge. Moving to defence was the obvious one for him, since I had become head coach and would lead more on the attacking side. Catty was an ideas man. I had worked alongside him with England, and I wanted to be challenged by people who would make me think. Like me, he could talk rugby all day.

Perhaps the most important lesson that I took from 2019 was in regard to our mindset. With the benefit of hindsight, I felt that we had not coped with the pressure and attention of becoming the number one side in the world. It felt like we had been happier as the underdog. *Why do we not want to be number one?* Changing that mindset was going to be important. It was going to involve two things. First, we had to put ourselves under pressure internally: I wanted us to relish being under pressure. And I needed to challenge the players about why it did not sit easily for us to be number one.

Winning is more important to me than you could imagine. When I was a player, the only thing that mattered was winning silverware; I was obsessed by it. But with more life experience, I understood that there was more to the game than that. I remembered the moments when we had been up against the odds, dealing with five injuries going into a cup final, terrible weather conditions or poor refereeing decisions, or facing formidable opponents. Any side can lose a game. You are never in control of absolutely everything. You are only in control of being consistently good and of how people within your own group perceive you. Those moments when you knew you had given everything you had together meant more than any result or trophy that I won. I wanted the Ireland team to connect with the supporters and make them proud of the type of rugby we were playing. The most powerful thing in sport is when a team comes together and is achieving more than the individual parts realize that they can. When they are involved in something that they are owning and love doing, then it no longer is a job, or even hard work. Then it becomes something special to be involved in. For me, that is what the gold standard should be: chasing your potential.

I would create scenarios to make games seem even more pressured than they were, just to see how we would react and whether we could perform under that pressure. That is how we would evolve our mindset.

Whenever you are in a Test week, the game you are preparing for is always the biggest thing ever – but then the following week the next game becomes the biggest. My own experiences as a player – like playing St Helens on a Good Friday, or a Test match against Australia in rugby league, or rugby union for England against Ireland at Croke Park – had taught me that there was always something bigger or better coming down the track.

My job was to paint pictures and create scenarios to push us to levels that as individuals we probably didn't believe were possible. Growing our own internal expectations would be as important as winning the Six Nations. That is how we would get better.

As a player, I had experienced being on a winning roll, of not knowing how to lose. I had seen some players not understand why we were winning. It is when you suffer a loss, and you have to figure out why and get back on the horse, that you see the true character of a player.

I looked back on my own career. The environment at

Wigan had been brutal; driven and unbelievably hard and only about earning respect. At Saracens under Brendan it was ultra-positive, and you couldn't get stuck into one another. But it was also very successful. I thought the ideal balance was somewhere in between, with a little bit of everything thrown in.

I wanted us to be critical of ourselves after victories as well as defeats. It is the perfect time to do it, when everyone is in a good mood, and you can go even harder on the details of how and why we could have done things better. Just like when John Monie gave Steve Hampson a bollocking after he had scored three tries for Wigan, my view is that if you don't keep the pressure on maintaining standards even when you are flying high and winning, then things can very quickly unravel. The players need to know the reality, irrespective of the result.

If I let things slide, it would be my fault that the team started sliding. I had to be truthful with them at all times. If I am full of praise for a performance that was not up to standard, even though we might have got away with it and won the game, then it is only natural that the players will think that is what 100 per cent looks like. But the reality is that then we would be starting the week at 80 per cent, thinking that we were at 100 per cent. The week after, that 80 per cent could have dropped to 60 per cent of where we should be. The best teams improve like a coiled spring. At the start when they are winning, the curve is upwards, and the player thinks he is performing really well. But the best ones say to themselves, *How do I make myself even better?* The good ones catch themselves and go again back up the curve. The players who keep falling back down the other side are the ones who say to themselves, *Why is this happening to me? I am doing what I have always done; it is not fair, I am not to blame.* And they end up back at the bottom.

I wanted players who aimed to keep rising. Everyone loves a pat on the back, but the smart ones smell the bullshit. There is nothing worse than flattery, because it is meaningless. No, I would be honest with them. I would let the players know where they were at, where the team was, and how we were going to go forward. That is how we would get consistency to aim for the performances we were after.

* * *

I wanted honesty to be a two-way street. My philosophy was that if anyone has got something to say, then they should say it now. I guess it was a reaction to my experience with England in 2015. As hard as that was to take at the time, and tough for families too, I would be mad if it didn't help shape my thoughts.

Going into the Six Nations, we might have five training sessions to get up to speed. If I was explaining something to a player and they didn't understand, I needed to know now.

At our first gathering for a mini-training camp in December 2019, I told the players that there would be no such thing as a stupid question. 'I need to know what you are thinking,' I told them. 'Because if you are not quite sure about something, then we probably haven't coached it right. Or if you completely disagree with something, there might be an explanation that puts you back on page straight away. Or you might have an answer where I say, "You've got a point," and then I have to be big enough to change my mind.'

I wanted to shift the sense of responsibility to the players. I wanted them to feel like this was *their* team. I wanted them to own it. To feel that we were all working together. I asked them: What did *they* want a Six Nations performance to look like? When they turned up on Monday morning after a game on the Saturday, what did they want the review to look like?

I didn't want players to be whispering in corridors: 'What are we doing? I don't get that.' It takes a big man to admit he doesn't understand something, particularly in front of a group. When you get feedback you don't like, it's easy to say to yourself, *He just thinks I am shit.* But I wanted the players to be able to deal with feedback and to know that there was no agenda other than getting better as a team. There would be no laughing if a player was big enough to put his hand up and say, 'I don't understand what we are trying to do.' I told them not to hold anything in, but to speak their mind. I needed to know from day one that they understood what we were trying to do and own it and drive it on together.

When it came to selection, I told the players there would be a fresh start. The move to a new training base in Dublin, at the Sport Ireland campus in Abbotstown, helped. It was a fantastic facility, planned by David Nucifora with the backing of the IRFU and Sport Ireland. I wanted to make sure that when we returned to our hotel at Carton House after training that the work was done, and the players would have a bit of time for themselves.

We would harness the best of what had gone before, but this would be a new team. I would draw heavily on my own experience as a player when I had been left out of a team. As a coach, it is easy to think it is obvious that you have selected the best side and that everyone else should just get on with it. But I knew some players would feel a decision was unjust. So after every selection, I personally made sure that the only people I spoke to were those who were not selected. Sometimes it would be just a two-minute conversation, because they accepted the decision. Sometimes it would be longer, when they wanted to know what they needed to do to improve. But I vowed to make sure that I listened to them and gave them feedback so at least they knew where they stood in my thinking.

'I want you to come with an opinion,' I added. 'Make sure you come into work not just looking to conform. When you come to work, I want you thinking about how you can add to your team.'

I knew that if we could get buy-in like that, then the players would know that this was their team.

Next, they needed to know who would be their captain.

* * *

In early January I rang Johnny Sexton and asked if I could pop over to his house for a word. He was the outstanding candidate for the captaincy, and I told him as much over a coffee in his kitchen. I knew how much it meant to him to captain Ireland and how determined he would be to do a good job of it, even more so because he was thirty-four. I knew he was not just doing it because it was a high honour; it meant far more to him than that.

'Let's just see how it goes for the Six Nations,' I told him. I could tell that he immediately took that as a serious challenge. I could sense him thinking, *OK, I'm going to show you, Faz.* But the truth was, it was never in doubt. I knew he would be the perfect leader to drive standards and show the younger players what was needed. He would have seen it himself from players like Brian O'Driscoll and Paul O'Connell, just as it had been handed down to me as a kid at Wigan from the senior players.

As a young player, when you start playing as a professional you don't know how you are going to act or perform until you have done it. It is the same as an assistant coach, and now I was finding out that it was exactly the same as a head coach. No matter how much prep you have done or how hard you have worked to get to that point, it is never the way you think it is going to be. I was 100 per cent learning on the job. I remember David Nucifora saying to me right at the start that I was going to have a lot of people wanting my time so that they could do their jobs properly. I had to get my head around the big-picture stuff and all the planning that is required. I learned that no one could function properly unless you give direction to them.

The coaching was the easy part. That is the bit I loved. I classed myself as a head coach, not a director of rugby who sat behind a desk organizing and drawing up plans. I was a coach who wanted to get out on the training field, but I also had to plan for the medium- and long-term. Around 70 per cent of my time was taken up with planning, organizing, selecting and getting the story right. But even if my coaching time was now in the minority, I felt it was far more powerful to be on the pitch to fast-track how we were going to do things, how we were going to play the game and how we were going to live our lives in camp.

I knew if I wasn't true to myself, then I was going to come unstuck. I understood that there were a thousand things that we were already good at, so there was no way I was going to ditch them. I made sure that all that intellectual property from Joe's time stayed exactly where it was, and I would evolve bits and pieces from there.

I selected a thirty-five-man squad for a training camp in Portugal in January 2020. We only had five sessions to prepare for our opening Six Nations game against Scotland at the Aviva Stadium, but I wanted us to take the first steps in evolving our game plan. I knew it was going to challenge the players and might have an impact on our results early on, but it was an ambition worth fighting for.

If I were to sum up what I tried to put in place, it was about making every player accountable. I wanted to get the most out of the team by having all fifteen players involved in every element of the game. It is all centred around decision-making. People talk about playing heads-up rugby or playing what you see. But it depends on what you are looking for.

Heads-up rugby might sound like a free-for-all. But it is not. It must have a structure in and around it. Look at the best footballers in the world: they could play in their dinner suits because they have seen it all beforehand. I wanted our team to know not only what was unfolding, but also what was going to unfold, so that they could be ahead of the game.

Sometimes players are described as great offloaders, or as running great lines. Those things don't just happen, and they're not just about talent. They are built on an understanding of the game and they depend on the interplay of teammates. For every element of the game, you've got to understand how it happens as a group, how you make it work as a group.

The plan was to educate players on what a good decision looks like, and what you need to do to be able to execute it. It was exciting because the game is forever changing in front of your face. With some coaching drills, all you're doing is learning the drill. But if a player is to learn about decision-making, he has got to learn about how teams can vary the tempo at which they play, how to assess the space in front of the defence, and how to manipulate defenders. When our players saw a picture, I wanted them to be thinking how to move people around and make something out of nothing.

I wanted all of our players, including the front-five forwards, to be comfortable on the ball, to be decision-makers in their own right, and for our system to always offer them options. Make the right decision and we might just open up space to chase after. I'd seen plenty of teams where the ball-carrier takes the ball in, and three or four players hit the breakdown – and then those players are not able to offer themselves to work hard in attack or defence a phase later. It was not right to be attacking or defending with just eleven or twelve players because the others were not accountable. I wanted to attack and defend with fifteen.

I knew we were asking a lot of them. It was something very different and required a lot of understanding. It wasn't highly structured, but it required drilling into the smallest details to allow that to happen.

I've heard loads of coaches say that good players make good coaches, and it's true. But the part that I love about coaching is a little bit of that in reverse. Of course you need good players who have a good attitude, who want to understand and want to be a brilliant team player. But there is nothing better than seeing a team that has not got the best players win a big game.

In training, the key was setting up different situations and forcing the players to make decisions. We would play twelve defenders against fifteen attackers, or seventeen defenders against fifteen attackers. This would force them to find space, and when there wasn't any, we would ask, 'What are you going to do now?' It was a way of developing game understanding, and the flow of seeing space early and playing to space early. When you are training in that way, there are thousands of decisions to be made the whole time. That is not the case in small-sided games, when you're working on something specific.

I am sure some of the players were thinking, *This is different, this is going to take some time.* But I could see that the lads were enjoying it and with time started to believe in it and own it. I knew it would not necessarily translate into results straight away, but I think the players and coaches all knew that success would come with time. What I did know was that if the team did not believe in what was happening behind the scenes, then I would be dead in the water as head coach even if we were getting results.

I wanted our players to be able to play what was in front of them, but to reach that point requires unbelievably deep preparation. An opponent might come up with ten different ways to play against us. We had to be good enough instinctively to scan and say, 'That's the picture, I have seen it, and we are ahead of the game.'

20. The Ripple Effect

When I was a young coach at Saracens, I once showed the players a video of Chris Ashton, who at the time was scoring tries for fun for Northampton Saints. All Ashy cared about was scoring. He would do *anything* to score tries. The amount of knockbacks he would have received by following moves, running inside lines but getting nothing in return was remarkable. But he found a way.

Ashy would have learned that instinct when he was a young full-back playing rugby league at Wigan Warriors. What he probably didn't realize is that his finishing prowess had been influenced, indirectly, by the great Ellery Hanley. Ellery scored a record sixty-three tries in his second season at Wigan in 1986/87 by being mentally ahead of the game and relentlessly following the ball. But his impact went way beyond the scoresheets.

A young Shaun Edwards saw at first hand Ellery's scoring feats and was smart and talented enough to copy him. It was infectious. In a match against Leeds during the 1991/92 season, Martin Offiah set a Wigan record by scoring ten tries. Martin was unbelievably quick and could score on the outside against anyone, but he had learned to follow the ball as well. He and Shaun were both hungry for it. A few months later Shaun matched his record, scoring ten against Swinton in a cup match.

That art of scoring would have been passed down to Kris Radlinski, who in turn would have been the inspiration for

Ashy. Ashy was unbelievably fit, and although his top-end speed was not extraordinary he had great speed endurance, and his fitness to just keep going was matched by his hunger to score tries. Ellery, Shaun and Martin were fit, but what set them apart from others was their mentality. And what they created was a ripple effect, even subconsciously, for the younger players.

Now that I was Ireland head coach, I wanted the best of the standards that had been set under Joe to be passed down through the squad in a similar fashion. Through my own experience at Wigan, I knew that a group benefits massively if you have got brilliant senior players who show the younger ones the way.

I would not be disappointed. For our opening game against Scotland, I decided to hand Caelan Doris his debut. He had been in good form for Leinster, and I felt he had earned the chance to start. To accommodate him into the back row, I switched CJ Stander to the blindside flank, which meant that Peter O'Mahony, who had played at No. 6 against New Zealand in the World Cup quarter-final, started the game on the bench.

At the time, Pete was one of our senior leaders. I spoke to him during our camp in Portugal before we flew back to Dublin. I explained that Caelan had been showing up so well that he deserved the chance to start, that someone had to give way, and on this occasion it was him. Now of course Pete wanted to play, but he also wanted what was best for the team. That is what good leaders do.

That evening, I went back from training and saw Caelan on the computer, looking through video clips and being as diligent as he could be. But who was showing him the stuff that he needed to see? It was Pete. Being the best version of a teammate you could ask for. The decision to rest him would have hit him hard. I know how much it mattered to him, but I also know he expected me to be honest with him and make decisions that were right for the team. And there he was, helping out his team-mate. Seeing that, I knew we were in a good place.

* * *

We made a solid start to the 2020 Six Nations, beating Scotland and Wales in Dublin, but then had a bit of a wake-up call by losing 24–12 to England at Twickenham. I was more interested in how we were progressing towards what we were trying to achieve than in the results themselves, and what I learned was that after the first three games we still had a load of work to do.

On the Tuesday after the England defeat, we were at Abbotstown for a training session when we were told that our match against Italy was going to be delayed because of concerns about the coronavirus. We finished training and then went out for a team social in Dublin because we didn't know when we would be together again. It was a brilliant opportunity for bonding. The pressure was off, and the players were able to come out of themselves a bit more and have deeper conversations.

As a coaching team, we tried to make good use of the free time. There were numerous Zoom calls and personal development sessions, and the relationships among the coaches were strengthened. We could really drill into the details and plan for the future. With the Six Nations postponed indefinitely, we had a lot more time to have deeper conversations about where we wanted to go and how we wanted to get there, and reflect more deeply than we would usually be able to about our first three games.

When I named a thirty-five-man squad in mid-October ahead of the resumption of the Six Nations, lockdown restrictions made it impossible to develop my focus on inclusion, engagement and encouraging players to be themselves. Players had to eat just three to a table in the dining hall, it was impossible to hold meetings, and with everyone wearing masks it was difficult to assess facial expressions. Gym sessions took twice as long because the players had to keep wiping down all the equipment they were using.

It was hardest for players who were deemed to have been close contacts of people with Covid: they had to stay away even if they had no symptoms. It was hard to prepare from one day to the next, with players constantly dropping out of training. It was a tough time for everyone, but one of the concepts I wanted to drive home was that we must never give ourselves an excuse not to perform. If you whinge and moan at a situation, then you are only giving yourself a way out.

We encouraged the players to open up, to speak freely about what was on their minds, to share their feelings and their vulnerabilities. Bring your personalities, I told them. Behave like you would at your club, because that is what has got you here. I told them I wanted them to be the best version of themselves, and if they didn't know what that was, then my door was open for a chat about it. I wanted everyone to feel like they could be themselves in camp.

Everyone except for Johnny Sexton.

I didn't want him to be himself. He was intensely driven and committed, and that was at the heart of everything he had achieved. But now that he was captain, he had to change. Behind closed doors I told him just that.

'What do you mean?' he asked.

'You need to be more like a chameleon. You need to play the game to get people onside, if it is winning you are concerned about,' I told him.

Perhaps I recognized a bit of my younger self in him. I was unbelievably demanding of high standards when I was a captain. I had been committed to doing all the extra training, not just because I loved it but also because of the ruthless example that had been set by the senior players when I was a fourteen-year-old starting training at Wigan. When I was captain, if someone told me I was doing something wrong, then the hairs on the back of my neck would be standing up straight away and I would be saying, 'How dare you?' Some of the things I did as a captain I am now disgusted by. At times I behaved like a spoiled brat.

Johnny had been the driver of the team as the fly-half, but before taking up the captaincy he hadn't needed to be especially philosophical or empathetic. Now, as a new captain, he was learning on the job. There was more weight on his shoulders with things he had to do during the week. I knew it was tough for Johnny at the start, as it was for me as a new head coach.

I explained that he needed to connect with the players. He needed to realize that everyone was different, and what made them tick could be completely different from what made him tick. He had to work that out. Build relationships with his players as a captain by understanding the best way to motivate them and get the most out of them as individuals.

There are some players who are nowhere near as good as they think they are, but they are a tiny minority. The rest probably don't believe they can do unbelievable things that are out of their comfort zones. The key is to be able to get them to aim miles higher together as a team. And to do that, you have to develop all sorts of soft leadership skills.

I never had the softer skills when I was a captain. I learned that I needed to change if I wanted to become a successful coach. I would go on to say this to a lot of our top players, not just Johnny – guys who were so committed, so driven and so emotional and who probably couldn't understand why others were not as committed.

If I'd tried to coach the Ireland team using the approach I took as captain at Wigan, I would have been dead in the water. Standards still matter – that has not changed in thirty years – but the method of teaching has changed dramatically. You have to know your student and what makes them tick. The teacher is no longer the sole source of information. The art of coaching has become so much more about empathy, guiding and influencing. Those same attributes are what make great captains today. And it was my job to recognize that and help Johnny reflect on his leadership.

What was so impressive about Johnny was that he realized very quickly that he needed to change, and he went on to become a brilliant captain. He learned how to treat people in order to get the best out of them. The improvement from day one until he retired was remarkable, and in my opinion it also made him a better player, because he was more complete.

* * *

When we eventually faced Italy in October 2020, we won comfortably, leaving us in contention to win the title in our final game against France in Paris. We needed a bonus-point win to claim the championship but in the soulless atmosphere of the empty Stade de France that night, we gained something far more valuable. We lost a game we could have won, and our 35–27 defeat handed the title to England.

A bit was made in the press about Johnny shaking his head when I took him off with twelve minutes remaining, when we were chasing the game at 28–20. But Johnny's reaction didn't bother me at all. That was just passion overflowing. It showed me how much he cared.

No, the big lesson learned that night was by Caelan Doris and Hugo Keenan. Hugo was one of a number of new faces I had brought into the squad when the Six Nations resumed, and had made his debut in the victory over Italy. Caelan was returning to the starting back row having picked up a head injury after only five minutes on his debut against Scotland. Both were in good form and had earned the right to start.

But both players afterwards realized the scale of the difference between provincial rugby and a Test match in the Six Nations. After the game, they both admitted that, although they thought they had been ready, in reality they had been nowhere near. Some players might have insisted they had prepared well, but those two were mature enough to admit they had been way off and that something had to change.

From that moment, both of them massively improved how they prepared through the week. The way they got into good habits just took off. They were helped by the standards that were set by the likes of Johnny and Pete. Caelan and Hugo would go on to become shining examples for others to follow, and the knock-on effect of that was priceless. I would have taken the defeat just for that because of how it influenced them and others who came after them.

* * *

The Autumn Nations Cup followed as a replacement for the fixtures against the southern hemisphere sides that had been cancelled because of the pandemic, and our results continued to be mixed: a win over Wales, a defeat by England, a below-par win over Georgia and a victory over Scotland. In the run-up to the 2021 Six Nations, pressure started mounting in the media. Some said that it would be a make-or-break year, while others questioned our reliance on Johnny at fly-half.

That only intensified when we lost our opening game to Wales, after Peter O'Mahony had been sent off in the four-teenth minute. Then at home against France, we squandered too many scoring opportunities and lost 15–13. The best we could finish now was third place. But I remained defiant.

'You either embrace the pressure or you get buried by it,' I said after the game. 'I enjoy it; it makes you feel alive. You know that when you are taking the gig on. I believe if you've not got pressure in your life, it's not living anyway, so it goes with the territory, I suppose.'

But I was a realist too. I understood why questions were being asked. This was my first job as a head coach, and we were losing games. I understood the deal. But David Nucifora, who had the courage to give me the job, could see the progress we were making behind the scenes because he was connected with the camp. I knew it was coming together and took confidence from that. The players and coaches all knew it was coming too.

The addition of Paul O'Connell to the coaching staff at the start of the year had been a positive step. For the first year, Simon had combined coaching line-outs and defence, but he wanted to focus on defence so I brought Paulie in. I wanted someone who could run the line-out but also tell it like it is about what it takes to be an Irish forward, and Paul epitomized that. He had cut his teeth in coaching positions with the Munster academy, Ireland Under-20s and Stade Français, and he was another big voice, another personality that complemented our coaching team.

We went on to win our next three games, culminating in a 32–18 victory over England at the Aviva Stadium. Another third-place finish, but this time I felt we were in a much better place. The players were starting to have the balls to back themselves in attack when they saw something was on.

There are so many moving parts in attack that it always takes more time to organize than a defence. I worked with Mike Catt, our backs coach, to align our philosophy. The players were starting to execute what they saw in front of them, rather than be hesitant in the moment. At international level an opening can be gone within an instant. Through repetition of our training, and greater understanding, we had more confidence of how to challenge defences and break them down, even when the opposition was trying to disrupt us.

* * *

Warren Gatland had been named as head coach again for the Lions tour of South Africa, and once more asked me to be part of his coaching team. It was an honour to be considered again, but I had to focus on our summer tour and progress how we were trying to play and create more depth in our two home games against Japan and USA, which had replaced our scheduled tour of Fiji.

Of more significance was Gats's decision not to take Johnny on the tour. It was my job as coach to help pick Johnny up again. We drew up a plan to take him through to the World Cup in France in two years' time. Not just Johnny, but also Conor Murray, Keith Earls, Cian Healy and Peter O'Mahony. We wanted to help give them the longevity they would need to be at their best in France. There was no point just getting through to the World Cup: we wanted them to be the best version of themselves.

It involved working with their provinces on their conditioning and their rest. At times we were able to take them out of the provincial set-up and send them away for a week or two to fast-track a body of work. It is one of the best things about Irish rugby: everyone has the best interests of the players at heart, so the medical and coaching staffs are able to work together on situations like this.

I was devastated that the pandemic had forced the cancellation of our tour to Fiji. I felt it would have been a fast-tracking experience for our younger players, because it would have been completely different from what a lot of them would have been used to. I spoke with Nuci, and together we came up with the idea of adding extra games to our tour of New Zealand the following year. We were due to play three Tests against the All Blacks, but we decided to be bold by adding two games against the Māori All Blacks as well, and taking a larger squad. We wanted to make it like a mini-Lions tour of our own. People thought we were mad, but we thought it would be a great opportunity to give ourselves the ultimate test one year out from the World Cup.

I knew it would be critical that we worked on our positional depth charts over the next two years. In Ireland the schools and amateur systems connect brilliantly with the professional game, but the numbers are still the numbers. We are not South Africa, England or New Zealand. I made a comment once about 'little old Ireland' when we were being compared with New Zealand. Someone pointed out that the two countries had roughly the same population, but that is

irrelevant because the only thing that matters is the partici-
pation numbers. Our numbers are similar to Wales, Scotland
and Italy. New Zealand's are far higher.

At times I had to trust my gut and look at players who
might not be first choice at their province but who could
play the way we wanted to play. Jamison Gibson-Park was a
good example. He was second choice for Leinster when we
gave him his first cap. We also saw that Tadhg Beirne could
switch from the back row to the second row.

It was that sort of thinking that prompted us to talk to
Andrew Porter about switching from tighthead prop to loosehead. He was too good a player to be sitting on the bench
behind Tadhg Furlong at Leinster, and we needed more loosehead options. Andrew had begun his career at loosehead, but
it took big balls by him to make the switch. Some people
think that moving from tighthead to loosehead or vice versa
is not a big deal. But the two roles are vastly different. It was
his decision in the end, and Leinster facilitated the switch. He
did unbelievably well.

I picked him at loosehead prop for the opening game of
the autumn series against Japan. Jamison started at scrum-
half and his scanning ability, vision and endurance matched
the way our game was evolving. We won the game 60–5
against the side that two years earlier had shocked us at the
World Cup.

I was pleased with the depth we were building in certain
positions. Ronan Kelleher had emerged at hooker, and then
Dan Sheehan came along and started pushing Ronan. People
started asking if Caelan's best position was at No. 8, rather
than the blindside flank, and that was then pushing Jack
Conan, who had been the starting No. 8 for the Lions.

The following weekend we played the All Blacks. It was

the first time that four of the backline – Jamison, Hugo, Andrew Conway and James Lowe – had faced them. We won 29–20, our third win over New Zealand in five years. And Caelan Doris was man of the match.

It was described as a statement win and an endorsement of the new system we had put in place. But I felt we were only just getting going. I couldn't wait to get to New Zealand the following summer.

21. The Inspiration

In November 2013, when I was part of the England coaching team, we were preparing to face New Zealand at Twickenham when the *Daily Telegraph* ran a story about what had been written on a whiteboard in the All Blacks' team room in the Royal Garden Hotel in Kensington. Among the motivational messages, one stood out. It declared: 'We are the most dominant team in the history of the world.'

The story created a bit of a stir, but what struck me was the response of Steve Hansen, the All Blacks head coach, who defended his side against accusations of arrogance. 'Look at it another way,' Hansen said in a press conference a few days later. 'England are looking to be number two in the world, and we are striving to be better than where we are, even though we are at number one. That's the place we're in, and we are happy with it. If you don't look to improve yourselves, you are going to go backwards. You're striving for the perfect performance.'

I had a lot of respect for what Hansen had said. They hadn't been arrogant; their messaging had been done internally, and I loved the philosophy behind it. When I read the article, I thought to myself, *Fair play*. Because they were *doing* it. They were the best. Even though rugby wasn't the biggest sport in the world, if anyone knew anything about rugby, they would know that the All Blacks were the best. If you are already number one in your own sport, the next target can only be becoming the best team in world sport. That internal motivation was why they stayed at the top for so long, just like Manchester United back in the day, or Brisbane Broncos in Australia, or Wigan when we were at our best.

It got me thinking about what my Ireland side wanted to stand for. I would often ask players: 'What is it that we are striving for? Just to be good?' I wanted us to think bigger than that. Maybe even bigger than just chasing results. I wanted us to *inspire* the nation. I asked the players how they wanted to be perceived, how they wanted to connect with the supporters, how they wanted to play the game, how they wanted to *attack* the game. I told them to imagine what it would be like if we won the World Cup. What would it do for rugby in the country? Why shouldn't we aim for the stars? I wanted the players to own the concept and then drive it on even further.

When I started to hear comments about how the Ireland camp had become more 'fun' since I had become head coach, it used to wind me up. 'That could make people think we are soft,' I would complain, largely to myself. But they would have been so wrong. Just ask the players.

Yes, it mattered to me that players looked forward to going into work: if they hadn't, it wouldn't have been good for learning. But I was only trying to do it my way. I wanted the players to love what they were doing because they were striving to be the best, on a journey together, pushing themselves and each other – not just because it was fun. Of course it was important to lift the mood at times. Working under pressure in an environment that is constantly intense is not good for anyone. We would work hard, bloody hard, but I always tried to mix things up to keep the environment fresh. I wanted the players to know that I cared about them and their development.

When you are a player, you are in your own thoughts all the time, focusing on training, diet and recovery. *How am I going to be at training today? How do I want to play this weekend? How is that going to add to the team performance?* But as a head coach, you have to think of everyone. How they are feeling as individuals, when to pick people up, when to push them. Sometimes there had to be an element of bad cop, if I noticed that anything was slacking. Occasionally that would involve a roasting, but you had to choose your moment. Do that more than twice a year and it loses its impact.

I wanted families to be involved, too. I had benefited so much from sharing my journey as a player with Owen, and latterly as a coach with Gabriel. When the players celebrated a first or a fiftieth cap, we would make sure the families were able to share the moment during the week.

If we were going to inspire the nation, first we had to inspire ourselves.

* * *

I first heard about Mack Hansen from Andy Friend, who signed Mack for Connacht from the Brumbies before the 2021–22 season. Mack had been born and raised in Canberra but qualified for Ireland through his mother, who is from Cork. I watched some videos of him before he arrived in Galway and was immediately impressed.

He had quite a bit of experience at No. 10, and Andy originally thought of him as a full-back, but he ended up playing him on the wing. Mack was deceptively quick, and good both in the air and in contact. What I liked most about him was his desire to get involved and be connected: he was not content to sit on his wing. And that was just what I wanted – a player who would go looking for the ball and could make things happen in attack. In our system, it is not enough for wingers simply to be finishers.

He started well at Connacht, so I invited him to join us for training in November 2021. I guess I wanted to see if he would sink or swim. He came into the camp and seemed to understand immediately what it was about. He had a calm presence and a hunger about him to keep improving.

When James Lowe was unavailable for our first game of the 2022 Six Nations against Wales, I felt Mack was ready to show us what he could do. He did just that, winning the man-of-the-match award in our 29–7 victory and then scoring a brilliant try, plucking the ball out of the air above his head from Joey Carbery's restart, in our narrow defeat against France in Paris in round two. We had found another one.

The defeat in Paris would cost us the chance of a Grand Slam, but we finished the campaign with the Triple Crown, defeating Scotland in our final game. England had a man sent off in the second minute and some people felt that we made hard work of our numerical advantage, as we didn't settle the game until we scored two tries in the final ten minutes to win 32–15. But I don't think it is easy to play against fourteen men. Playing against thirteen makes a difference, but with fourteen a team can still organize itself and players often raise their game because they have been galvanized by the adversity. That's when you see players with character step up, and England stepped up against us.

The Triple Crown used to be a big deal for Ireland, but it didn't seem to mean as much as it once had. I guess that was a sign that the fans' expectations had risen. So had the team's.

* * *

In New Zealand, along the route between our hotel and the training pitch, we were met by electric billboards flashing messages slating us and telling us what the All Blacks were going to do to us. I thought it was brilliant. This was what touring was about, and it showed that we *mattered*. It was something that I had wanted for Ireland: to earn a bit of respect from the best teams in the world. And I knew the only way we would kick on was to put ourselves under pressure.

We brought an extended squad of forty on the tour. It included five uncapped players, while a further twelve had fewer than ten caps each.

Because of Covid, we had not toured since the trip to Australia in 2018, and five massive matches across three weeks was exactly what we needed. The pandemic was still wreaking havoc on our preparations, however, because of the restrictions in New Zealand. Throughout the tour we always seemed to have seven or eight players who had to isolate, and when the injuries started to mount we found ourselves stretched to breaking point at times.

We had put ourselves under a lot of pressure by adding the two Māori fixtures. At one stage I remember a few members of the staff asking if we had been mad to undertake such a venture. After we lost to the Māori in Hamilton in the opening game of the tour, conceding four tries in the first half, the media were starting to ask the same question.

But one of the benefits of going through the challenges of the pandemic was that we had used it to enshrine a 'no excuses' mentality. If you start using excuses, then you are giving the team an 'out' for not performing. There would be no excuses.

After the game, I said to Keith Earls, who had played on

the wing, 'See you at training tomorrow.' He looked at me as if to say, *Are you serious?* and waited for a second to see if I was going to say anything more. I didn't. He had played the game on the Wednesday night; now, with people dropping like flies with injury or Covid, I needed him to play in the first Test on Saturday. 'Yeah, no problem,' he said. His response epitomized our spirit. Players knew they had to give everything because their teammates needed them. Doing things out of the ordinary was the aim of the tour, to see what types of characters we had. Not just players but also coaches and backroom staff.

Jeremy Loughman was stood down for twelve days after suffering a concussion against the Māori, and Cian Healy had gone off with what looked like a serious leg injury. We were also without Finlay Bealham – a tighthead who had played loosehead earlier in his career – because he had Covid. If Cian's injury ruled him out of Saturday's Test in Auckland, it would leave us with just one fit loosehead prop, Andrew Porter, in the squad.

We began to scour New Zealand to see if there were any Irish-qualified players who might be able to do a job for us at prop. David Nucifora said he knew of an Irish player, Conan O'Donnell, who had played around twenty times for Connacht over a four-year period before travelling to Japan and then New Zealand, where he was currently playing for Northland in the Mitre 10 Cup, New Zealand's provincial competition. Nuci phoned him and the following day he turned up at training. It was as if he had won a golden ticket for Willy Wonka's Chocolate Factory when we introduced him to the players. He couldn't believe he might be playing for Ireland. But just an hour after he arrived, Nuci took a call from O'Donnell's club physio. O'Donnell, he said, had suffered a facial fracture a couple of weeks earlier and under no circumstances was he to be allowed to join our training. He was supposed to be sidelined for a few months.

'Why didn't you tell us you had a fracture in your face?' Nuci asked him.

'I thought it was my choice,' he replied. He had been that desperate to play for his country. He was devastated when an hour later he was back on the road, heading home.

Mick Kearney, our team manager, then made contact with Michael Bent, the former Leinster and Ireland prop, who had retired from professional rugby the previous year and was living on his farm in Taranaki and playing the odd game for his province. He joined us for training. Meanwhile, we sent for Ed Byrne, the Leinster prop, to fly out from Ireland, but his flight was delayed and he didn't arrive in time for the Test match.

Thankfully, Cian Healy was passed fit to take his place on the bench, but Michael Bent was on hand during the warm-up just in case. In the end we asked Andrew Porter to play the full eighty minutes.

We lost 42–19. Once again, we had been hit by a fast start, with the All Blacks scoring four tries in seventeen minutes in the first half. We lost Johnny in the first half after he came off for a head-injury assessment, and although we were confident he would be OK for the second Test, the scenario that lay ahead of us now could not have been more testing of our character.

Privately, I was upbeat. Even though we had been absolutely slaughtered on the scoreboard, we were held up over the line four times. If we had taken our chances, it would have been a completely different contest. When I review a game, I always watch it from the perspective of the opposition head coach, and it was clear that we had caused them problems.

I told the players that we should take a huge amount of confidence from the defeat. If they had won but played poorly, I would tell them that we hadn't met our standards. But in defeat, even this heavy defeat, the reverse was true.

Johnny had to go through return-to-play protocols, which he passed, but even so I told him not to play if he had any doubts. He wanted to play. We did some work on our set piece and our defence in transition, but otherwise we just needed to be more ruthless in our finishing. We had also been doing a lot of work with Gary Keegan, our performance coach, on 'staying in the moment'. Fundamentally, this was about taking emotion out of our game, being level-headed and asking each other what are our jobs were and how we were going to go about them. And that proved critical in the second Test in Dunedin. The All Blacks received two yellow cards in the first half, and then after half an hour Angus Ta'avao was sent off for making contact with the head of Garry Ringrose in a tackle – but we still only led by 10–7 at the interval. *Stay in the moment, lads.* And they did. Andrew Porter went over for his second try of the game before Johnny's kicking took us to a 23–12 victory, Ireland's first against the All Blacks on New Zealand soil.

We headed to Wellington with the chance to make more history by clinching the series. But first we had to face the Māori side again on Tuesday. Some of the players had to play on two days' rest including Mack Hansen, Conor Murray and Joey Carbery. Keith Earls was a worthy captain.

Our 30–24 victory was a further boost to our confidence ahead of the Test series decider, but perhaps the biggest cheer in the changing room afterwards was for Michael Bent, who had come off the bench for the final four minutes of the game. We had selected the retired thirty-six-year-old as we did not want to risk involving Finlay Bealham, who had arrived back with us the day before the second Test after being out with Covid. I was as proud of our performance in that game as any on the tour, because no one knew the challenges that had to be overcome behind the scenes.

The biggest challenge was yet to come. We knew we were going to face the very best from the All Blacks in the series decider. If it is rare for them to lose two games in a row, that is even more true in New Zealand. They had a full-strength side and would be gunning for us: the ultimate test. It was everything that I wanted from the tour.

I know South Africa have won back-to-back World Cups, but to me, the All Blacks have always been the standard-bearers. I reckon the Springboks would agree. Our 32–22 win in the series decider remains my favourite as Ireland coach.

This time we raced into a lead, with tries by Josh van der Flier, Hugo Keenan and Robbie Henshaw, and we led 22–3 at half-time. But inevitably the All Blacks came back at us hard, with three tries in twenty minutes. *Stay in the moment.* We were up by three when a try by Rob Herring, from the back of a line-out maul, clinched the series. I can't tell you how much it meant to us. I knew that it almost certainly wouldn't be done again: it was expected to be the last proper three-Test tour because of plans to restructure the Tests between northern- and southern-hemisphere teams, starting in 2026.

The idea behind making the tour so difficult for ourselves had been to prepare for the World Cup in France the following year. But what we had achieved here, against all the odds, was probably the toughest thing to do in world rugby. We had beaten the All Blacks in a series away from home, and not only that, we had come from behind to do so. In the dressing room afterwards, some of the boys were in tears, even senior pros like Pete O'Mahony.

22. The Shirt

On our journey to Murrayfield to play Scotland in the 2017 Six Nations, the Edinburgh police had taken our team bus along a different route than usual. We found ourselves stuck behind some marching bagpipers and got to the ground fifteen minutes late. We lost the game, and the impact of the pre-match delay had clearly irked Joe Schmidt, who brought it up with the media afterwards. 'We arrived at the stadium about ten or fifteen minutes late and we were late for most things in the first half,' he said.

It was an example to me of why we had needed to become more resilient. I wanted us to be able to cope with anything that was thrown at us, and revel in the adversity. Professional sport can be unfair, cruel even. However much you plan and prepare, there are always going to be last-minute problems, injuries, refereeing decisions that go against you. The best teams just get on with it.

I once told the players a story from when I was playing for Wigan. On our journey to Leeds, we got stuck on the M62 going over the Pennines, and we were running so late that we had to get changed and have our warm-up on the bus. We got to the ground ten minutes before kick-off and didn't even go into the changing room. We quickly finished our warm-up on the pitch and then went on to win comfortably against a good Leeds side. It was an example of what you can achieve if you have the right mindset, I told them.

Our experience in New Zealand had proven just that. The

challenge had been so extreme: the injuries, Covid, constant travel and playing against the best team – a team that had been gunning for us – on their home patch. Out of their comfort zones, the players had achieved something they probably never thought possible. It had been a turning point. There was no going back.

We selected Ciarán Frawley, Joe McCarthy and Cian Prendergast, who had all featured against the Māori All Blacks during the summer, in a thirty-five-man Emerging Ireland squad for a short tour of South Africa in September 2022. It was tricky for the provinces to give up that number of players at the start of the new season, but we saw it as a brilliant opportunity to bring in a group of largely uncapped players and see if they could handle the pressure of training and getting up to the level required to be an international within a week or so. Nuci and I saw it as an important step to give opportunities to a wider group so as to build depth going into a World Cup year.

Our first Test after going back to number one in the world rankings – a position we hadn't held since 2019 – was against South Africa in Dublin that November. We held on for a 19–16 win despite a late surge by the Springboks. Then, after beating Fiji, our preparations against Australia were disrupted when Johnny was forced to pull out of the game with a calf injury that he picked up doing the warm-up. Jack Crowley – at the time a youngster who had only just made his debut off the bench against Fiji – was now facing his first start against the Wallabies with little time to get his head around it. But he was still expected to perform, and I loved the way he rolled his sleeves up and got on with it.

It was a priceless experience for him and the squad. Jack finished the game confident that he could cope at this level, and his teammates knew it too. Dealing with what might be deemed 'oh shit' moments is far more important than just getting a result. It was a scrappy game, but Ross Byrne, who hadn't even been in the initial twenty-three, was on hand to land a late penalty for a 13–10 win.

I felt the players were becoming more accountable, working hard in attack and defence to offer themselves to the team. That gave us greater freedom to take different options, so we could become unpredictable but within an organized structure. I would love having conversations with Mike Catt about how we could evolve and keep the opposition guessing. That is as exciting as it gets for me. *Where can we make a difference? How can we make a difference? How is it going to happen?*

You can't stand still, because everyone else is always evolving. But you need to get the balance right and not tinker too much. It is very hard for the lads to come in and pick up something new in just five training sessions before a Test match, so we strive for simplicity and clarity; but getting there can be complex. The players need to understand how and why it works, and that's when they take ownership of it. Rugby union is a complicated game, but when the players are able to do something instinctively, and know that they will have support to back up their decisions, it can become beautifully simple.

When we reassembled in January for the 2023 Six Nations, we wanted to continue our project of inspiring the nation. I felt we had grown enough as a group to be bold in our ambition and state internally that we wanted to go for the Grand Slam.

The challenge was that if you lost your first game, then the question would be: *Where do we go from here?* But we had got to the point where I felt we could cope with that extra pressure.

We were the number one side in the world rankings. If we did fall at the first hurdle, then there would be a reason for it, and addressing that would become our narrative.

I put the idea across to the senior leadership group. They were up for it, and then we told the rest of the players so that we could start owning it together. 'Let's go after it,' I told the squad. Everyone was on board. Mack Hansen even made a promise to the lads that if we won the Grand Slam he would get a tattoo of my face on his thigh. It takes all sorts. There are not that many Mack Hansens, that is for sure. I knew if we got there it would be so rewarding, but not as rewarding as the journey.

* * *

When our team bus arrived late to the Principality Stadium in Cardiff for the opening game of the championship, this time it bothered no one. It was just as well. Because in this, of all years, our resilience would be tested to the limit.

Warren Gatland had returned as head coach of Wales, and we expected a big bounce from them. We hadn't won in Cardiff in the Six Nations since 2013, and I carried a few war wounds myself. I had lost an Anglo-Welsh Cup game with Saracens there back in 2008, and four years earlier had lost to St Helens there when playing for Wigan in the Challenge Cup final.

Our pre-tournament preparations in Portugal had hardly gone smoothly. Tadhg Furlong was ruled out with a calf injury, so Finlay Bealham had to come in for his first Six Nations start; Johnny had just returned after undergoing surgery for a facial injury in January. Then, on the eve of the game, Jamison Gibson-Park and Cian Healy had to withdraw because of injuries. With the roof closed and a fevered atmosphere, it was a real test of our resolve, but we won the game comfortably in the end, keeping the crowd quiet with an explosive start and then showing patience to clinch the bonus point in the final ten minutes.

We knew the game against France in Dublin the following weekend could decide the title. They were the defending Grand Slam champions, and ranked number two in the world.

Gary Keegan was now with us full-time during competition windows and we had made real progress with our mindset as a group, in terms of being able to stay in control of our emotions and focus on the next task. I knew that what I did next could put all that at risk, but it was something I felt I had to do.

* * *

I had been intrigued about why no one ever spoke about the history of rugby on the island within the squad. I have Irish heritage, which can be traced back three generations to Longford, while Colleen's family also has strong Irish roots. I guess my interest first took hold when I played for England against Ireland at Croke Park. When I moved to Dublin, Vinny Hammond, our high-performance analyst, gave me a book on Irish history, and reading it only made me even more intrigued.

But when I asked a few older heads in the game, the answer I got back was: 'Don't go there.'

Undeterred, I kept on digging and reading more books, and the more I learned about Irish rugby, the more I realized that talking about the story would be anything but rocking the boat. It was something to be treasured and shared.

All the way through partition and the Troubles, the sport had never wavered. It was a game that had always been played throughout the island and had brought people together. Clubs from Northern Ireland would travel to the Republic and vice versa, crossing the border, even in the face of real adversity, for the love of the game and playing for Ireland.

I wanted to celebrate the fact that our sport shone like a beacon even in the darkest of times. The connection never broke. To me that made the Ireland shirt the most powerful in world sport. You hear about other iconic shirts, but in my eyes they don't even compare.

This was something that deserved to be brought into the light and talked about. I wanted the players to be able to share what they felt and hear other points of view, because perceptions are often influenced by individual experiences. Everyone always says they are proud to play for Ireland, but you have to understand why. That is what interested me, more than anything.

A few years earlier, Brian O'Driscoll and Craig Doyle had made a fascinating documentary called *Shoulder to Shoulder*, which explored how the Ireland team had crossed the divide throughout the Troubles. So, on the Monday night before the France game, I asked Drico and David Irwin, who had played for Ulster, Ireland and the Lions in the 1980s, to speak to the squad. Davy, along with Ulster and Ireland teammates Nigel Carr and Philip Rainey, had been caught up in an IRA bombing near the border when they were travelling down to Dublin for an Ireland training session for the 1987 World Cup. Nigel Carr never played again because of the injuries he sustained. We also invited Paul Rouse, a professor of history from University College Dublin, and Craig chaired a question-and-answer session. The whole squad and staff gathered in our team room at Carton House.

After being sacked by England, I wasn't permitted to coach another Six Nations team for six months. I joined Munster as a consultant, and spent some great time with their head coach, Anthony Foley. His sudden death later that season was a terrible blow. [Inpho/Donall Farmer]

When Joe Schmidt offered me the job of Ireland defence coach, I jumped at the chance to work with him. I had to do a lot of detailed work to convince him of the need for a complete change to Ireland's defensive system.

[Inpho/Dan Sheridan]

When we played the All Blacks in Chicago in 2016, Joe's message was that if we got ahead in the match, we had to keep playing – something Ireland had failed to do in 2014. This time the players did keep playing, and secured a historic win.
[Inpho/Dan Sheridan]

Celebrating the Lions' victory over the All Blacks in the second Test in 2017, with Johnny Sexton, Conor Murray and my son Gabriel.
[Inpho/Billy Stickland]

Johnny Sexton had been a leader in the Ireland team as fly-half for many years before he became captain at thirty-four. In the captaincy, his leadership only got better.
[Inpho/Dan Sheridan]

In 2022, after Ireland won a Test against the All Blacks in New Zealand for the first time ever, the challenge was to kick on and win the series. We did, and it was brilliant to savour the moment with Bundee Aki and lots of Irish supporters in Wellington.
[Joe Allison/Getty Images]

At the start of 2023, we were clear that we were targeting a Grand Slam. We rode some adversity along the way, but achieved our goal with a victory over England at the Aviva Stadium.
[PA Images/Alamy Stock Photo]

With Springboks captain Siya Kolisi after our narrow victory in the group stage of the 2023 World Cup.
[Inpho/Dan Sheridan]

With Sam Cane after the quarter-final against New Zealand. We went behind 13–0, then dragged ourselves back into a brilliant match. It was a huge disappointment to fall narrowly short, but I felt we were in a good place.
[Inpho/Dan Sheridan]

It's not easy to defend a Six Nations title, but we bounced back quickly from the World Cup to beat France in Marseille in the crucial opening match, and weathered a one-point loss to England before wrapping up the title against Scotland in Dublin.
[Inpho/Dan Sheridan]

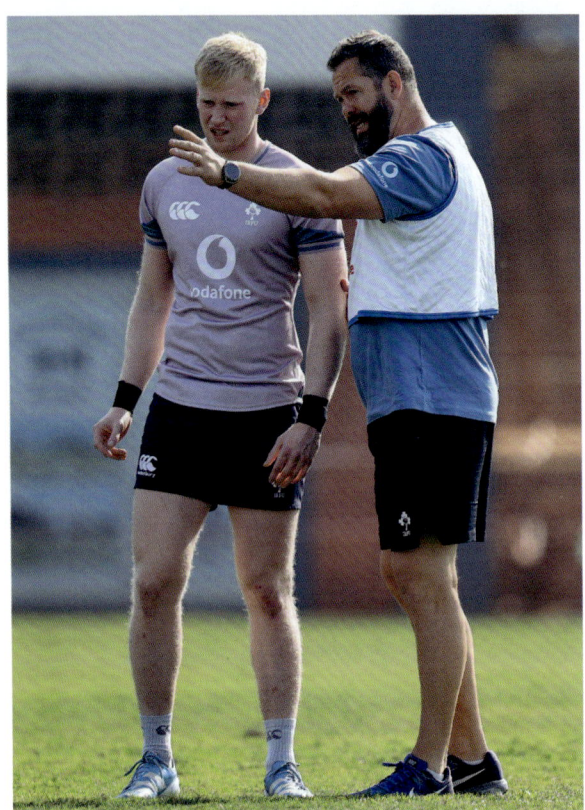

With Hugo Keenan absent, I asked Jamie Osborne to make his international debut against the Springboks in Pretoria. He played well, and then he was man of the match in our dramatic victory in the second Test in Durban.

[Inpho/Dan Sheridan]

With tour captain Maro Itoje and Ieuan Evans at the announcement of the British and Irish Lions squad for the 2025 tour of Australia. For a rugby coach, leading the Lions is as good as it gets, and I jumped at the chance.

[Inpho/Dan Sheridan]

The dressing room before the first Test in Brisbane. The players had bought in fully to the Lions concept, and we felt we had given ourselves the best chance to win, but they had to go out and do it. And they did.

Even when we went behind 23–5 in the second Test, I backed us to win. After we won the match and the series with Hugo Keenan's last-minute try, I felt proud of how the players had come back to get what they deserved.

Celebrating our series win with my son Gabriel, who was part of the camp during the Test weeks.

At Owen's wedding to Georgie, with Colleen and our daughters Gracie (*left*) and Elleshia.

Our grandchildren: Owen and Georgie's sons Freddie (*left*) and Tommy.

Colleen's dad, Keiron, and my dad, Peter.

I just stood at the back and let the night unfold. It was more than I could have hoped for. Drico and Davy spoke about their experiences. Davy described what it was like to be an Ulster player playing for Ireland at the height of the Troubles, and the sacrifices and risks that were involved. Brian talked about what he had learned from talking things through deeply with Rory Best while making the documentary. James Ryan spoke about his great grandfather being in the GPO during the Easter Rising in 1916 and what that meant to him.

One by one others stood up and spoke about their personal experiences and perspective. Some players who never thought they would speak about it were inspired to do so by the honesty that was in the air. *Think about what the jersey has done for the country, what it means to the people. We need to represent the jersey properly.*

Keith Earls was one of the first. He said he would get pats on the back when he was getting into a taxi for not singing 'Ireland's Call', the anthem that is played alongside 'Amhrán na bhFiann', the Irish national anthem, at home games. 'Ireland's Call' was written by Phil Coulter before the 1995 World Cup in recognition that players from Northern Ireland also represented the Ireland team, and it is the only anthem that is played for away matches.

Earlsy admitted not singing 'Ireland's Call'. For him it had been 'Amhrán na bhFiann' or nothing. 'I am embarrassed,' he said. 'Now I know the truth about the shirt and what it is all about.'

Once Earlsy had spoken, the ice was broken. It was an incredibly moving night. I held the shirt up and said: 'This is the most powerful shirt. It is not a brand; it is not a gimmick. It stands for peace and unity, because of everything that it has been through.' From then on, we carried one of the original Ireland team jerseys around with us, a tiny thing, as a reminder of that night.

The boys said they could have played France the following day after what we experienced that night. When it came to the game on Saturday, I could see a few guys had tears in their eyes during the anthems, and I wondered if we had overdone it. We had worked so hard to that point on taking the emotion out of our game and being level-headed in our decision-making. But then I thought, *It's more important than a game. It means so much to them, and if we are emotional then so be it.* I would have taken a defeat that day to be able to get to that point, because that was the beginning of our story. From then on, I would use snippets from that night and make sure that we kept bringing it up, using it in different ways to fit the feel of the group.

When you have ambitions as an individual, they are nowhere near as big as your ambitions can be when you come together as a team. You can always find something far bigger and better than yourself. It is the job of us all to find what that is.

* * *

Despite my fears, we didn't lose against France. It turned out to be an epic Six Nations encounter. We embraced the pressure of the occasion.

What surprised me was just how expansively France played. Usually they play a long-kicking, territorial game and then hit you on the counter-attack. But this time they played a lot more from inside their own half. Hugo Keenan, James Lowe and Andrew Porter scored first-half tries, but it was not until Garry Ringrose touched down in the final ten minutes that we saw them off. Our 32–19 win ended France's run of fourteen wins and set a new national record of thirteen successive home victories.

After defeating Italy in Rome, we headed for Edinburgh. There was no delay to our bus this time, but by half-time I was laughing to myself, such was the dire situation we faced.

Both our hookers, Dan Sheehan and Ronan Kelleher, had to come off with injuries, while Caelan Doris and Iain Henderson also went off hurt inside the opening twenty-five minutes. A part of me thought it served me right for wanting chaos to test ourselves.

Losing the two hookers forced us to cobble together a new front row, as we desperately didn't want to go to uncontested scrums. We had registered Cian Healy, our loosehead prop, as a hooker. He had scrummaged enough there over his long career to know what he was doing, and having a prop go into the middle of the scrum immediately gave us extra heft. We actually won a penalty at the next scrum.

Meanwhile, we were able to break the glass on another emergency back-up. Josh van der Flier is a fantastic athlete, and when he had spare moments during our camps he would practise line-out throwing, just in case. Craig Casey, one of our scrum-halves, is also brilliant at throwing in. Josh did a fantastic job with the line-outs, and at half-time Fogs and Paulie tried to give Cian a crash course in his new duties at hooker. He could scrummage all right, but we had to fit him into all the set-piece plays that he had never run before as a hooker. For example, he would never have had the ball at the back of a maul and played it quickly from there.

We had to hope that our collectiveness would allow us to find solutions among ourselves. I must be mad, but I loved it. 'This is brilliant,' I said in the dressing room at half-time. To me the beauty of it was seeing everyone working so hard in all the chaos to try to restore a bit of order. We had nothing to lose now. From the outside it might have looked like the coaches applied strokes of genius, but believe me, it was not that. It was the players finding a way, both in the dressing room and out on the pitch. That is when you know you have a good group.

Cian got stuck into his new roles and Josh's throwing was superb. Having led 8–7 at half-time, we pushed on for a 22–7 win.

We were one game away from the Grand Slam now, and that brought its own pressures. The fact that it was England in Dublin only added to the sense of occasion. But in sport there are never guaranteed endings, or fairytale finishes. That is why we love it so much. Ireland had spoiled enough Grand Slam parties for England over the years for us to know that Steve Borthwick's side would be desperate to beat us. They would arrive in Dublin with an edge. We had to find ours.

We had not given way when England came to win a Grand Slam on our home ground in 2017, but how would we react when we were the side with the chance to win something?

England played well, as I expected. Even after they lost Freddie Steward to a controversial red card, they did a great job slowing the game down with spoiling tactics. Two penalties by Owen had put England in front before we hit back with a try by Dan Sheehan, and we made hard work of putting them away even with the extra man. Tries by Robbie Henshaw, a second for Dan, and another by Rob Herring eventually secured a 29–16 win.

It was a fantastic achievement for the players to deliver a Grand Slam when they had gone into the tournament with the pressure of being world number one. I was delighted too for the senior players, like Johnny, for whom it was his last appearance in an Ireland jersey at the Aviva Stadium. He had already announced he would be retiring after the World Cup later in the year. I knew how much it meant to the supporters as well. This was only Ireland's fourth Grand Slam title.

But I knew we hadn't played well at all. It is my job as head coach to see the reality and I wasn't happy with our performance. We hadn't played. We hadn't been ourselves. We hadn't gone after them the way we had done so magnificently against the All Blacks in the third Test. Silverware is one thing, but the most important thing to me is meeting our own internal standards. The easy thing would have been to gloss over a poor performance. But if I did that, the players would know that I wasn't being honest with them. We told them the truth. We had to learn from this. We had to understand why we hadn't performed if we were to do justice to the shirt when we headed to France for the World Cup.

While the rest of Dublin celebrated long into the night, I went back to the hotel around 9 p.m. to spend time with Colleen and the family.

23. The Pride

When Jamie George scored a try for England from the back of a maul late on in the Grand Slam game, Johnny Sexton, who had joined the maul to try to stop their momentum, suffered a groin injury as it collapsed over the line. He needed surgery and wouldn't play again that season.

And when Johnny missed our warm-up games against Italy, England and Samoa because of a ban he picked up after the Champions Cup final, it inevitably led to questions about our over-reliance on him and our succession planning. Why had I not brought a younger player through as our first-choice out-half during the previous three years? Had I been too loyal to a player who would be thirty-eight at the World Cup?

In truth, the reason Johnny was first choice was not because I was too loyal; he was there only because of his standards and drive.

Johnny looked after himself, and the way he managed the captaincy made him a more complete player. He was never going to simply stand aside as he approached the end of his career so that others could take over. And I was never going to drop him while he was still performing at such a high level. You benefit massively as a group if you have got brilliant players who are showing others how it should be done.

If you look at the players in the Ireland squad who are in their late twenties or early thirties, I can tell you that not one of them would still be there if they didn't have the ambition to improve. Not one of them would say they are comfortable. They can't be: their peers won't allow it. That is how it has to be. It is the same in any successful organization. That drive and competition have to be at the heart of it. When it comes to selection of a player whose inclusion I see as a 50/50 call, I might tell him that and see how he reacts. If he has still allowed it to be a 50/50 call later in the week, then whose fault is that? But if he turns it into a 70/30 call, then the player has picked himself.

I will never rule someone out purely because of age – at either end of the spectrum. If the attitude, ambition and performances are there, I will pick the player on merit.

When young players come into our training camps, I often have to tell them to stop being so respectful of older players. You don't have to be everyone's best friend. The established players might think, *He's a good bloke*, and, *He's allowed me to stay ahead of him*, but they won't respect you.

In our camp there is no hierarchy. We don't have play-ers who are twenty-three or twenty-four waiting their turn behind twenty-seven- or twenty-eight-year-olds. If someone can show us that he is good enough, then he's old enough. Irish players in their early twenties are not inexperienced. I have seen myself the pressure they are put under in big games in school competitions: they are brought up with it. The ones that come through quicker are the ones who say, 'I am not just going to fit in, I am going to try to make it happen.' That is what happened with Caelan Doris and Hugo Keenan. The ones who work it out pretty quickly tend to have longer careers.

And the younger players benefit from seeing what it takes from the senior players. Look at what we have now:

287

competition between four or five fly-halves who are going to fight it out over the next few years. And that has a lot to do with the standards set by others.

* * *

There is only one Mack Hansen, and it turns out he is a man of his word. I am not sure too many of us took him seriously when he promised to get a tattoo of my face if we won the Grand Slam. But one afternoon my phone beeped with a message from Mack, with a photograph of my tattooed mug, on his upper quad. Apparently, he and Bundee Aki had been in the gym and decided to send it to me to see what I thought. For a bit of craic, I decided to sit on it for a day and not text him back, just to let him stew. Mack was left thinking: *What have I done? Maybe he hates it.* The following day I put him out of his misery and messaged him back. I knew it was just a bit of fun and it didn't bother me at all. Each to their own.

It was a light-hearted moment that underscored the spirit in our camp. We knew there would be a lot of attention on us going into the World Cup in France, but again the idea was to embrace it. Our ambition to inspire the nation had begun a couple of seasons earlier, and this would be the moment to take the connection with our fans to a new level. We would draw energy from them and attempt to make them proud of us and the jersey. With the World Cup so close to home, we knew that tens of thousands of Ireland supporters would make the journey. Our job was to keep winning for them.

We beat Italy in our first warm-up match in Dublin. Then, in the build-up to our second game, against England, I found myself answering questions about Owen. He had been sent off for a high tackle on Taine Basham during England's 19–17 win over Wales at Twickenham in their opening warm-up game. The RFU appealed the red card, and an independent Six Nations hearing overturned it. World Rugby then appealed that decision. The appeal had yet to be heard at that point, but Owen had already been stood down by England for the game against us.

Usually when I am asked about Owen I just bat the questions off, but the red card, the decision to overturn it, and the World Rugby appeal had created a media circus. Some of what was said was aimed directly at Owen, and appeared to be personal.

I told the press conference that I thought the attacks on Owen had gone too far. 'I'd probably get his mother up here to do an interview with you, and you'll see the human side of the bullshit that's happening,' I said. 'Or maybe get his wife to write a book on it, because then you'll probably see the impact that it's having on, not just the professional player, but the families and the human side that goes with it.'

* * *

When I named the team for our opening World Cup group game against Romania, I faced questions about whether Mack had not been selected because of a disciplinary issue. I had earlier made a comment about the distractions the players had faced when we were based in Biarritz in a hotel on the beach for our final warm-up game against Samoa. I said some people hadn't handled those distractions brilliantly, and we had talked about it internally as a group, but that had nothing to do with my selection against Romania. Mack was never going to start the game. We wanted to give Keith Earls more game time, but I probably gave the story more legs by questioning one of the journalists who kept asking about it.

I was more bothered about our slightly below par display against Samoa, and we went with a strong side from the outset against Romania in the searing heat of Bordeaux. Johnny was back and we needed to give him game time from the off to get him up to speed for our crucial third pool game, against South Africa. The number of Ireland fans who turned up made it feel like a home game, and that was important because you can no longer take any match lightly in the World Cup. With bonus points available and points difference potentially deciding which two sides will qualify from the pool, you have to aim to put on a big score. The heat was brutal, hitting the high thirties in the middle of the pitch, and we were just glad to get under way and rack up a few points. Some questioned whether we should have put out pretty much our first team from the start, but given the order of our fixtures we had to generate momentum going into the defining games against South Africa and Scotland. The selection strategy might have been different if the order of fixtures had been different. At least our sharp performance in the second game, against Tonga, allowed us to make changes early in the second half. Twenty tries in two matches was a decent start ahead of our game against the Springboks.

We had tried to turn our training base in the city of Tours, in the Loire Valley a couple of hours' drive south-west of Paris, into a home from home. It was a fantastic place and the municipality made a big effort to make us feel welcome. You knew you were in a World Cup, a stark contrast to 2015 when I was with England and we were stuck in Pennyhill Park with no tournament atmosphere. Families were able to come out during downtime, and the lads loved it. The backroom staff did a great job of setting things up. The players could cycle to training from the hotel, and we had a big marquee with a team room. The IRFU had provided us with amenities such as a pool table, a golf simulator and table tennis for the lads. The atmosphere was fantastic.

When we travelled to Paris for the South Africa game, it felt like the city had been taken over by the Irish. There were green shirts everywhere. The pubs and bars were packed, there were fans scrummaging in the streets, and when we got to the Stade de France there was already an electric buzz.

The Springboks were the defending champions, and had moved up to number two in the world rankings while we were still top. We knew they would come hard at us. All the chat was about their decision to go with seven forwards on their bench. I joked that I had been considering going with seven backs and one forward, but that John Fogarty, our scrum coach, was having none of it. We knew what was coming, with their 'bomb squad' and aggressive line speed in defence. Our job was to keep them guessing where we would come after them.

We had a tricky enough start, losing a few attacking line-outs. But we were good enough and calm enough to work things out in the face of adversity. Our physicality was spot on, with Ronan Kelleher leading the way by smashing into Damian Willemse, and our defence was superb. It is not often you see Eben Etzebeth picked up and driven back, as James Lowe managed to do at the start of the second half to win a turnover. We had a bit of luck too, with the Springboks missing four kicks at goal. They could have snatched the game at the end when they had an attacking line-out, but again we found a way to hold them up. There were only two tries in the game, a brilliant finish by Mack in the first half, while Cheslin Kolbe put the Springboks in front soon after the interval. It was proof that you don't need a big score for an epic game. Penalties by Johnny and Jack Crowley were enough to secure a 13–8 win, sparking phenomenal celebrations from the Irish supporters, with the Cranberries' song 'Zombie' booming into the Paris night.

We had a two-week break before the Scotland match, as we headed back to Tours and gave the players a few days off to spend with their families.

* * *

I know I will get slagged off for saying this, but I thought our final pool game against Scotland was as big as, if not bigger than, any other game we would face at the World Cup. I say that because if we had lost that game without picking up a bonus point, we would have been out, and in most of the scenarios in which we lost with a bonus point, we were out too. I regarded this as the first of our knock-out games. The message was, *Scotland are a dangerous team. Lose and we are going home, lads.*

We had a setback during the week when we lost Robbie Henshaw with a hamstring injury. Stu McCloskey, another centre who had done well for us, came onto the bench. We also had the focus of Peter O'Mahony's 100th cap, and the number of Ireland supporters in Paris seemed to grow by the day. No one wanted to go home, and our explosive start reflected it. We had a four-try bonus point before half-time and stretched the lead to 36–0 before Scotland scored two late tries.

It was our seventeenth successive Test victory, a national record. We hadn't lost since the first Test in New Zealand, over a year earlier. Back then, we had fired the players up ahead of the second Test. 'These lot don't even know your fucking name, make sure by the end of tonight they know who the fuck you are,' I said. Then, before our victory in the third Test,

I told the players: 'They know your name now, but they still don't know who you are. They don't respect you.'

Going into the quarter-final fifteen months later, I hoped we had their respect now, and they certainly knew who we were. But I also knew what was coming.

* * *

I have heard the story that I should have taken Johnny off, that his legs had gone by the end. Another one is that I should have rotated the squad more during the pool stages to keep us fresher for the quarter-final. Another one is that we choked. That the pressure of getting beyond the quarter-finals for the first time in World Cup history overwhelmed us.

The story, in my eyes, was a very different one. In the build-up we had been calm and focused. My job was to make sure the team knew what they were trying to achieve and how they were going to do so. The players honestly believed they could win, and that made the defeat harder to take. It was difficult not to see it as an opportunity missed, but the All Blacks were pretty good at believing in themselves as well. I know more than many that nothing gives you the right to have it all your own way.

I have no doubt that New Zealand had been preparing for this moment for a long time. Joe Schmidt had joined Ian Foster's team the previous year, and people talked about the influence Joe had on their attack, and about the inside knowledge he had on us. But Joe had not worked with Ireland for four years, and things had moved on. We were a different team. We knew they would have some tricks up their sleeves, but my thinking was that we had to be good enough to cover all bases. You can fall into the trap of being over-analytical and trying to predict what is going to happen. You have to be instinctive enough to be able to adapt in the moment: that is the art of top-class sport.

In our run of victories, we often got off to a fast start, but this time New Zealand did the same to us, going up 13–0 in the first quarter. That can happen to any team – and what tends to follow when New Zealand start so well is that they go off and win the game by forty points. But in the next sixty minutes we had the balls to drag ourselves back into it. We got rid of the errors we'd made in those first twenty minutes – not just individual mistakes but team errors – reset ourselves and attacked the game for the next hour. I cannot tell you how proud I was of the players for having the guts and skill to give themselves a chance of winning such a huge game against a world-class side. Bundee Aki's try gave us a foothold, and Jamison Gibson-Park burrowed over just before half-time to reduce their lead to a single point. We were calm, and finding solutions on the hoof under the most unbelievable pressure. Will Jordan scored and again we responded, winning a penalty try as they collapsed our driving maul.

With fifteen minutes to go, it was 25–24 to the All Blacks and they had Codie Taylor in the sin bin. Jordie Barrett kicked another penalty to make it 28–24, but in the seventy-second minute our maul was driving over their line again. Somehow Barrett managed to get himself under Ronan Kelleher to hold him up.

I still believed we were going to do it, because we had worked so hard getting to the point of staying calm and delivering when it mattered: we had done it time and time again. And why would I take Johnny off? He was dictating the game.

The night before the game, I had done what I always did: challenge myself to consider different scenarios. *What would I do if X, Y or Z happens?* I always write it all down to stimulate my thinking. But a head coach has to have a feel for the game as it is actually unfolding, and I am always guided by what is going on in front of me. There's no alternative. It's pointless saying before the game that, for example, Andrew Porter, Tadhg Furlong and Dan Sheehan are only going to play for fifty-five minutes. You need to judge if the player is really tired. Also, a rigid pre-match plan can impact a player's mentality. If you keep taking them off after fifty-five minutes, they can come to think that is all they can play for. The way training sessions are now, everyone should be able to play for eighty minutes. At the other end of the spectrum, it might look harsh to take a player off after thirty minutes. But either decision can be right, if it arises from a good reading of the *feeling* of the game.

You might start thinking about taking off your out-half in the last twenty minutes, even if he is playing well and even if he is your captain, because of the effects of fatigue. But between the sixtieth and seventy-fifth minutes, the game was stop-start and Johnny was firing on all cylinders. He was our general, our captain, and he knew from vast experience how to manage the game. There was no point during those fifteen minutes at which Johnny appeared to be labouring.

We had a goal-line drop-out with 75:28 on the clock. That turned out to be the last opportunity to make a substitution: after that, the ball was in play continuously for just under seven minutes. Our final attacking set lasted five minutes and twenty seconds, during which we went through thirty-seven phases and advanced sixty metres, to within ten metres of the New Zealand line, before we were penalized at a breakdown. Every player on the field was struggling as that passage of play wore on, and Johnny has said that by the end of it his legs were gone. Of course, by then it was too late to make a substitution. And it was thanks to his excellence as the orchestrator of our attack that we came as close as we did.

Imagine us scoring the try and getting the game done. Would anyone have been asking about our decisions then? It all becomes irrelevant, doesn't it? It made me proud to see how delighted the All Blacks were to hang on and win the game and regard it as one of their best wins. It made me think we were in the right place.

There has been a bit of a fuss made about exchanges after the game between Johnny and Rieko Ioane. But it's just sport, isn't it? People claim they don't want to see things like that, yet they love it at the same time. It showed me how much the players cared, and sometimes, when something means so much, you can lose the run of yourself. I should know, I've done it plenty of times myself!

It is hard to describe the emotion in the changing room afterwards. I knew how much the players had put into it, their hearts and souls and more, and I was so proud of them. They just didn't want to go home, or lose the connection they had made with the fans, because it had been such a wonderful ride.

Amid the despair I had one more job to do, to make sure I did justice to Johnny and Earlsy, who were both retiring. I had been talking to Keith over the previous two years about when he was going to step down, but he had not said anything publicly. At the start of the week, I had to broach it with him. 'Look, Earlsy,' I said to him, 'I know you don't want to hear this, but if we lose at the weekend, we have to announce it to the players.' I only said it because he deserved to have a send-off after his last game.

I didn't realize how tough it would be to find myself

standing in front of a changing room of distraught players with the job of giving him and Johnny a nice bottle of
fine wine each. Both men deserved better. I still think back
now about the scene. There were plenty of tears, which just
showed how much it meant. I knew it was one of those situations when I had to man up and get it done. *Those words still
needed to be said, we still needed to give them each that nice bottle of
wine.* You have to, don't you, because losing is part of life. I
stayed with the players as long as I could until I was called off
to do the post-match press conference.

* * *

After the game, I did what I always do and watched it back as
if I was the opposition head coach. When you do that, you
tend to find that the opposition had made as many errors as
your own side, but because they won nobody cares.

What I know is that we had been pretty good consistently
over a number of years because we learned as much or more
from winning as from losing. If you only focus on the result,
it can mask poor performances. And if you don't know why
you are winning, that is when you can suddenly fall off a
cliff. We had won some incredibly important games while
making the same number of mistakes, but people didn't see
them: they thought it was an unbelievable performance just
because we won by a point or whatever.

Our World Cup dream was over, and all we had left was
ifs, buts or maybes. It was a game that should really have been
a semi-final, but for the lopsided nature of the draw. Fair
play to Ian Foster, he and his team delivered. They would
have been waiting for that moment since the series the previous year.

When I stripped away the emotion of the night, I realized

there was still much to be proud of. I don't know if I am cold-hearted, but it didn't take me long to get over the defeat. Of course, I was gutted at the time, and even more so for the players. But there is something bigger than winning. I know my sixteen-year-old self would never believe that, but time has taught me differently.

If our ambition had been to inspire a nation, then judging by the incredible atmosphere in the stadium that night, and the scenes across Paris and back home in Ireland, then I think we did an OK job. People will have their own opinions, and some would maybe rather that the nation had been miserable all the way through the tournament but we'd won the quarter-final. I disagree. Think of the interest that had been generated about rugby. It raised the profile of the sport and hopefully led to more young people getting involved.

Our support in France had snowballed into a juggernaut that was the envy of world rugby. That told me that we had been doing something right. We wanted people to love what their team was about, what it stood for, the role models that the players became. It was just about being the best version of themselves and connecting with the nation because of that. These things don't just happen: you have to work on them from both sides. That World Cup will be an abiding memory for me for the rest of my life.

* * *

Once again I found myself at the semi-finals of the World Cup as a parent, not a coach, and once again in a rush to book hotel rooms for the family and sort out match tickets. Just as they had done in Japan four years earlier, England had reached the last four, having beaten Fiji in the quarter-final, and now faced the Springboks. The circumstances, however, were completely different from Tokyo. Owen had just been through a tough time after completing his ban. He had been booed by some supporters during games. In France, the crowds boo all the time – they are just being passionate about their own players. I don't know whether the English fans started to boo because they were copying the others in the stadium, but whatever, I can tell you it was tough.

Colleen and I tried to support Owen as best we could during the tournament and act as sounding boards. It says a lot for his character that he was able to lead his country with all this going on in the background. He kicked four penalties and a drop-goal against South Africa in the rain in Paris, and England almost reached another final, but for a last-gasp penalty by Handré Pollard.

When Owen returned home, he took the decision to step back from international rugby. As parents it was heartbreaking for us to see what he had gone through.

We told him he had more than earned the right to do whatever he wanted, and if that was how he felt, we supported him 100 per cent. He had nothing to prove in rugby any more. It had become a question of whether he needed international rugby in his life, or if it was more important to be happy, not just for himself, but for his family. That he made the decision he did showed just how big the problem had become for him. Even as parents we didn't know the half of it. That was the hardest part for us. It would be the same for anyone. I could say what happened didn't surprise me, because of everything that had gone on. But if I am honest, it did surprise me because I knew how much he had put into it. It just shows how bad things had become in his eyes.

Sadly, we have a history in England of people getting

bored and knocking others down. People forgot what Owen had done for his country: 112 caps, and England's record points scorer. In other places they celebrate what has been consistently good for them as a nation over a period of many years. Whereas in England we try to get rid, don't we?

24. The Truth

I met Ben Calveley, the chief executive of the British and Irish Lions, in a lovely little hotel off the beaten track in Pembroke Street in Dublin. I had heard all the rumours linking me to the Lions head-coach job for the tour of Australia in 2025, but I knew nothing myself until Ben had called a couple of days earlier asking to meet.

It was early in November 2023, and my mind was already full of plans for the upcoming Six Nations. Everyone was talking about a World Cup hangover, but I just didn't get it. If we were still feeling sorry for ourselves a couple of months after our defeat by the All Blacks, then there would be something wrong. I couldn't wait to get going again.

When Ben offered me the Lions job, I accepted without hesitation. The Lions had been part of my life since 2013 and I saw it as an unbelievable privilege and honour: as good as it gets. I was able to say yes straight away because I had already done a lot of thinking about it since Ben first messaged me. Once I knew I had the support of the IRFU, everything was done in no time.

It was a prospect unique in professional sport, putting a team together entirely from scratch. Building a coaching and logistical staff from the ground up and choosing a squad of players would be one of the most exhilarating experiences of my coaching career.

I later told Ben that I didn't want to take a twelve-month

sabbatical before the tour, but that I would prefer to coach right through 2024, to take in the autumn internationals. Andrew Goodman was replacing Mike Catt in our coaching team ahead of the summer tour to South Africa and I wanted to be there as he got his feet under the table. I would love to have coached the 2025 Six Nations too, but that was not possible.

After Johnny's retirement, I had to appoint a new captain. Doing that is not just about what I want: the player has to want it too. The job can be taxing, and the media and public scrutiny increases. Some thrive in that environment, others hate it.

Peter O'Mahony was the obvious choice, a player who would embody our desire not to miss a step after the World Cup. I had no intention of dismantling the squad and starting again as we began a new four-year cycle to Australia 2027. We just don't have the number of players to do that even if we wanted to. But that does not mean we ignore forward planning, identifying new players and looking at ways of introducing them to our squad, and using the Emerging Ireland tours as a way of giving them greater exposure to the national set-up. I knew that Pete, as Johnny had done before him, would set the standards for the younger players coming into the squad. People would ask, 'Why is he still picking Peter O'Mahony or Conor Murray?' It is about the way guys like that make the squad feel. You don't have to be a superstar to play that role: it could be anyone who has the right character and gets it. Leadership is mostly about respect.

It was a sweet coincidence that our opening game of the 2024 Six Nations took us back to France. With the Stade de France unavailable because of preparations for

the Olympics, we headed to Marseille and to the Stade
Vélodrome, where England had beaten Australia in the
quarter-finals of the 2007 World Cup. It is a stunning
venue, and I knew what it meant to the French nation. We
made just four changes from the side that had lost to the
All Blacks, but the sense of renewal came with first Six
Nations starts for Jack Crowley, Joe McCarthy and Calvin
Nash – and they all stepped up. I couldn't have hoped for
a better response from the players from the quarter-final
exit. Our 38–17 victory was something of a statement
performance.

We backed it up with a big win over Italy in Dublin, and
when we defeated Wales 31–7 in the third round all the talk
turned to our chances of making Six Nations history by winning back-to-back Grand Slams. England had opened their
campaign with narrow wins over Italy and Wales, but then
had lost to Scotland at Murrayfield, and faced questions over
their game.

With their backs to the wall, they knew they had to produce a performance at Twickenham. They came at us with
an edge, as if their lives depended on the result. They threw
everything they had at us. That is the beauty of the Six
Nations: the narrative changes every week and in a one-off
game we were always going to get England not far off their
best. We were not at our best ourselves.

England thoroughly deserved to win, with Marcus Smith's
last-minute drop-goal sealing a 23–22 victory. It had been
another great game, an intense Test match and one that we
learned lessons from.

We faced Scotland in Dublin in the final game of the
championship, knowing that a win or a draw would secure
the title for us again. Scotland made life difficult for us, and

we seemed nervous in attempting to get the job done. We led 7–6 at half-time, thanks to a try by Dan Sheehan, and it was not until Andrew Porter scored that we had a bit of daylight between us, after Tadhg Furlong and Robbie Henshaw had seen tries ruled out.

It had been a remarkable season. We would all have loved to win the World Cup, and there was disappointment too that our Grand Slam bid had failed, but winning a Six Nations title is bloody tough. It was only Ireland's sixth of all time, and doing it back-to-back made it more special. My job is to try to push Ireland to do things that we shouldn't really be expected to do. If those things become the norm, then surely that is a good place to be.

* * *

The tour of South Africa offered the chance for more evolution. I selected a thirty-five-man squad, including three uncapped players: Sam Prendergast, Jamie Osborne and Cormac Izuchukwu. Even before we flew out, their media was talking the Tests up as a battle for supremacy. The Springboks had moved to the top of the world rankings after their World Cup triumph against the All Blacks, and we had dropped into second place. The two games were sell-outs, and Rassie Erasmus was in good form, having a go at naming my team ahead of the first Test.

For us it was the end of a season that had begun thirteen months earlier when we had assembled for our first World Cup camp. But I was determined that our standards would not drop. There was a good edge going into the games. I had to laugh when someone sent a clip of the Springbok hooker Bongi Mbonambi in their World Cup documentary saying that Ireland saw them 'as a little country in the corner of Africa' and that we thought we could compete with the rest of the world 'with all the best facilities and training grounds'. We may have good facilities, but I have also been to South Africa and seen how many big stadiums they have.

Our selection for the first Test in Pretoria caused a bit of a stir when I named Jamie Osborne, who usually played centre for Leinster, at full-back for his international debut. But that was no biggie for me at all because I had seen him play at full-back for Ireland Under-20s and we often train against the Under-20s. I knew he could catch a high ball – I had seen him do it time and time again in training – and I knew that he had the organizational and ball-playing qualities that we want in our full-back. It was not even a risk. Hugo Keenan was out – representing Ireland in the Sevens competition at the Olympics that summer – and it was good to see if I could find someone new. If it didn't work, so be it. Pretty quickly, when you put a young player in a position like that, you discover how anxious they are going to be and whether you are asking too much.

It was the same when Jack Crowley had to start against Australia in November 2022 after Johnny pulled out in the warm-up. People said Jack was only a kid. He wasn't a kid: he had been training with us for a while, and had been on an Emerging Ireland tour and gone back to Munster knowing what was needed if he did get another call. Jamie, similarly, had been in our group for two years. The first time he had come in, he was shy, but we could see he had a great skillset. Then when he came again – when there was an injury, or we needed numbers in training – he became more confident in himself. He had been part of our World Cup training camp the previous year and came close to making the squad. I can understand how someone watching him for the first time playing at full-back on his debut could have thought it a surprise selection, but it was nothing new for Jamie.

He gave a good account of himself, scoring a try in the first half, but we lost the game 27–20. To make matters worse, Dan Sheehan ruptured his ACL, an injury that would sideline him for six months. It was the first time the Springboks had beaten us for eight years.

It was one of the few occasions when I gave the players a real roasting afterwards. Everyone seemed to think we had done all right, that we had run them close and performed OK at high altitude. But I had to tell them how it was. They knew I wasn't shouting for shouting's sake. If I gave the fluff, some might think they had got away with it. They had to know the truth. For their own sakes. I told them we had been nowhere near the best version of ourselves. 'I know you thought you were not far off them, but we were way off where we need to be,' I said.

What annoyed me was that we had not been in front of the game. We were playing reactively, and in fits and starts. I didn't think we were being brave enough to push our game to the limit, and that's not good enough to win against a full-blown South African side in Pretoria. I held myself to account, too. I had not got the preparations right.

As a player I always thought, *How do I want this to look on Monday morning after the game when we are doing the reviews?* And what I learned through experience is that often when you played a game that you might have been shitting yourself about because of the pressure or the quality of the opposition, it was never what you thought it was going to be. I would spend the night after the game thinking about all the things I wished I had done and I'd wake up the next morning wanting to play the game again, because I had made it out to be something that it was not. The lesson was that, however big the occasion or however strong the opposition, you always had to attack games, to try to make things happen. That's what I wanted our players to do in the second Test. Attack it. Go after them.

I decided to make Caelan Doris captain for the second Test, as I brought James Ryan into the second row, with Tadhg Beirne switching to the blindside flank and Pete dropping to the bench. It was the start of the changing of the guard. Caelan had captained the side against Italy in the Six Nations, and I had seen enough leadership potential in him to want to give it the opportunity to flourish. I had to have a similar conversation with Pete to the one we had back in 2020 when I gave Caelan his debut, except this time Pete was the tour captain, and I knew how much it meant to him. I also know that he expected me to be honest. He accepted the decision because he was a team player, and he went about the week helping Caelan be the best captain he could be.

The second Test was a hell of a match. I couldn't wait to see how we would react, and I was pleased at our intent from the start. Ronan Kelleher made a few big hits and carries early on, and the players were having the balls to be themselves. We got a decent lead, they fought back, we held on to give ourselves the opportunity to win, and Ciarán Frawley kicked those two dropped goals at the end to win the game 25–24. Ciarán showed great courage to have a go under pressure, and the drama of the finish meant it was heralded as another great win for us as it ensured the series ended in a 1–1 draw. But in the cold light of day, when I analysed the game, there were still loads of things we should have done better.

* * *

I made Caelan captain for the autumn campaign. He had come so far from that day against France four years earlier. Now he was unbelievably well prepared, thoughtful, in control of his emotions and the team's emotions. And it was good that Pete would still be around when Caelan was captaining the side for his first competition.

The All Blacks were coming to Dublin battle-hardened off the back of their Rugby Championship campaign. There had been great excitement about the fixture, our first meeting with the All Blacks since our World Cup defeat, but it was nothing like that contest. We were poor, we looked uncooked and seemed too desperate, which led to too many unforced errors in a 23–13 defeat.

After a narrow win against Argentina, I tried some new combinations for the Fiji game. Jack Crowley had started the first two autumn Tests, but I decided to give Sam Prendergast his first start at fly-half. We had given Sam twenty minutes off the bench against Argentina when the game was on the line, and he had impressed me with his level-headedness and confidence. His potential had earned him an opportunity to see if he could kick on. Sam was only twenty-one but he understood what was expected. When I asked him how he thought he played against Argentina, he was thoughtful about what he had done well and what he had done badly. He was a young player trying to find his way, and I liked how he ran the team during the week. The prospect of him and Jack Crowley driving each other on was an exciting one. The noise generated about their rivalry was just that. They are two good lads working hard and I knew they would both become better players because of the competition between them.

We also gave debuts to Gus McCarthy and Cormac

Izuchukwu, while Jamie Osborne got another run at full-back. I love the process of identifying players and bringing them in to see if they can handle the pressure of training with the national team. Then I enjoy seeing whether someone like Sam can come in and make it *his* team with players that he is not with every day at their club. Then, when you think the player is ready, put him in a decent side to see if there really is the potential to become a Test player of the future.

On the flip side, I also find it fascinating to see the reaction of a player who misses out on selection. Some players become disheartened because of the disappointment and then give up because of how that made them feel. Others thrive on disappointment and try to prove a point, not just to others but to themselves.

Everyone makes mistakes, everyone gets things wrong, everyone has a bad game. But I judge a player's character by how he responds. I look for the ones who tend not to let it happen again the following week, and I also take an interest in how they make the people around them feel. Depending on the character, sometimes there is no need to leave a player out: even though he played really poorly, I knew he wasn't the type to let the same thing happen again. And sometimes, when you tell a player he isn't starting, his reaction makes you wish you could pick him five minutes later. But then they should have been at that level in the first place.

We finished the autumn with two games that may not have attracted great praise, but I took as much satisfaction from them as any of our so-called 'big wins', such as the second Test against South Africa. I know that might surprise some people, but there were moments in both those performances that I knew would be important for our development towards the 2027 World Cup.

Against Fiji we had chopped and changed, and tried new combinations, but won comfortably. Then, against Australia, I had heaped the pressure on the players because of the IRFU's 150th anniversary celebrations that weekend.

Joe Schmidt had been appointed Australia head coach back in January and his return to Dublin made headlines. It was my last game in charge of Ireland before I became Lions coach, when I would be going head-to-head with Joe, and hence an opportunity for the Wallabies to lay down something of a marker.

We trailed 13–5 at half-time, but we found a way to win despite the pressure with a late try by Gus McCarthy. I know the match reports said we scraped home, but it was another important experience. Each game takes its own course, and how you handle each moment and then each period is down to the experiences you have had together. The critics might have labelled our autumn campaign patchy or underwhelming, but we finished with three wins from four, and more importantly we were growing as a group again, with increased competition for places as we tried to fill the hole left by the retirement of senior players.

We weren't playing well, weren't reaching the standards we'd set ourselves, and that was disappointing. I felt a few players had come into camp not ready for the step up to Test rugby and I told them that was not acceptable.

But I wasn't worried. Every team goes through dips, and we were dealing with significant change. We had a new young captain and new staff – Aled Walters had joined us from England as our head of performance, and Andrew Goodman was now in charge of attack. We had handed out four new caps, including in the key decision-making position of out-half. I liked what I saw of Sam Prendergast, and I liked Jack's reaction. We were evolving.

When you live and breathe a job, it is strange to step away from it for a while – but that was what I had to do now. Nothing other than the honour of coaching the Lions could have made me do it.

25. The Lion

Standing on the stage at the O2 Arena in London, for a moment I wondered just what I had signed up for. I am a coach, not an actor. Yet here I was, in a suit, live on Sky Sports, with an audience in front of me and millions watching at home.

This was the day the British and Irish Lions squad was to be announced. To my left, standing in the wings, was Maro Itoje, the England captain, who seconds later would be revealed as my captain for the tour. During the dress rehearsal, one of the directors had asked Maro to make sure he walked out slowly. I knew Maro would have no problem doing that. But the run-through had not helped with my nerves.

Even after all these years, moments in the spotlight do not come easily to me. There are times when I have to be in an advert for the commercial team with Ireland or pose for a photograph, and while I understand why it has to be done, I absolutely hate it.

I know I need to challenge my perception. The game would be dull if every team consisted of fifteen players like me. I like watching the characters who enjoy performing off the pitch. I admire their bravado. But it is just not me. I would rather be watching a game than sitting for a photoshoot.

As the show got under way, my thoughts were with the players who were in contention for selection. Many of them were sitting with their teammates in their clubs across the four nations. It took about half an hour to get through the interviews with Maro and me before the squad was announced, and I felt for the players who had to wait it out.

I had phoned Maro a couple of days earlier to ask him if he would captain the tour. That in itself had proved something of a challenge. I had already phoned his Saracens head coach, Mark McCall, to ask what their training schedule was. I wanted Maro to be on his own when I made the call. I wanted to make sure he was in the right place and had the space to savour the moment.

I phoned him at 3 p.m. I was at Dublin airport, waiting for my flight to Heathrow for our final selection meeting with the coaches. Maro answered, but the signal was bad and he started to crack up. I hung up and tried again. When he answered, I said, 'Would you like to be the British and Irish Lions captain?'

His reaction reminded me of just what it means to the players. I know some are reluctant to say publicly that playing for the Lions is the pinnacle of their career, but most players see it differently once they have been involved. This is the best of the best. And now Maro had been given the honour of leading them.

Earlier in the day I had also called Caelan Doris. That had been a very different conversation. We had received the results of the scan on the shoulder injury that he had sustained in Leinster's defeat by Northampton Saints in the Champions Cup semi-final. Before his injury, my shortlist for the tour captain had consisted of him and Maro. We felt that either of them would do a brilliant job. What happened to Caelan the weekend before we had to pick the captain and the squad is why I like to leave selection decisions until the very last minute. Now there was no decision to make. Caelan needed surgery and would be out for several months.

I was devastated for him, but I knew he was strong, and he would get over his disappointment and use it in the right manner.

* * *

I had started thinking about my selection as soon as I had been asked to do the job back in November 2023. I was well aware of the huge honour it is to be Lions head coach, and of the responsibility that comes with it. I owed it to everyone to make sure I did my homework to get the best people.

My first task was to assemble a core team to get the project off the ground. It was a new experience for me. I felt more like a director of rugby than a coach. The first person I advised the Lions to appoint was Charlotte Gibbons, the long-standing and highly regarded senior team operations manager with England. She joined as the operations director. My next two appointments were Vinny Hammond, my head analyst with Ireland, who knows exactly how I work and has been on a couple of Lions tours before, and Aled Walters, who had recently joined Ireland from England as head of athletic performance. With these three in place, we could start planning and organizing. We were off.

Another key appointment was David Nucifora, who had left the IRFU after the 2023 World Cup and was now working as performance director with Scotland. His recruitment was a slow burner at first, because the Lions had not previously employed someone in the role that I wanted him to do.

His official title was general manager of performance and he was involved in contracting the staff I wanted. He could also oversee the staff, to allow me to get on with coaching. On Lions tours it is very hard for the head coach to keep across everything because touring involves so much travelling and so many games. The high-performance team, the analysts, the coaches, the backroom staff and commercial team all need to know what the others are doing. They need support, and they also need to support the team. Nuci was key in overseeing all of this. Even before we had left for Australia, his appointment had already proved to be the best thing we'd done. He does this kind of work in his sleep.

Once we'd got the remaining heads of department in place, I asked them who they wanted for their own teams. Then I would play devil's advocate: 'Why? Are you sure they are the best?' I also asked, 'Are you sure they're going to muck in and not work in silos?' I had been on tours before when coaches and staff departments worked in isolation, but that's not my way of doing things. For me, all teams should work together, not just look after themselves.

Once we decided we were going to invite someone to join, I insisted on making the initial phone call. I felt that was the right thing to do. I wanted everyone who was going to work on the tour to feel how I had felt when I was asked to be head coach. I loved making those calls and hearing the reactions: *Are you taking the piss? Are you sure? I can't believe it, oh my God you have given me goosebumps.* There was no mention of financial reward. These people would do it for nothing, as we all would. And it was not for the kudos either. It was because they knew the appointment was the pinnacle: the best of the best.

We went on a recce trip to Australia in January 2025. Seeing the training pitches, the hotels and the stadiums made everything feel real. The pandemic-related travel restrictions in 2021 meant that it had been eight years since supporters had been able to travel for a Lions tour. I imagined what it would all look like when the sea of red arrived.

With the core of the Lions logistical staff taking shape, I wanted to give myself a bit of space to consider who I wanted on my coaching team. Previous head coaches had appointed their assistants before the Six Nations, but I wanted to see how that tournament went. If you get things set in stone too early, you can't undo them. What if I had appointed a defence coach or attack coach from a national side and their team ended up having a poor Six Nations? Or if I had over-looked someone who had excelled?

The most important thing for me was to get all the back-ground work done first. It was exactly the same with the players: you can't really justify any type of selection unless you've done all the homework and fully understand the dynamics of what makes the individual and the team work. It takes a bit of time, so patience is the key, because once you make a phone call, you can't pull it back.

Both the Lions and the IRFU were brilliant in how they let me get on with things, but stepping back from Ireland – as is required of a Lions coach – and watching the 2025 Six Nations was a torturous experience for me. I am a coach, and I wanted to be coaching, not sitting in the stands watching the games. In my view, if you are picked to be head coach, you should be trusted to know when to put your Lions hat on. If they can't trust you, then I don't think you are the right coach for the job anyway.

Still, my 'sabbatical' – I hated that word, people seemed to think I was on holiday – was a great opportunity for Simon Easterby to step up as head coach. I could have brought in a defence coach to cover Simon's usual role, but I felt that requiring Simon to bring a new person up to speed would have been disruptive. Simon had looked after our defence for four years. He could do it standing on his head. Imagine him bringing someone in and him having to say, 'That's not right, we don't do it like that.' You would end up wasting more time. I also think it is important that every head coach has a hand in all aspects of coaching anyway.

Ireland opened up with victories against England, Scotland and Wales to win the Triple Crown again. We were in the running for another Grand Slam. But the dynamic of the Six Nations can completely change from year to year. The key match of the 2024 Six Nations had been our victory over France in Marseille. Now, in round four, France were coming to Dublin, needing a win to stay alive in the championship.

Over the past five years we had worked really hard on staying 'neutral' during matches: not letting mistakes bother us, getting back on the horse and staying positive in the next moment. Early in the second half, we were ahead 13–8 when France scored a try. In the build-up, I felt that Peter O'Mahony had been taken out illegally by Thibaud Flament, but no penalty was given and the try stood. We also lost Calvin Nash to the sin bin for a high tackle in the same move. It was a double blow – a controversial try against us, and a yellow card – but our reaction was not good enough. We allowed France to score again within a couple of minutes when Louis Bielle-Biarrey scored a great try and then the floodgates opened. That can happen when you get two good sides going at it. We had done something similar to them in Marseille the previous year. The French learned from that performance, and we learned from the defeat in Dublin.

It is why the Six Nations is such a brilliant tournament. France had not just fought back from the Marseille defeat to us, but also from losing by a point at Twickenham a few weeks earlier. Their bonus-point win set them up to finish ahead of England and ourselves on points.

Many people thought that Ireland finished the Six Nations campaign with a bit of a slump, and overall there was a feeling that the quality of the players across the four nations I had to select from for my Lions squad was not as good a vintage as for previous tours.

But my job was to take the emotion out of it all and understand the reality. And the reality was very different.

* * *

I know about every professional rugby player in the world. It is my job to know about them. I watch games all the time. When I watch a game live that I am not involved in, I like to use it as a coaching tool. I ask myself in the moment: What would I do tactically? At half-time, what would I be saying in the changing room to both sides?

When watching a game live, it is impossible to see everything. On Mondays and Tuesdays, I will review the weekend's games on my computer. It can take up to six hours for each match.

In international rugby, the broadcaster's match agreement includes a commitment to provide six angles of play to the coaches' box. These are then uploaded to a world server, which is shared with every nation in Tiers One and Two. That means that we all have access to six angles of every international game.

I never rely on an analyst's edit. I know some coaches who receive footage from an analyst that shows clips of the line-outs, counter-attacks, turnover balls, penalties, etc. But I need to know the story of the game and why things have happened.

I want to know if a player has worked his balls off (or not). Did he scan properly to see what was in front of him? Was he ambitious enough to play to space? Why did he give that penalty away? Was he distracted by something that had happened two minutes earlier?

When people say that a player won so many line-outs or gave so many penalties away, or that a side only converted five out of ten entries to the twenty-two, it is not good enough to say 'these are the numbers'. It is about understanding the why.

The sort of analysis that goes into picking a Lions squad is different from the analysis I do when preparing for a match. You can't get everything you need from watching matches. I wanted to know what made a player tick, what his attitude was like, his dedication, what type of team player he was. I needed to know whether he was a pain in the arse or great to be around. The playing side is part of it, of course, but just as important, especially on a tour like this, is that you have to be selfless. There is no truer saying than that misery finds misery. Not having two misery guts in the first place makes it harder for them to find each other.

Everyone is different, and I have no problem with that. But I wanted players who would pull in the same direction, even if there is disappointment for some of them individually along the way. I wanted players who could understand what we would be trying to achieve together. Getting to that point doesn't just happen by chance.

I obviously knew the Irish lads well, and I had worked with some of the players from the other nations on previous Lions tours and when I was with England. For those who I knew less about, I made inquiries. I would phone their teammates, and coaches who had worked with them in the past. I spoke with the three national head coaches – Steve Borthwick, Gregor Townsend and Gats – and then Matt Sherratt after he took over from Gats at Wales. These were people I had competed hard against in the past, and would resume competing against the following year. I loved that they were open and honest enough to help me form proper opinions about players.

When you are a national head coach, the provincial or club coaches tend to push their players forward. But as Lions head coach, I didn't get that from the national coaches. When it came to one-on-one conversations, they knew not to bullshit me. This wasn't just because they are decent people but also because they would not be doing their players justice. I loved their honesty. I had multiple conversations to back things up and try to get a balanced view. I was also able to draw on opinions from our analysts, who have known many of the players for years. By the end of the Six Nations, I had drawn up a long list of around seventy players.

Before starting to whittle the number down, I turned my attention to appointing my coaching staff. My criteria went something like this: 1) they had to be good people; 2) they had to be unbelievably good at their jobs; and 3) I needed to know they could deliver what I wanted them to deliver.

There is so much to do on tour, and I knew I was going to be pulled from pillar to post. I needed coaches who could address the players when required to save my voice. There were lots of great candidates for the coaching jobs, and I had conversations with people who were disappointed that they were not involved. I just needed to know that I could be allowed to coach to the best of my ability, and that the team could be prepared the way that I thought it should be done, and I knew that the people I had selected could deliver that. Look at all the Lions selections over the years. Look at the tours that have gone well and the ones that have not. The most successful ones happened when everyone was on the same page.

The Irish guys I named in my coaching team – Simon, John Fogarty and Andrew Goodman – were there because they ticked all the boxes: I had experience of working with them, they are good lads, and they are bloody good coaches. Later I also appointed Johnny Sexton. We needed a kicking coach, and although Johnny had little coaching experience, he *gets* the Lions. Many of the players selected would not have experienced the demands of a Lions tour before, and Johnny's experience would be crucial.

Richard Wigglesworth was doing a great job with England, and I knew his personality would be a great fit for us, having coached him at Saracens and England. It was the same with John Dalziel, Scotland's forwards coach.

An even split between the four nations was never a consideration for me – nor for previous coaches. For me, it was about who could deliver and who deserved it. If in four years' time I am lucky enough to do this job again, the split might be lopsided in a different direction.

I said to the coaches that no one would be able to pick us apart, because we would agree on how we were going to move forward, and everyone would know what everyone else was doing. That way we could integrate as if we had been coaching together for years.

I could not have been happier with the coaches I selected. They all mucked in together right from the start. There were no egos. Take Wiggy, for example. He was England's senior coach, and while I asked Andrew Goodman to be lead backs coach, Wiggy was happy to work with him. Each of the coaches had specific roles and responsibilities, but I told them that they weren't to think that these were their areas and no one else could go there, or that they couldn't go and help people in other roles. I told them they had to find ways to make sure they were integrated, so that the players could see 100 per cent that we were all on the same page. We were Lions coaches.

* * *

We had a couple of days in London before the announcement of the coaching team at the end of March, and after that we caught up every couple of weeks, whether it was on a Zoom call, or a couple of days that we had at the K Club, a golf resort in County Kildare. I felt both relieved and excited to be able to finally blurt out all my plans to them, start discussing selection and how we were going to play in Australia.

From then on it was non-stop. We all drew up our own squad lists, which could change on a weekly basis. I felt it was important to see how players reacted in the final part of the season. I decided we would select around thirty-eight players but knew that we would probably have to bring some more out later in the tour, depending on injuries, to cover specialist positions.

While looking at the various potential versions of the squad that we considered during the spring, I never totted up how many players we were considering from each of the four nations. It is the same with Ireland. People talk about Leinster's domination, but I have never thought about squad or team selections in terms of how many players we have from each province.

I made it clear to Ben Calveley that I had no interest in picking anyone because it was deemed politically correct to do so. How could I look a player in the eye and tell him he was not selected only because of the country he was playing for? I would not be doing the jersey justice.

There had to be no bias whatsoever. And that included the consideration of whether to pick Owen.

I couldn't shy away from that decision professionally. I wanted to bring him, despite his difficult and injury-disrupted season in Paris. I knew he would add the type of leadership skills we would need with a squad containing only a handful of players who had been on the last proper Lions tour, in 2017, when there were midweek matches. This would be Owen's fourth tour, including the last one in Australia in 2013. I knew he would get it immediately and would help bring the best out of the others around him.

Every other coach favoured picking Owen too. Ordinarily, that would have been it: we would have simply named him along with the others. But I knew it was not yet a done deal. I told the coaches I would have to ring Owen first. I needed to know whether he wanted to go and what he thought about stepping back into the international spotlight after all he had had to put up with during the 2023 World Cup.

This was a very hard phone call. When I asked Owen if he would come, he broke down in tears. He said he did not think it would be right for him, for the squad, or for me as head coach.

It was a tough thing to hear. I told him to think it through, to take his time, and if he changed his mind then I would put him on the standby list to cover an injury.

At the press conference at the O2 Arena after my appearance on stage, I was asked if Owen had been under consideration. Obviously, I didn't feel I could tell the full story.

'Owen was in the conversation, obviously, an experienced player like that, looking for his fourth tour and with his leadership qualities,' I said. 'But it got to a point, like with a few others, where he is still trying to find his way back to fitness. There are thirty-eight picked, which leaves a couple of slots open for us down the track, if and when needed. Owen and a few other guys would be in that type of bracket.'

I read some of the coverage about the squad selection and thought to myself, *If only you knew . . .* I understand that people have to have an opinion, but I could not get distracted by the bullshit. Those people had not done their homework like I had. And I had stayed true to myself and the team.

* * *

We didn't have to wait until we had arrived in Australia to experience the sea of red. Dublin was awash with Lions jerseys on the glorious summer's evening in June when we played our pre-tour game against Argentina at the Aviva.

I know some people are sceptical about the concept of playing Lions matches at a home venue, but to me it was a special night. Across the city, English, Irish, Welsh and Scottish fans gathered, all supporting the same team, and the Argentinian fans added to the colour and atmosphere. I loved it. I also knew it would be a difficult game for us. Argentina are a good side and would be pumped to have a crack at the Lions, their first fixture against us since 2005.

We had taken the players who weren't involved in end-of-season finals to Portugal for a week-long training camp to begin the bonding process and start to share details of how we were going to play and the standards we expected. It's unusual to conduct a training camp with just twenty-four players. We would be used to being able to train with fifteen players against fifteen. But I knew from previous tours that sometimes there's a team playing in a midweek game and you've only eight fit lads to train against. That's the beauty of the Lions. You're ad-libbing, doing things differently all the time.

Argentina were the perfect warm-up opponents for us, and it was brilliant that so many supporters could have the chance to see the Lions play and start getting excited about the tour.

We lost the game, failing to score in the final quarter. Argentina hit us on the break twice, and that was the game. But I was actually buoyed by the performance. Yes, there were too many errors, but I thought we played some really good stuff at times, given the stage we were at in our development.

I knew it was a decent start for us, but I didn't want the players to know that. I used the press conference after the game and the post-match interviews with the broadcasters to let the players know that higher standards would be needed on tour. The message to them had to be: 'This is the Lions, that is not good enough.'

The newspapers all carried headlines like 'Andy Farrell angry at Lions display'. Perfect. I wanted the players to take note and believe that what they had produced was not the right standard, even though privately I had been quite pleased with much of the performance.

I will often use media sessions to speak indirectly to my players and make my point to them. The players, like coaches, say they don't read the reports, but they all do. Sometimes, if a team is lacking in confidence, then it is my job to stick up for them. This time, even though I was not angry, I wanted them to believe that I was.

The message that I wanted to set for the tour was that here was a chance for the players to make history. No Lions side had ever won back-to-back series against the same country. Thanks to the achievement of the 2013 tour in beating the Wallabies 2–1, we now had that opportunity. I wanted the players to walk towards the challenge. I wanted them to be aware of both the privilege they had been given and the responsibility that was on their shoulders.

I also told them I wanted them to be the best teammates they could be. That is what would matter most. I wanted the players who were not in the twenty-three-man squad for each game to do everything they could to help those who were. I wanted every training session to count. I knew I had selected good characters; I wanted them to be themselves. I also knew that in this highly competitive environment some players would surprise me. Some would thrive, and get to a place they would not have thought achievable, while some might find the environment a challenge and struggle with the expectation.

Also, some would inevitably fall over with injuries and have to be replaced. We had our first casualty before we played Argentina, when Zander Fagerson had to withdraw with a calf injury. It was a tough call to make, but he was determined to crack on with his rehabilitation to make sure he was fit if needed for the business end of the tour.

Then there was a call that almost reduced me to tears. It was to Finlay Bealham. He had missed my first call, and when he answered on my second attempt, he was in the gym, training with a few of the Connacht lads.

I said: 'Is everything OK? How's your fitness?' I'd already given him a heads-up that if Zander was not quite right, I would need him for the squad to face Argentina. Now, I was telling him that he was not only in the squad for the game in Dublin, but he was coming on tour. At first, I could hear no sound at all on the line. Then, when I heard how emotional he became, I almost welled up myself.

* * *

The tour party left Dublin on three separate flights. Coaches and those players who had not been involved against Argentina were on the first two, while those who played in Dublin travelled a bit later, to give them as much post-match recovery time as possible. Aled Walters, our head of athletic performance, Graeme Close, the head of performance nutrition, and Ben Pollard, our strength-and-conditioning coach, gave each player a personal plan for minimizing the impact of jet lag. Graeme told me that it usually takes up to ten days to recover from the sleep disruption caused by travelling across seven time zones. His target was to reduce that to four days. It was still a tough week for players and staff, but I didn't want to give anyone an excuse not to perform. We had to hit the ground running.

We decided to use the tour games to get some cohesion in our attack. That is what takes the longest time to develop. I've seen coaches start a tour playing tightly at first and then begin to open up their game, but we wanted to play expansive rugby from the outset. If we got that connection before the Test series then we could tighten it all back up, knowing that we had the ability to open up in the locker.

Good players own the plan and implement it their own way, and as coaches we did not want to be too prescriptive. Obviously, you need a bit of structure to get everyone on the same page, but we didn't want to be an easy side for the opposition to work out, and that meant being a little bit unpredictable at times.

I also made it clear that I wanted the players and the coaching staff to speak their minds. If somebody had a better idea than me, then we would go with that. Working together like this would make the journey more powerful. It creates a good environment when no one cares who came up with an idea in the first place. I wanted everyone to feel that this was their team.

It was important to remain open-minded about selection as we went. We had to be ready for every situation. On the 2017 tour of New Zealand, Liam Williams and Elliot Daly played in the midweek game against the Chiefs and then made it into the Test team on the Saturday. We wanted the players to know that everyone had a chance.

It became clear from the outset that the Super Rugby teams had put a lot of time into preparing to play us. Western Force opted to keep the ball on the pitch, and that suited us, because it allowed us to work on our attacking game. We didn't want to kick penalties for points, we wanted to build our connections and work on our fitness. It was a promising start, with Finn Russell stepping up at fly-half.

I had read before the tour that people wondered if Finn was my type of player, but I was impressed by him. He is a down-to-earth lad who trains hard and is good fun off the pitch. His family were with him on tour from when we arrived in Perth, which showed to me how much it meant to him to be a Lion. He has matured a lot and proved to me that he could remain focused through a game: he didn't tire of doing the right things. Henry Pollock also made an impact, showing he was not afraid to get involved, helping set up two tries, while Joe McCarthy delivered the type of performance that would press his claims for a place in the Test side.

Tomos Williams picked up a tour-ending injury in the act of scoring his second try. It was a cruel blow. I had been really impressed by him. He was a good character and a galvanizing force. Ben White, who we called in as his replacement, had been close to making the original squad. We had to ask Alex

Mitchell to play a lot of rugby until Ben arrived from New Zealand, where he was touring with Scotland.

I felt Finn Russell would benefit from starting again four days later against the Queensland Reds, and he did. But we lost another key player in Elliot Daly, who fractured his arm. Elliot had been excellent for us. I knew him well from the previous Lions tours and his hunger to stay at the top had not diminished, even though he had been in and out of the England team. He is a glue-type player, a genuine man who does whatever is asked of him. Nothing fazes him and he does a lot of things well in a lot of different positions, which makes him an ideal Lions player.

There wasn't a like-for-like replacement available for Elliot: no one who had so much versatility across the backline *and* so much experience of Lions tours. The early weeks of the tour had given us time to see who could step up as cover in different positions in the backs. For example, Tommy Freeman was able to run at 13 and full-back, while Sione Tuipulotu also ran at 13 and Mack Hansen could cover the back three. But our options were more limited at inside centre. When I saw Bundee Aki pull up with a sore calf during the Reds game my immediate thought was, *If he has pulled his calf, we are in the shit here.* Thankfully it was just cramp, but if he broke down that would leave us with just one inside centre in the squad. It focused our minds.

Everyone agreed that Elliot's replacement should be Owen. We knew that he would be able to get up to speed quickly, knew what it took to be a Lion, and he would give us cover at inside centre as well as at fly-half.

We had lost a lot of experience with Elliot going home. Owen had experience of three tours and would have a positive impact all round, in a squad with lots of first-time Lions.

329

We knew he would make other players feel better about themselves, and he already had a good relationship with many of them, including Finn Russell. He had been quietly training away at home and was now clear of the concussion symptoms that had brought his season with Racing 92 to an early end.

When I rang him, this time he was ready to come. He was in a better place, and with the tour already up and running he hoped that his inclusion would not be such a big deal. And he knew we needed him. It was a short phone call and a relief to hear how much he was up for it now. 'Yeah, I'll get ready, get packed and ready to go,' he said.

Elliot said to me that while he was gutted to be going home, the fact that it was Owen who was replacing him made it less hurtful. He said the same to Owen.

I had expected a bit of a reaction to the decision but hoped that people had moved on from the negativity that had been previously directed at Owen. Sadly, in some cases I was wrong. The easier decision for both of us would have been not to go there. But we had to do what was right for the team.

* * *

Before he flew home, I asked Elliot to read out the team announcement for the game against the Waratahs in Sydney. It was a mark of respect for his contribution on three Lions tours.

Owen joined us the following evening. Before he had even arrived there had been a negative reaction to his call-up in the media.

'There has been a lot of that nonsense for some time,' I said at a press conference. 'That was in the past. We all just need to move on and embrace what the Lions is all about and what we have got coming ahead.'

It seemed like many people had not moved on. It was hard to take some of the things that were written, including that Owen would be a disruptive influence on the squad, particularly the other fly-halves. Some things were written that I won't forget. It was tempting to tell those people what I really thought of them, but I could hardly talk to the group about being calm under pressure if I was losing my shit!

Owen fitted in just as I knew he would, having already been on three tours. It didn't take him long to get up to speed. He worked well with the other out-halves and centres. By the time we got to the Test series, all the noise from outside had died down.

Inevitably, we had to deal with more injuries along the way, further stretching our resources. Hugo Keenan had been dealing with a minor calf issue when he came out to Australia, and when a stomach virus ran through the squad in Perth it seemed to affect him far more than it did the others. He was desperate to play but had to pull out of the game against the Reds on the day because he just wasn't right. Although he had no weight to lose, he dropped around six kilograms during his illness. He wanted to play but didn't want to let anyone down. He came up to me in tears. 'I don't know what's wrong with me, but I can't do it,' he said. He did play the next game, against the Waratahs, but he was still well below par. It showed to me what the Lions meant to him that he kept going.

In our victory over ACT Brumbies in Canberra, Blair Kinghorn injured his knee after just twenty-five minutes, and Garry Ringrose took a knock to his head that would result in him having to stand down for twelve days as part of the concussion protocol, ruling him out of contention for the first Test.

Our 48–0 victory over the AUNZ side in Adelaide proved particularly costly. Mack Hansen picked up a foot injury and Luke Cowan-Dickie, was knocked out. Neither would play again on tour. Losing Mack was a real blow, as he was coming back to his best form and definitely would have pushed for a place in the Test side on the wing. We called up Jamie Osborne as cover for Blair and Mack.

Luke had also impressed us, and, given that hooker is a specialist position, we had to move swiftly to call up a replacement, as we knew it would take a few days for the new guy to recover from jet lag. We wanted to bring in Jamie George. He had been very close to being selected in the original squad, and with his experience and set-piece strengths would be a great asset to us. The problem was that Jamie was due to start for England against Argentina in a game that was to kick off several hours after our game had finished.

I knew that calling him up immediately would disrupt England's plans. But I also knew that if I let him play for England, and then he picked up an injury, I would not have done the right thing by the Lions. I phoned Steve Borthwick, the England head coach, and he understood my position. He also did not want to stand in Jamie's way.

Jamie's journey from San Juan in Argentina to Brisbane took forty-seven hours, but he was like a kid in a candy store when he arrived. 'I would have swum to get here,' he said. It was just the sort of spirit we wanted.

We delayed announcing Mack's injury because we didn't want to let the Australia camp know he would be struggling for the first Test, but we brought in Darcy Graham as cover. We also called up cover for each of the positions in the front row: Ewan Ashman, Tom Clarkson and Rory Sutherland. For match day, we would need three players at each of these specialist positions: the starter, the substitute, and a standby who could step in to play if someone was injured before kick-off. If we got even one injury to a prop or hooker in a Test week, we'd have to scramble to bring in a player from the other side of the world, to arrive jet-lagged and with no chance to prepare with the group. Calling up Ashman, Clarkson and Sutherland was necessary insurance for these specialist positions before the Test series. It also gave us extra cover for the match against the First Nations and Pasifika XV in Melbourne, which was scheduled for three days after the first Test in Brisbane.

We wanted to make sure these players felt valued, particularly in light of the controversy that surrounded the call-up of six new players at a similar stage of the 2017 Lions tour of New Zealand. The six had been with the Scotland and Wales squads on tour in Australia and the Pacific Islands. There was a view that they had been chosen for their geographical proximity to New Zealand rather than for their qualities as players, and also that late call-ups somehow went against the ethos of the Lions. And, sure enough, some of the same criticisms were made against our call-ups, though it was not nearly as noisy as it had been in 2017.

I knew that nothing we had done was undermining the Lions. If we hadn't called in the extra players, we could have gone into the second and third Tests totally compromised.

I got a bit short with a journalist in a press conference after I read that he had described Tom Clarkson as Leinster's 'third choice' tighthead prop. We called Tom up because we felt he was our next best option. The lad had improved out of sight over the previous six months. I know we had involved other props during our pre-tour training camp in Portugal, but that was because Tom was playing in the URC Grand Final for Leinster, where he had been amazing against the Bulls. In the semi-finals the Bulls had destroyed the Sharks' all-Springbok front row in the scrum. But the Bulls' front row got nothing out of Tom in the final. Nothing. He is tough, he has got good skill. 'Has anyone watched him over the last six months?' I asked in the press conference.

I loved seeing people who had just come in doing well. Ben White was pushing hard for a Test spot. Jamie Osborne fitted in quickly and was impressive. He was not just another Irish player coming in, like some people said: he was the next cab off the rank at a time when we had a number of injuries in the back five. His versatility in playing centre and full-back was invaluable.

The Test side was starting to take shape. I had an idea of what it might be, but I meant it when I said I was keeping an open mind. And the players needed to know that.

People looked at the side that defeated the Brumbies 36–24 in Canberra as the 'Test side'. But there were still ten days to go before the first Test in Brisbane, and when we travelled to Adelaide for the game against the AUNZ XV, I was genuine when I said that some players were still pushing for Test places. We won 48–0 and played some of our best attacking rugby of the tour.

The side had been captained by Tadhg Beirne. He had not been at his best early in the tour, but I knew he was a big-game player. A guy might look good in a free-flowing fifty-point victory, but in a Test match the intensity is at a completely different level. Tadhg had delivered for me again and again with Ireland, and his work in the set piece and on the floor as a jackal and as a ball-playing 6 would also complement Jack Conan at No. 8.

I had similar feelings about Tom Curry: another big-game player who had been trying to find a bit of form. I felt Tom's work rate and physicality, particularly off the ball, could make our team tick in the Tests.

With Garry Ringrose out of the first Test with concussion, we also had to make a call in the midfield. The Scottish combination of Sione Tuipulotu and Huw Jones offered greater cohesion, particularly with Finn Russell at out-half, and they had played well together in Adelaide. Bundee would bring us power off the bench.

Meanwhile, Hugo had shown enough to nail down the full-back position. He was another player I knew I could trust to deliver when the pressure was on, even if he was still not 100 per cent after his illness.

Owen had come on with half an hour to go in Adelaide and looked sharp. But with Blair unavailable, we needed full-back cover, so Marcus Smith took the 22 jersey.

We wanted to make sure there were no surprises in terms of the Test selection, so when we did a walk-through on Monday in Brisbane we made it pretty obvious which direction we were going in. What impressed me so much was the reaction of the players who were not in the starting XV to our training session the following day. They asked some serious questions of the starters, which was great because it pointed to things that we needed to fix. I loved it. It showed to me that the group were as one.

I loved being back in Brisbane. I was asked by some of the Australian reporters about my memories of playing there with Wigan back in 1994, when we beat the Broncos to win the World Club Challenge. 'This seems a little bit bigger,' I said. 'This is huge. This would mean the world to me to beat Australia.'

And I meant it. Don't get me wrong: when I was a nineteen-year-old and we won there, it was huge for me and for Wigan. But if you fast-forward thirty-one years, coaching the British and Irish Lions at the Suncorp Stadium looked like that on steroids.

One of the things I love about Lions tours is the old faces that come out of the woodwork. I couldn't meet up with all my old friends because I had a job to do, but it was nice that people were reaching out, and the messages brought back memories of the good old times. In Brisbane I bumped into Gorden Tallis, one of the toughest Australian players I had faced back in the day. 'Hey, Gordie, what are you doing here?' I shouted across the street. 'Flippin' heck, Faz, good to see you,' he replied. We had a good catch-up. He recalled how everyone used to talk about Queensland being underdogs ahead of each State of Origin rugby league game against New South Wales. 'We never, ever saw it that way,' said Gordie, who had represented Queensland many times and was known as the 'Raging Bull' for his aggression in games. I got Gordie a couple of tickets for the first Test. His words were a reminder that for all the talk that we were heavy favourites to win the series, Australia would not see it that way.

On the Thursday night before the first Test, we organized a surprise cap ceremony for the players. We had delayed doing it because so many of them were winning their first Lions caps and we wanted to make the presentation when their families were there. We posted it on the family WhatsApp group, and some brought their flights forward just to be there. In some cases, the players didn't know until they saw them in the room. We did the cap presentation first, and then family members presented the shirts to those who were in the Test squad. It was so moving. Three or four families who couldn't make it had recorded video messages as well, and for some it involved remembering loved ones who had passed away. All sorts of individual stories came up. Everyone felt connected and that they were in this together.

Including families in this tour was so important to me. When I was a player with Wigan, wives and girlfriends were not allowed in the team hotel and the boys would have to sneak off to see them. I wanted the players to feel supported in the environment and to be able to share their experience with their loved ones, so we ensured there was a large family room in each of our hotels where they could meet.

Colleen and Gabriel had arrived in time for the first Test, and Elleshia and Gracie joined us in time for the last two. Gabriel came everywhere with me. He might walk into a selection meeting, sit down and grab a drink, or go and join a PlayStation game with the lads. The reason I allowed Gabriel to be around was that I wanted the players to see me as a father, and therefore as a person, not just as a rugby coach. It also brought a bit of normality amid all the seriousness, and I hoped it would help everyone to be more relaxed.

In the team talk I'd given to the squad the previous day, I'd wanted to address the elephant in the room: the fact that we were favourites. We had to embrace that, walk tall towards the challenge. I told them we had a chance to make history and that this was a moment they should enjoy because it was something they had earned. 'All you need in life is a big opportunity to do something special,' I told them. The players had to know that the reason they were here was because of a lifetime of work.

'All that matters is your belief. It doesn't really matter whether you're an underdog or whether you're a favourite. It's what you really believe that matters and who you are doing it with.'

If players were feeling pressure, then we needed to talk about it and get it out in the open. The more that you talk about things, the better you understand how you are going to attack the challenge.

I have never been as concerned about spying as some coaches are, but we had not held our captain's run sessions at the stadiums on the eve of the game until the first Test in Brisbane.

Frustratingly, we were allowed to have only thirty players training on the pitch at the Suncorp Stadium. It was the first time that we hadn't had the whole squad mucking in together: eight or nine lads had to sit in the stands watching. No one batted an eyelid that there were twenty-odd members of staff on the pitch. It didn't make any sense. And it was the opposite of what we were trying to do through the tour.

On the pitch, I made a point of speaking to the three back-row forwards – Tadhg Beirne, Tom Curry and Jack Conan. I backed them but I also challenged them. 'How are we going to go about attacking this?' I asked them. 'What does it feel like? If I am saying you are a big-game player, what is it that you are going to bring?'

They didn't let us down.

* * *

I was intrigued to see where we were at. We felt we had given ourselves the best chance to win, but we still had to go and do it. At the spiritual home of Australian rugby, I knew it was not all going to go our way.

Our decision to play expansive rugby early in the tour and then tighten up our game played out perfectly in the first half. Tadhg Beirne and Tom Curry did what they had promised to us and each other by bringing a physicality that the Wallabies found difficult to handle. Right from the kick-off, Tom smashed into Australian prop James Slipper with a tackle. And when the slow ball was passed to Joseph-Aukuso Sua'ali'i, Tadhg was waiting to pounce, winning us a penalty. Finn Russell knocked over the three points and we were up and running with less than a minute on the clock. We couldn't have hoped for a better start.

The Wallabies fly-half Tom Lynagh is a fine young player, but we knew that if he didn't have a platform to play off, he would run out of options. I was impressed with how we controlled the game. From a tactical point of view, our half-backs were superb. Jamison Gibson-Park's kicking was tremendous, and a 50/22 from Finn Russell set the tone of the game. Jack Conan and Ellis Genge got us over the gain line. With the front-foot ball, we scored good tries by Sione Tuipulotu, from a brilliant pass by Finn, and Tom Curry, who powered over from close range. When Dan Sheehan scored again to put us ahead 24–5 at the start of the second half, we looked on course for a big win.

But then we let them back into the game. We started giving away penalties, and under pressure we were losing a few collisions. Tries by Carlo Tizzano and Tate McDermott made the final score of 27–19 much closer than it should have been. Perhaps collectively we eased off a bit because we felt the job was done. But that was not good enough. We had talked about being 'next-moment focused' at all times.

I knew that if Will Skelton and Rob Valetini, who had both just come back from injury, were added to the Australian pack in the second Test, we would face a much sterner physical challenge. And Australia would be fighting for their lives.

Joe McCarthy, who had been a big physical presence for us, had to go off with a foot injury. He had been brilliant since our first game against the Western Force, and although we didn't know it then, it was the last we would see of him on the tour.

We had to fly to Melbourne on Sunday and start preparing to face the First Nations and Pasifika XV on Tuesday night. It was the pinch-point of the tour, and it felt like lunacy to attempt to run two teams in training during the week. We trained together on the Monday, then the lads who were not playing on Tuesday evening trained that morning. And those involved in the Tuesday match couldn't train on the Wednesday.

Yet there was part of me that loved the challenge. I couldn't wait to see the boys get their chance to play on the Tuesday night and I reminded them this was an opportunity to force their way into the Test side. It was a brilliant game, and gave us an insight into what was to follow in the second Test. The FNP side had only just been thrown together for a fixture to replace the Melbourne Rebels, who had gone out of business in the previous year, but they were proud to represent their cultures and communities.

I named Garry Ringrose on the bench. He had passed all his return-to-play protocols and was firmly in my mind to come into the Test side along with Bundee Aki. When you put someone on the bench, you should always expect that they might have to play from the first minute. In this case, Garry had to play for just over an hour because Darcy Graham, who scored a try in an impressive start, was forced off after sixteen minutes with an ankle injury that would end his tour. That he left the field in tears showed just how much it meant to him, and he stayed on in Australia with his family.

It might not have been ideal for Garry to play for so long, but he did really well and it solidified our view that bringing him into the Test side was the right thing to do. I can understand why people on the outside might have said our midfield in the first Test had done well. The team had played good rugby, and it had been a free-flowing game. But we also saw things that needed to improve.

Owen captained the side and played the full eighty minutes. He earned his place in the squad for the second Test. I knew it was not a problem for him to play twice in a week, as he had done so plenty of times before on the three previous tours. Jac Morgan also really impressed us, as did Blair Kinghorn. Even though Blair threw a couple of intercept passes, we didn't feel the pressure of the occasion – or of coming back from a knee injury – had got to him. He was just trying to be himself. We got both Jac and Blair off nice and early, along with James Ryan. All three had played their way onto our bench, with Ollie Chessum stepping up to replace Joe McCarthy in the second row.

Some of the guys who kept their places in the team were lucky to still be there. James Lowe knew he had been a bit off, but he had played big so many times for us. Sometimes knowing what a player *could* produce outweighed recent form – as it had with Tom and Tadhg in the first Test. But we had also been true to our word when we said that those involved against the FNP XV could put their hands up for Test selection. A number of guys did, and were rewarded.

When we finished our training session at Xavier College on the Thursday, Garry Ringrose came up to me and told me that he didn't feel right. Even though he had passed all the

return-to-play protocols and had not sustained any apparent knock to his head on Tuesday, he felt some concussion
symptoms. (Later, when watching the training footage back,
we discovered that he had sustained an accidental blow.) I
was gutted for him. He had yet to play in a Test match for
the Lions, and now he had to pull out of the biggest game
of his life. It was one of the most courageous things I have
seen. I knew the easy thing for him to do would have been to
keep his concerns to himself, but he did the right thing for
himself and the team.

Garry's withdrawal meant that Huw Jones retained his
place at outside centre, with Bundee at No. 12.

We asked Martin Johnson, the legendary Lions captain of
the 1997 and 2001 tours, to present the jerseys for the second
Test. He told the players about the perception that the Lions
took their eye off the ball in the second Test in Melbourne in
2001. They had won the first Test in Brisbane, and were leading at half-time in the second, but went on to lose the game
and narrowly lost the third Test in Sydney.

But Johnno told them the reality. They hadn't eased off.
They had started the second Test really well, but lost the run
of themselves after two quick tries by Australia in the second
half. Johnno told them that what people on the outside don't
realize is that when you get to the business end of the tour,
when the series is on the line, is when the Lions players are
patched up at the end of a long season. It all comes down to
mindset, of being able to will yourself into going again.

I knew our players were out on their feet too, but it was
important not to talk about it. We didn't want to give the
players that narrative, even subconsciously. We kept telling
the players that they were in great condition and how brilliant it was to have got to the business end of the tour in

such great shape. We needed to make them believe, because we were asking them to go places physically and mentally that many of them had not been before in their careers.

I know the French can't grasp the concept of the demands of a Lions tour. They think it is madness. But these guys have grown up watching it and wanting to be part of it. And now, despite the physical and mental demands, they were saying: 'Wow, how good is this?' It is the same for the staff and coaches. I told the players that the second Test would be the biggest game of their lives. And I meant it. But in my mind, the players had already proved to themselves by their effort and commitment that they were true Lions, even if Australia played unbelievably well and beat us. I knew the perception on the outside would change if we lost the game, but in my mind one result would not change what they had achieved together over the last eight weeks.

* * *

We had spent eight months planning for the tour. But planning isn't everything: you also need to have an ability in the moment to *feel* what needs to happen. In the week of the first Test, because of all the meetings that we had, I held back a presentation I had planned. On the Friday before the second Test, it felt right to shorten our captain's run – we just did a short walk-through at the stadium – and use the time to show the squad a video message from Katie Taylor, the legendary Irish boxer.

A couple of weeks earlier, Katie had beaten Amanda Serrano, the Puerto Rican boxer who holds the record for the most world championships won in different weight classes by a woman, having held nine major world titles across seven different weights. It was the third fight in a trilogy. The first, in 2022, had been the headline contest at Madison Square Garden – the first time a women's boxing bout had headlined there. It went down as fight of the year, and the greatest of all time for women's boxing. Taylor and Serrano were both nice and calm at the start of round one, not pumping with sweat like some fighters, and they lasted the ten rounds. Katie got rocked in the fifth but still won the sixth and seventh, and went on to take a split decision.

As some people questioned the judges' verdict, Katie's response was: let's go again. And she won again, this time unanimously, with 45 million people watching on Netflix. But because it went ten rounds and some people thought there was nothing in it, she went again. And won again.

It got me thinking about the journey we were on, trying to win a three-match series. I told Gary Keegan, our perform-ance coach, about my fascination with Katie's achievement. Gary was previously Irish boxing's high-performance man-ager, and he was able to contact Katie and ask if she would record a video message for the squad.

Before the first Test I had briefly mentioned the challenge of a prize-fighter having to deliver on their own in the ring. 'We think we are in a pressurized situation, but there is always someone who is being challenged more than you,' I said. 'For a prize-fighter, everything is on the line. What does that look like? What do you have to do? You've got to be calm if you want to be at your best in the tenth round. You've got to make sure that you're calm enough in your warm-up, so that you preserve your energy, so then you can think clear on your feet. That's not all going to go your own way.'

Now, in the changing room at the MCG in Melbourne the day before the game, I felt the time was right to share the video Katie made for us.

'The first thought is acknowledging the privilege of being part of big games,' Katie told the squad. 'There is no right to win. It must be earned, every game, every fight, every tackle, every minute. The second thought I want to share is: calm my nerves. Every athlete knows there are so many variables on any given day, and for reasons I can't fully control. Sometimes I feel sharp and strong, and my timing is perfect. Sometimes it isn't and this can lead to performance anxiety. But regardless of those things, some of which are hard to control, I know that even if it isn't pretty, I am 100 per cent confident that I will go to the trenches if necessary. That's a controllable. And that's a matter of will. So, here's my message: prepare to win by skill, but be ready to win by will.'

The players sat speechless. 'Just have a minute to think about that, lads,' I told them. 'There is someone who has put everything on the line.' I knew they were ready to do the same.

Out on the pitch, during the walk-through, I spoke to our back row again. 'People tell me you are not able to back that performance up,' I said to Tom Curry. I told Tadhg Beirne that people didn't think he could play well in two games on the trot. I asked Jack Conan that if he thought he'd had a good game in the first Test, and how was he going to be bigger and better this week. Finally, I asked Jac Morgan what he was going to add to the group from the bench.

I just wanted them to realize how good they were, in case they were reading some of the comments being made about them. I did the same with the centres and the wingers.

MCG stands for Melbourne Cricket Ground. It is a vast stadium, with a huge oval playing surface. We decided to lift the mood and take the pressure off the players by having a game of cricket. Aled Walters got the bats.

It was backs against forwards. If you missed the ball twice, you were out, and people got out pretty quickly. Even though the backs won, the man-of-the-match by a mile was Finlay Bealham. Now, Finlay would struggle to ride a bike, but he kept smashing sixes.

* * *

Like Katie Taylor in the fifth round of her first fight against Serrano, we were rocked midway through the first half. Australia stormed into an eighteen-point lead with three tries, the last a thrilling sixty-metre effort from the restart. At half-time we trailed 23–17, after tries by Tom Curry and Huw Jones late in the half. Keeping calm was the key message as the players entered the dressing room at half-time.

Australia's first-half performance had not surprised me. They are an unbelievably proud sporting nation. I have played against them often enough to know that. I knew they would come back hard at us after the first Test, particularly with Will Skelton and Rob Valetini back in their pack. Have a look at the tackles that we had missed. They were a bit to do with us, but it was a lot to do with the type of athlete that they have and the quality in their backline.

They had had a great set-up in place under Joe Schmidt for the previous eighteen months and had made significant progress. We might have hit them hard in the first half of the first Test, but I knew they would react in the way that they did with the series on the line. I had often been in that situation myself, playing in teams that went 1–0 down in a three-Test series. It is do or die.

In 1997, Great Britain lost the first of a three-game Super League Test series heavily at Wembley. In the second Test, at Old Trafford, we delivered the best version of ourselves, because we had to. That is why the Wallabies' performance was expected.

We held the Wallabies in huge respect. It has always been that way and always will. It was embarrassing for me to hear people question whether the Lions should tour Australia in twelve years' time. Every team has ups and downs over the years, but Australia is a leading rugby nation and it was ridiculous to suggest that they should be struck off. And, of course, Australia is also a brilliant place to tour. We were having the best time of our lives there. The second half of the second Test was about to make it even more special.

'Even if it was 23–5, I would still back us to win,' I told the players. Our problems were glaringly obvious. Our lack of discipline and being second best in the collisions had allowed Australia to get the momentum and belief that they needed. But the couple of tries we'd scored just before half-time would have put a bit of pressure back on them, and we had some easy fixes. I knew we could win with our skill. Even though Lynagh landed his third penalty in the fifty-fourth minute to edge his side to nine points in front, and it took a massive tackle by Tom Curry on Sua'ali'i to scupper another try-scoring opportunity, I was confident that if we could gain enough entries into their twenty-two, we'd get the scores we needed, as we'd been successful in that area most of the night.

When Tadhg Beirne crashed over for a try and Finn Russell nailed the touchline conversion just before the hour mark, we were just two points down and looked on course to push for victory.

But Australia dug deep. Carlo Tizzano won a turnover penalty on his own line after Finn had kicked a monster penalty to the corner.

347

With ten minutes to go, Blair Kinghorn made a break down the right, and we piled into the twenty-two, but Will Stuart was penalized for an extra roll on the ground after being tackled. Lynagh kicked the penalty to touch, but at the subsequent line-out Maro managed to get his hands on the ball in the maul and force the turnover. We had a scrum on the left-hand side of the pitch about thirty metres out. It was a great attacking platform, but the Wallabies seemed intent on running down the clock by ensuring the scrum had to be reset a couple of times.

To add to the drama, we then had the remarkable scene of Will Stuart having to swap boots with Tadhg Furlong on the sidelines.

In the final training session before the game, I had noticed that Will's boots were in terrible condition. 'Will, your boots are taped up,' I said.

'I've only brought one pair with me, but I only need them to get through a few more sessions and they will have done a full season,' he replied.

Now, in the biggest scrum of his life, his boots had split.

The ref at least stopped the clock to allow him to put his new boots on. But Will's boots are a size twelve and Tadhg's are only a size ten. Facing the biggest scrum of his life, he stuffed his feet into Tadhg's boots and got on with it.

Meanwhile, Bundee was receiving treatment for cramp, but he was prepared to go again. When the ref turned the clock back on, the final scrum ate up another minute. But I felt calm. And I knew that, if the players stayed calm enough, there was still time to score. Tadhg Beirne's try had involved fourteen phases, and there was no reason we shouldn't replicate that. And in wasting those minutes, the Wallabies had taken away their chance to have a go back at us if we did take the lead.

Eventually, we got a free kick and Jack Conan made some ground. Then Will Stuart, despite his crushed feet, made some more up the left. We attacked again, with Tadhg Beirne driving on, but Bundee was cramping up again, and the ball went forward from a carry by Ellis Genge. Scrum to Australia, just outside their twenty-two. Bundee took a carb gel and a drink and carried on. Lynagh cleared long, and Hugo Keenan launched a high ball, but a huge clearance kick by Jake Gordon took play back inside our half.

The clock was at 77:21 when Rónan Kelleher threw the ball into our line-out. Fourteen phases later, Hugo Keenan raced over for the try that would win the match and the series. It was one of the proudest moments of my coaching career. This was the moment we had trained for. This was a band of brothers going about their work, even though their limbs were aching and their lungs burning.

There was no panic, only calmness as they stretched Australia first up the right-hand touchline, then down the left, a carry by Bundee up the middle, then right again, then left again, with Will Stuart somehow finding a way to carry through two tackles. When Tadhg Beirne cut back inside two defenders to take us deep into the twenty-two, it was on. Finn Russell doesn't do drop-goals, so we kept playing: Kinghorn up the right again, Beirne another carry. Finn's composure at the end was remarkable. He looked left, then cut back to the right, knowing that if he was tackled the game would have been lost. But James Ryan was on hand to take the pass and charge on.

In the background, Hugo Keenan, the player who earlier on the tour had spent twelve days on the toilet with a stomach virus and shed six kilograms, found the energy to run from the right-hand touchline in an arc to the left side of the pitch. The Wallabies defenders were stacked on the other side, unaware. But Jamison was aware. The clock had entered the eightieth minute when he fired his pass fast and wide, perfect for Hugo to run onto. With Jack Conan outside him, Max Jorgensen, the Wallabies wing, had to stay out. Up in the box I screamed for Hugo to pass it to Jack, but Hugo knew better. He backed himself to take Len Ikitau on the outside and scored. We'd done it.

But as the players celebrated, Harry Wilson, the Wallabies captain, approached referee Andrea Piardi, urging him to review the final breakdown. Jac Morgan had cleared out Carlo Tizzano. It looked fine to us, but Tizzano had held his head as he fell dramatically backwards. Piardi reviewed but declared it a rugby incident.

Afterwards, Joe Schmidt and some Australian pundits insisted it should have been a penalty. Listen, I understand why they would. It means so much, and they had lost the match and the series in a devastating way, on the last play. But if Jac's clearout was a penalty, then how many penalties went unwhistled in that match, and in every other match? The law says a guy going in for a poach can't have his head below his knees anyway, which was the position Tizzano was in.

Earlier in the game their scrum-half Jake Gordon had gone over for a try that, in our view, should not have been awarded because the ref was obstructing Andrew Porter. If it had been a player rather than the ref, it would definitely have been called as obstruction. On one of the angles we could see, it was clear that the ref had been in the way, and we were shouting on the microphone to ask him to have a look at it. Andrew went over to Maro, and Maro spoke to the referee, but the officials didn't even question it. How that happened, I don't know, but we had to live with it.

Whether or not Tizzano was being dramatic, I don't know. But he got four experts – the ref, the assistants and the television match official – to review it, and they all said the try should stand. Andrew Porter should have done something similar to make sure they looked at Gordon's try again.

But none of it mattered now. Our immediate reaction was sheer relief. And pride at how the players had held on and come back to get what they deserved. We scored five tries to Australia's three, and in my eyes it should have been five tries to two. We were worthy winners.

In the coaches' box, I shouted: 'We are off to Coogee!' We had a day out planned at the beachside suburb in Sydney with our families, with Monday and Tuesday morning off, whatever happened. But the night was not yet done. We had media duties to fulfil, although the players were only interested in celebrating. Back in the changing room, I couldn't get a word in edgewise. Then Jamison picked up his white plastic chair and asked the lads to follow him as he walked back out onto the pitch. They wanted to celebrate and feel together what they had just done. The ground staff wanted to get on with mowing the pitch because they had an Australian Rules game on the next day, but it just showed what it meant to the players. We had won the series scoring eight tries in two matches, which was more than the Lions had ever managed in a three-Test series. The whole squad brought out their chairs and sat in a circle as Hugo, whose nickname is 'Barry', re-enacted his try. The area where he touched down was renamed 'Barry's corner', at least until the rugby posts were dismantled.

* * *

There were moments in the third Test when my mind went back to my eleven-year-old self, playing a rugby league game at Saddleworth Rangers in Oldham in hail so thick that you couldn't see through it. Everyone must have been thinking 'Flippin' heck, what are we doing? Why are we even playing?' But it was the only way I know. For those players who loved it, and I was certainly one of them, you'd stay out in any conditions.

In the coaches' box at the Accor Stadium in Sydney, we couldn't even see what was going on because the windows had steamed up. And when we wiped it clear, the rain was so heavy that you still couldn't see the game. Hats off to Australia, they managed the biblical conditions better than us.

We could have no complaints. After the game in Melbourne, the lads had gone to celebrate at a venue we had booked for them, while the staff went back to the hotel with our families. I think we had a better time than the lads did. I like just relaxing and taking it easy, chewing the fat over a couple of drinks.

The following day we flew to Sydney and went straight out to Coogee, with everyone dressed in their civvies apart from John Fogarty, who wanted to wear his Lions gear so he would be noticed. But no one went mad.

After two days off, everyone was back at it on Tuesday afternoon. There was no sense of tapping out from anyone, and watching how the players not involved in the twenty-three-man Test squad went about their work made me as proud as anything we had achieved.

We lightened things up in training by playing a version of 'Squid Game'. We had considered whether to freshen up the squad for the final Test, but we felt the players were ready to go again. The only changes were promoting Blair onto the left wing ahead of James Lowe, while James Ryan started in the second row in place of Ollie Chessum, and we added Ben Earl to the bench as one of six forwards.

We couldn't lie to ourselves. We had set out to win the series 3–0. I reminded the players they were like a prize-fighter. It was on the line again. Why go for just one fight? Why go for just two fights? If there is any doubt, everyone wants a trilogy. That's why Katie Taylor kept turning up. That's why we had to turn up again.

We had made sure that we had looked after the squad, freshened them up physically and mentally, and by the time we did the walk-through on Tuesday and the one main session we had on the Wednesday, everyone looked as good as ever.

We would all have loved to see a dry day and the rugby that both sides were capable of playing, but that is not always possible in Test match football.

Australia played better than us. They played in a product-ive manner with the personnel they picked. We overplayed a little bit because we were trying to chase something when we didn't need to. Losing Maro and James Ryan, our two line-out lieutenants, both to head injuries, so early in the game certainly didn't help, but I thought Australia's defensive line-out was impressive on the night.

I know some people felt the thirty-eight-minute break because of the risk of lightning at the start of the second half might have favoured Australia. There was criticism that we had players sitting in beanbags and looking at their phones, while the Wallabies were working on their skills and reviewing their tactics.

The reality was very different. When you see the lads walk-ing around on their phones all the time, it is because they are looking at something they have been sent, such as video footage or maps of set-piece plays. Finn Russell is on his phone constantly, looking at this stuff. But even if he had just been chilling out, it would have been fine by me, given we were potentially facing an hour's break.

We had the beanbags put into the changing room because the day before we had been held up in traffic, so we decided to leave for the stadium earlier on match day. We wanted the players to be able to chill out and not get het up. If they started warming up too early, then they would be running out of juice or cramping up at the end of the game.

Before kick-off we had been told that the game could be stopped if lightning occurred within ten kilometres of the stadium, but nobody could tell us how long the break was going to be. At first it was half an hour, which is a long time for players to keep warming up. Then we were told forty-five minutes, or even longer. It was possible that the game could be called off. So we made a plan with our strength-and-conditioning group and medical group and were ready to go again.

In the second Test we'd had the chance to build ourselves back into the game after falling behind. But after the lightning break, when the Wallabies picked up that loose ball and ran off for a try by Jorgensen, there was no way back.

Afterwards, I addressed the whole group. The tour had been an unbelievable experience for everyone. It might sound corny, but all ninety-one of us there had had the time of our lives. We had a team of people who were not just good at their jobs, but who could also be selfless and muck in. It was a huge credit to the staff that a tour with so many moving parts had progressed seamlessly. Within all that, the players were fantastic in buying into the whole concept, even though three-quarters of them had never been on a tour like this before. To a man, they never whinged or moaned; they just got on with something that was miles out of their comfort zone.

The lightning break meant that by the time we got back to our hotel it was after one o'clock in the morning. The players went on to a place we had booked where they could celebrate together. I thought I'd go to bed straight away, because I was absolutely shattered, but after a bit of food and a chat it was 4 a.m. A few of us went to Manly the following day before the flight home.

* * *

When Colleen and I went for our first walk by the seafront on Sandymount after the tour, it caught a few people by surprise that we were home so soon.

I still had things to consider for the Lions review. I favoured naming the squad later in the season, when the biggest games are taking place: players are performing when it really matters. But in thinking about changes it is important that we preserve the romance and tradition of the Lions. A lot of it doesn't make sense, but that is why we all love it.

What I do know is that the future of the Lions must be guaranteed, no matter what else happens to our game. Ask any of the boys who went on this tour, and they will tell you why.

Acknowledgements

I would like to thank Gavin Mairs for his help in telling my story. When I first met Gavin, I got the immediate impression that he was dedicated to working out how to tell the truth of any story that he writes. His work ethic and understanding shine through in everything he does, and I couldn't have asked for a better person to help get my story out of me. To say he gets it is an understatement, and the time we have spent working on this book has forged a friendship that will last for ever.

I also to want thank Ciarán Medlar, who was instrumental in making this book happen in the first place and who is a constant source of advice. He has been a great support to me over the years.

Thanks also to Michael McLoughlin and Brendan Barrington at Penguin Sandycove for backing the project and for their professionalism, guidance and encouragement.

Finally, a huge thanks to my wife, Colleen, who has been by my side the whole way and has been a tower of support through the process of writing this book. It means the world to me that our family and future generations will be able to read the history of our life together.

Index

The Fate of the Sea Stag

Orkneyinga Murders V

by

Lexie Conyngham

First published in 2024 by The Kellas Cat Press, Aberdeen.

ISBN: 978-1-910926-95-6

Cover illustration by Helen Braid at
www.ellieillustrates.co.uk